# *The* **Business**

## INTERMEDIATE Teacher's Book

Antoinette Meehan, Fr... ...Emmerson

MACMILLAN

# Contents

| Introduction | p 4 |
|---|---|
| **1 Corporate culture:** Subject background | p 8 |
| 1.1 About business | p 9 |
| 1.2 Vocabulary | p 11 |
| 1.3 Grammar | p 13 |
| 1.4 Speaking | p 15 |
| 1.5 Writing | p 17 |
| 1.6 Case study | p 19 |
| **2 Customer support:** Subject background | p 21 |
| 2.1 About business | p 22 |
| 2.2 Vocabulary | p 24 |
| 2.3 Grammar | p 26 |
| 2.4 Speaking | p 28 |
| 2.5 Writing | p 31 |
| 2.6 Case study | p 33 |
| Review 1 and 2 answers | p 35 |
| **3 Products and packaging:** Subject background | p 36 |
| 3.1 About business | p 37 |
| 3.2 Vocabulary | p 39 |
| 3.3 Grammar | p 41 |
| 3.4 Speaking | p 43 |
| 3.5 Writing | p 45 |
| 3.6 Case study | p 47 |
| **4 Careers:** Subject background | p 49 |
| 4.1 About business | p 50 |
| 4.2 Vocabulary | p 52 |
| 4.3 Grammar | p 55 |
| 4.4 Speaking | p 57 |
| 4.5 Writing | p 59 |
| 4.6 Case study | p 60 |
| Review 3 and 4 answers | p 62 |
| **5 Making deals:** Subject background | p 63 |
| 5.1 About business | p 64 |
| 5.2 Vocabulary | p 66 |
| 5.3 Grammar | p 68 |
| 5.4 Speaking | p 69 |
| 5.5 Writing | p 72 |
| 5.6 Case study | p 74 |
| **6 Company and community:** Subject background | p 75 |
| 6.1 About business | p 76 |
| 6.2 Vocabulary | p 78 |
| 6.3 Grammar | p 80 |
| 6.4 Speaking | p 82 |
| 6.5 Writing | p 84 |
| 6.6 Case study | p 86 |
| Review 5 and 6 answers | p 88 |
| **7 Mergers and acquisitions:** Subject background | p 89 |
| 7.1 About business | p 90 |
| 7.2 Vocabulary | p 92 |
| 7.3 Grammar | p 94 |
| 7.4 Speaking | p 95 |
| 7.5 Writing | p 98 |
| 7.6 Case study | p 100 |
| **8 International trade:** Subject background | p 102 |
| 8.1 About business | p 103 |
| 8.2 Vocabulary | p 104 |
| 8.3 Grammar | p 106 |
| 8.4 Speaking | p 109 |
| 8.5 Writing | p 111 |
| 8.6 Case study | p 113 |
| Review 7 and 8 answers | p 115 |
| Grammar and practice answers | p 116 |
| Additional activities (photocopiable speaking and reading activities) | p 120 |

# *The* **Business**

## INTERMEDIATE

### Introduction

The objective of *The* Business is to help your students learn two things: how to do business in English and the language they need to do it. The new language and structures are presented in the Student's Book, the DVD-ROM provides language practice and extension and this Teacher's Book provides teaching notes and ideas, answers, recordings, subject background notes and additional reading and speaking activities. Below is a description of what you will find in each.

### *Student's Book*

#### The modules

The Student's Book contains 48 modules in eight units. Each unit deals with a key sector of activity in the business world. There are six different types of module:

#### 1 About business

These modules contain information and language for the topic area of each unit. The focus is on getting students to understand the topic and the general sense of the texts. The key topic vocabulary is dealt with in depth in the vocabulary module, allowing you to concentrate on developing reading comprehension skills here.

#### 2 Vocabulary

These modules build on the important words and phrases introduced in the previous module and provide thorough practice. There is a useful focus on phrasal verbs and collocations most commonly used in business.

#### 3 Grammar

These modules take a 'test-teach-practice' approach. A *Test yourself* page opens the module to focus on any areas of weakness; the target grammar is then modelled in context e.g. using short reading and listening texts; finally, controlled and freer practice in realistic business situations enables students to get to grips with grammatical concepts. If you wish, you can also use the *Test yourself* section after the practice exercises to check students' understanding of those. The grammar modules are supported by the *Grammar and practice* section at the back of the book.

#### 4 Speaking

These modules develop understanding and speaking skills in typical business situations. Language is recycled from other modules, but the focus is mainly on functional words and phrases. There are lots of group work and problem-solving tasks to engage students and encourage their fluency in using the target language in realistic situations. These modules contain pronunciation practice too, which is supported by further interactive practice on the DVD-ROM.

#### 5 Writing

These modules provide practice for the most important types of document students will need to write at work. Model texts are examined and used as a basis to write their own. Key writing sub skills are focused on in the process of the guided writing, such as using appropriate style and register, reformulating, ordering and expanding from notes.

#### 6 Case study

The case studies provide an opportunity for the students to apply all the language, skills and ideas they have worked on in the course of the unit. The case studies present authentic problem-solving situations similar to those encountered in business.

**Internet research**

Every module includes an Internet research task. The Internet provides almost unlimited resources for students to improve their English and learn more about business. These tasks direct them to interesting background and details on topics related to each module. The tasks can be set as homework and done before or after working on the module.

Note that words to type into the search engine are in *italics*. They should only be entered between quotes (" ") if quotes are used in the rubric.

## Other features

In addition to the eight main units, the Student's Book contains the following:

## Reviews

These units can be used in three ways: to consolidate language covered in the units, to catch up quickly on any lessons missed, and to revise before tests or exams.

## Additional material

This section contains all the extra materials students need to do pair or group work activities.

## Grammar and practice

The section gives a very useful summary of grammar rules with clear examples, but also provides further practice of the essential grammar points in this level of the course.

## Recordings

Full scripts of all the audio recordings are given for reference, allowing students to check or study the audio dialogues in detail. However, encourage students not to rely on reading them to understand the listenings.

## Wordlist

In the modules, words which intermediate level students may not know are in grey. Definitions of grey words are given in the wordlist, often with examples. Words in red are high-frequency items, which you should encourage students to learn and use. The others, in black, are words they just need to understand.

## *The DVD-ROM*

The DVD-ROM empowers students to continue improving their English autonomously, away from the classroom. It contains:

### Interactive workbook

This includes everything you would normally find in a workbook, and more; interactive exercises for vocabulary, grammar, writing and listening practice. There are also pronunciation exercises in each unit, which allow students to record themselves and compare the recording with that of a native speaker. Like the *Review* units in the Student's Book, the Interactive workbook can be used in three ways: to improve skills and consolidate language work from the Student's Book; to catch up on missed lessons; to revise for tests and exams.

### Video

Each unit includes an episode of a mini-drama illustrating the communication and people skills practised in each unit, with exercises to practise the functional language used in the video.

### Business dilemmas

There are four problem-solving games to allow you to review and practise functional language from the Student's Book. You could also try doing these in class with the students working in pairs to practise discussing problems and solutions.

### Tests

There are four tests, one for every two units. These allow students to check their progress through the DVD-ROM. If they do well on a test, they get 'promoted'; if they do well on all four tests, they become CEO!

### Business documents

There is a model document for each unit, including letters, invoices, CVs, etc. Each document includes annotations explaining the structure and key phrases, and a follow-up activity tests understanding of this.

### Grammar reference

Students can refer to this section any time for helpful grammar rules and examples.

### Class audio

This section of the DVD-ROM contains all the audio recordings from the Student's Book, together with scrollable scripts.

### Downloadables

The DVD-ROM includes a set of downloadable files for use outside the DVD-ROM or away from a computer. There is a downloadable and printable PDF of the answers to the Student's Book exercises; a Word file containing the text of each Business document; and MP3 files of all the Student's Book audio that can be transferred to an MP3 player or iPod for listening on the move.

## *Teacher's Book*

This Teacher's Book aims to make using *The* Business Student's Book easy. It provides ideas for lead-in activities for each unit, for further practice and for extension / personalization activities, as well as answers and recording scripts and additional, photocopiable reading and speaking activities.

### Subject background

Each unit begins with a page of background notes about the sector of activity in the business world that is dealt with in the unit. These subject background notes contain lists of useful websites that will provide you and/or your students with more in-depth knowledge and information about the topic of each unit.

### Teaching notes

The teaching notes for each module contain the following:
- Classroom procedure and task management notes.
- Ideas for lead-in activities in the *About business* modules.
- Ideas for further practice and extension activities.
- A full answer key for the exercises in the Student's Book.
- Full recording scripts for all the listening activities.
- Suggestions on how and when to use the *Internet research* tasks.
- Tips for tailoring activities to suit lower- or higher-level classes.

### Answer key for Reviews and Grammar and practice

The full answer key for the Review sections can be found after every two units.
The full answer key for Grammar and practice is at the end of the teaching notes for the Student's Book units on page 116.

### Additional activities (photocopiable)

There is an additional, photocopiable speaking and listening activity for each of the eight units after the *Grammar and practice* answer key. There are teacher's notes and answers for each photocopiable activity.

### Tips for using this book

**Answers**

The answers to all the module exercises are on a grey panel at the end of the teaching notes for each exercise. Items that are gapped/missing in the Student's Book are <u>underlined</u>.

**Teaching notes**

Words, sentences and questions in italics are items that can be read out to the class. Expected answers follow in brackets.  For example:

'Get students to guess these words:
*this means the same as bullying* (purchasing)
*when you pay someone money for working, you give them this* (salary)', etc.

Words, sentences and questions in *italics* and <u>underlined</u> are items that can be written up on the board. For example:

'If students are unsure of the words, write them in two columns on the board under <u>*adjectives*</u> and <u>*nouns*</u>.
<u>*high*</u>     <u>*height*</u>
<u>*wide*</u>     <u>*width*</u>
<u>*long*</u>     <u>*length*</u>'

**Terminology**

The following terms are used frequently and you may wish to remind students what they mean:

- Scan reading: to read something very quickly to get a general idea of its meaning or to find particular information. It is not necessary to understand every word.
- Skim reading: to read something very quickly to find the main point or particular points. As with scan reading it is not necessary to understand each and every word.
- Listening for gist: to listen to something to get a general idea of what it's about without focusing on specific information or language that's used.
- Brainstorming: to get lots of ideas from a group of students without stopping to evaluate suggestions. The best ideas / suggestions can be discussed after the brainstorming session. It's important to write up all suggestions however unusual they might seem.

**Additional activities**

The photocopiable reading activities can be used for revision, additional reading practice, or to fill out a lesson with a higher-level group.

The photocopiable speaking activities can be used for revision or to fill out a lesson with a higher-level group.

# Corporate culture

**W**hat is corporate culture? There are two answers to this question, one non-academic and one academic. In the non-academic approach, the basic definition of corporate culture is 'the personality of an organization', or simply 'how things are done around here'. It includes:

- core values and beliefs
- corporate ethics
- rules of behaviour.

Corporate culture can be expressed in the company's mission statement and other communications, in the architectural style or interior decoration of offices, by what people wear to work, by how people address each other, and in the titles given to various employees.

Then, there is the academic approach to corporate culture (often called 'organizational culture' in this context). There are many gurus in this field, and perhaps the best known is Geert Hofstede. He has developed a Cultural Orientation Model which classifies cultures based on where they fall on five continuums (highly simplified below):

1 Individual vs. collective
 (At what level in the organization is behaviour regulated?)
2 Power distance
 (Do less powerful parties accept the existing distribution of power?)
3 Uncertainty avoidance
 (Do employees feel threatened by ambiguity? How important are rules?)
4 Dominant values
 (What are the dominant values? Assertiveness? Money? Job satisfaction?)
5 Short-term vs. long-term
 (Do employees expect immediate or deferred gratification?)

Company culture affects employees in many ways. For example:

- the hours you work, including options such as flextime and telecommuting.
- the work environment, including how employees interact, the degree of competition, and whether it's a fun or hostile environment.
- the dress code, including accepted styles of clothing and things such as casual days.
- the office space, including things such as cubicles, window offices, and rules regarding display of personal items.
- training and skills development available to employees.
- onsite perks, such as break rooms, gyms, daycare facilities, etc.
- the amount of time outside the office you're expected to spend with co-workers.
- interaction with other employees, including managers and top management.

Another key issue is whether the company hierarchy is 'tall' (with many layers) or 'flat' (with few layers). This links to the issue of the delegation (or not) of responsibilities.

The importance of corporate culture is growing as the result of several recent developments, some of which are listed below.

- Companies are encouraging employees to be more responsible and act and think like owners.
- With the decline of more traditional communities (e.g. neighbourhoods) companies are filling their employees' need to belong to a community.
- Companies are encouraging teamwork.

For all these reasons, organizations need to make their culture explicit, and it is increasingly referred to in mission statements and emphasized in company-sponsored training and company communications.

Websites with background information on company culture include:
**http://humanresources.about.com/od/organizationalculture**
**http://www.answers.com/topic/organizational-culture**

For individual companies, look for the 'investor relations' button on the company website. Download the annual report and look at the CEO's opening comments.
Job seekers might be interested in how to research a company before an interview. Try sites like this one: **http://interview.monster.com/articles/compculture**

## 1.1 About business
## Work culture and placements

This module focuses on the culture of the workplace and the unwritten rules of behaviour that can be found in every organization.

### Internet research

Students can be asked to do this search before the lesson which will help with the lead-in discussion or after the lesson as a follow-up activity for discussion at the start of the next lesson.

An Internet search of *"work fun"* will reveal references to office parties and outings, celebrating employees' birthdays, competitions or contests in which employees win prizes, etc. However, having fun at work can produce benefits for a company. It can contribute to greater job satisfaction, help to improve productivity and morale, reduce absenteeism, and improve employee retention rates. Other factors that would make employees happier at work might be meaningful and challenging work; good people skills in their managers; a pleasant physical environment; good facilities.

---

**LEAD-IN ACTIVITY**

Ask students to tell you what their ideal workplace would be like. The purpose here is simply to get students thinking about the topic of corporate culture and what it entails. Encourage students to be as imaginative as they can and to talk about a range of topics: physical environment, working hours, managers, meetings, annual leave, physical environment, business travel, etc.

---

### Discussion

**1** Check that students know the meaning of *work placement* (a period of work, usually unpaid, that someone does in order to get experience in the world of work; also known as *work experience*, and in American English as an *internship*).

Ask students to discuss the questions in small groups. Useful words and expressions that may arise from this discussion are:
*to conform* (to follow generally accepted rules)
*to fit in* (to be in harmony with something or someone)
*to step out of line* (to behave in a different way from what is expected)
*to rock the boat* (to do something that causes problems or difficulties).

Take whole-class feedback.

**SUGGESTED ANSWER:**

It depends on company culture. New employees need to try to work out quickly what is expected in each of the three situations and to adjust to the company culture as soon as they can. To start off though, it's probably safest to dress smartly, not be the first or the last to leave the office, maybe make one or two contributions to a meeting, but more importantly to listen and learn at first.

### Scan reading

**2** Ask students to read the first two paragraphs of the article quickly, then to close their books.

Get students to explain what happened in the experiment.

Read aloud the three pieces of information that students have to find in the article. Remind students what *scan reading* is (see page 7).

Students open their books, and read the whole article silently. Help with new vocabulary, if necessary. Remind students to use the *Wordlist* on page 148 in the Student's Book.

Get students to compare their answers with a partner. Take whole-class feedback.

**ANSWERS:**
1   The experiment demonstrated how an unwritten rule is created.
2   Below are seven examples of unwritten rules.
    - Nobody should ever climb the ladder.
    - Working long hours is more important than achieving results.
    - The boss is always right, even when he's wrong.
    - If you're not at your desk, you're not working.
    - Nobody complains, because nothing changes.
    - Women, ethnic minorities and the over 50s are not promoted.
    - The customer is king, but don't tell anyone, because management are more interested in profitability.
3   New staff quickly learn when their ideas and opinions are listened to and valued, and when it's better to keep them to themselves; which assignments and aspects of their performance will be checked and evaluated, and whose objectives and instructions they can safely ignore. They learn from the way staff speak to management, to customers and to each other, and from the differences between what is said, decided or promised, and what actually gets done.

### Discussion

**3** Ask students to keep a list of points made in this discussion as they will be useful for exercise 6. After each question take whole-class feedback.

Question 1: Ask students to look at the unwritten rules they underlined in the article and to think about how companies can avoid them.

**SUGGESTED ANSWER:**

Organizations and companies can try to avoid negative unwritten rules by respecting commitments, giving and listening to feedback, defining and applying clear procedures, providing training to develop a positive work culture.

Question 2: Ask the whole class to describe the kind of work that goes on in each type of organization and to suggest some adjectives to describe them, e.g. a government department (*traditional, hierarchical*), a small public relations firm (*relaxed, informal*), a manufacturing company (*highly-structured, organized*).

**SUGGESTED ANSWER:**

A government department:
- Office etiquette: formal dress code, strict office hours, inflexible, subject to security constraints.
- Relationships with colleagues, management and clients / business partners: hierarchical and formalized.
- Autonomy and initiative: limited, strict procedures for everything.
A small public relations firm:
- Office etiquette: probably very informal, relaxed, flexible, results-orientated rather than time-conscious.
- Relationships with colleagues, management and clients / business partners: friendly and participative, little or no visible hierarchy.
- Autonomy and initiative: wide, but must be justified.
A manufacturing company:
- Answers will depend on national and corporate culture.

Question 3: Students' answers will vary, but aim to draw out the reasons for their answers.

---

### EXTENSION ACTIVITY

Ask students to compare the three types of organization in exercise 3 with their own companies or organizations or ones they know. Encourage them to mention the topics listed in exercise 3.

---

## Listening for gist

 **4** 1:01, 1:02 Remind students that they are listening for gist (see page 7). Get students to compare their answers with a partner after listening. Check answers with the whole class.

**ANSWERS:**

1 Alessandra was not accepted by her colleagues. David upset an intern.
2 Alessandra misunderstood the (unwritten) office rules on working hours. David assumed Monica would know to inform him she had a dentist's appointment, but she didn't; Monica misinterpreted David's friendliness as changing the supervisor–intern relationship.

---

### RECORDING SCRIPT

 1:01

I got my first placement in a PR firm in Paris, which I was pleased about, 'cos I'm really interested in communication and image management. We'd been well prepared, and our teachers had warned us about dress code, being on time, respecting our commitments … you know, all the usual things. But I had a problem I really wasn't expecting.

The first day, I arrived at 8.30 and I was a bit surprised because I had to wait an hour and a half for my supervisor to turn up. In fact, most people seemed to get in at about 11 o'clock – and by the time they'd had their coffee and read their mail, and so on, they didn't really start work much before 12. But everybody was very relaxed and very friendly. My supervisor gave me a project to work on and told me to be autonomous and take initiative, you know, which I enjoy. So, I thought, great, I can really do a good job here and, you know, make a really good impression.

Anyway, for the first two weeks I worked from nine in the morning to about seven in the evening. I didn't really talk to other people very much, because when they arrived I was already working, and when I stopped for lunch, they were all busy. My boyfriend wasn't very happy about me getting home late, but, like I said, I wanted to impress the company, and I've never been afraid of hard work. But then, after the first couple of weeks, people seemed to be less friendly than when I started. I couldn't understand why they were giving me these funny looks, especially when I went home in the evening. Anyway, in the end, I went and asked my supervisor what I'd done wrong. And it turned out that it wasn't the done thing to go home until 11 or midnight – and, because I left at about seven, I was breaking the unwritten rules. They all thought I was just some lazy student skiving off work! I mean, I knew I was the first to leave, but I'd been there since 9am, and I was working really hard, you know?! But as far as they were concerned, you couldn't do any work before 12, so being in the office from nine in the morning didn't count!

 1:02

I'm a department manager in the civil service. My office is just a few minutes' walk from the Houses of Parliament. Contrary to what you might think, we're actually very informal and friendly in the department – we're all quite young and everyone's on first name terms. We all have lunch together in the canteen and we'll often go to the pub for a drink together after work. We have one or two interns per year and we try to make them feel

at home and part of the team, and usually it's fine.

But, a year or two ago, I had a problem with a student I was supervising. At first, everything was fine. She was very bright and friendly, and immediately got on well with everybody. For example, the whole department was invited to her birthday party. But then, one day we had a bit of a crisis in the office. We'd got behind schedule on one particular project, which Monica, the intern, was working on, and my manager wanted a report for a meeting at 10am. Of course, Monica was the only person who knew where the file was – only that day she didn't arrive at the office until 10.15. In fact, she'd been to the dentist's, but she hadn't told me that she'd be late. Well, as you can imagine, I was pretty stressed out and I made it very clear that this was unacceptable. I suppose I sounded angrier than I really was. And Monica just burst into tears, so I had to tell her that, you know, that was unprofessional too.

Anyway, after that, things were never the same. She became very quiet and reserved and stopped socializing with the rest of the team. She wouldn't say anything in meetings and she didn't even eat in the canteen with us any more. Obviously, her work suffered and I don't think she enjoyed the placement. I tried to explain that I was her boss and that it was my job to tell her when there was a problem, but that it wasn't personal and it didn't mean we couldn't be friendly. But she didn't seem able to accept that. For her, a boss was a boss, and a friend was a friend, and you couldn't be a boss and a friend.

## Listening for detail

**5** Play 1:01 and 1:02 again. Pause the recording at appropriate places and ask students to use their own words to describe the mistakes each student and supervisor made.

**ANSWERS:**

Students' mistakes:
Alessandra's story: didn't ask about / was not sensitive to unwritten rules; didn't talk to colleagues
David's story: took friendly culture at face value; didn't accept criticism; didn't learn from the problem
Supervisors' mistakes:
Alessandra's story: didn't tell student about unwritten rules; gave student too much autonomy; didn't make sure student met colleagues
David's story: didn't explain local work culture; didn't keep enough distance from intern; didn't understand the intern's confusion

---

### EXTENSION ACTIVITY

Ask students to work in small groups and describe any experiences they have had themselves as an intern or as a supervisor. They should explain what happened and what mistakes were made. Each group then chooses one story to share with the whole class.

---

## Brainstorming and presentation

**6** Remind students what brainstorming is (see page 7). Students could use the ideas they noted down in exercise 3 to help them write the guidelines.

## 1.2 Vocabulary

## Work organization and responsibility

This module focuses on the vocabulary of organizational structure, roles and responsibilities, and employment.

### Internet research

Some possible results for this search might be: CIO (Chief Information Officer), CMO (Chief Medical Officer), COPE (Chief Officer for Planning and Environment), CTO (Chief Technology Officer), CSO (Chief Security Officer), CCO (Chief Compliance Officer – responsible for ensuring that a company and its employees are in compliance with government regulations and internal policies), CNO (Chief Nursing Officer), CPO (Chief Police Officer), CFO (Chief Fire Officer).

Students could do a search under *"Chief x-Officer"*. CXO is now frequently used as a generic term covering all Chief 'Something' Officers (x = something). Students may come across some humorous examples, such as:
CCO (Chief Chocolate Officer), CIO (Chief Intimidation Officer) and CXO (Chief Xeroxing Officer).

## Discussion

**1** Ask some students to read the words aloud and check pronunciation. Explain any new vocabulary, e.g. *subsidiary* (owned or controlled by another company) or allow students to use their dictionaries. Some answers may vary, especially in 2.

Check answers with the whole class.

> **SUGGESTED ANSWERS:**
> 1 foreman, supervisor, project leader, line manager, director (by hierarchical status)
> 2 section, department, office, branch, unit, subsidiary, division, company (by size)
> 3 task, job, assignment, project (by importance)

## Listening for detail

**2** 1:03 Ask students why organigrams are useful. In this context, it helps an intern to get a clear picture of the structure of the organization and where responsibilities lie. In other contexts, if the organigram is from a customer's company, it can help you identify contacts; if it is from a competitor, it can help you understand how they run their business.

Give students a few minutes to look at the organigram. Get them to try to predict the words that are needed to complete it.

Remind students that they are only listening for departments and job titles. Play the recording again if necessary. Check answers with the whole class.

> **ANSWERS:**
> David Darren = <u>COO</u>
> Administration: Monica Overstreet = <u>Office</u> Manager + two <u>accountants</u>
> Marketing and Sales: Bertram Newman = <u>Marketing and Sales</u> Manager + one art director, one <u>PR</u> officer and two salesmen
> R&D: Douglas Pearson = R&D Manager + seven <u>research scientists</u>
> Engineering: Herb Munroe = Program Manager + two software engineers and one <u>technical writer</u>
> IT and Technical Support: Roxane Pawle = IT Manager + one <u>web</u> <u>developer</u> and two <u>support engineers</u>

## RECORDING SCRIPT

 1:03

A: All right, Samantha, welcome to San Antonio. Now, I just want to give you an overview of the company and who does what, so you know who to ask when you need information, OK?

B: OK, Mr Newman.

A: And please call me Bertram, Samantha – we're very informal here in Texas.

B: All right, Mr New- er, Bertram. And, er, everyone calls me Sam.

A: Right, Sam. Now, as you know, my role is to manage Marketing and Sales; you'll be working with Jake, our Art Director, and Saidah, who's our PR Officer, but you're going to report directly to me. I'll introduce you to Saidah and Jake in a few minutes.

B: All right.

A: As I told you, we're a small company, so the organization is simple for the moment, but we're growing fast, so that's going to change as we hire new staff. For example, right now we don't have an HR department as such – Monica Overstreet, our Office Manager, takes care of personnel, so she's the person to see if you have any administrative questions.

B: Yes, I met Ms Overstreet last time I was here.

A: That's right. She also looks after finance, and she has two Accountants working under her. Now then, as you probably know, Warndar Technologies was founded by Merilyn Warner, our CEO, and David Darren, who's now COO.

B: COO?

A: Yuh. Chief Operating Officer. Basically, David runs the business on a day-to-day basis. Merilyn deals with strategy, and she's on the board of our parent company, so she's often away in Houston.

B: Uh-huh – and Warndar is a subsidiary of the Irysis group, right?

A: That's right. They took us over a couple of years ago. Anyway, as well as Monica and myself, there are three other department heads who all report to David. The woman we met just now in the corridor is Roxane Pawle. Roxane is in charge of IT and Technical Support. She's new – she joined six months ago when our old IT Manager resigned. He was appointed Head of IT at one of the big consultancy firms up in Washington. Nice job, but too much stress. They fired him after three months. He's working as a bar tender now!

B: Wow!

A: Yeah. Glad you chose marketing, eh? It's dog eat dog in IT. Anyway, Roxane has a web developer and two support engineers reporting to her. OK? Now, the biggest department here is R&D. We have seven research scientists in the lab, plus Doug Pearson who coordinates our development programmes. He liaises with me in Marketing and with our Program Manager, Herb Monroe. Herb manages the Engineering Department, and he's responsible for building our product package – CD-ROMs, user manuals, and so on. Herb has a team of three: two software engineers and a technical writer.

B: OK.

A: All right, I think that's everyone. Unless you have any questions, we'll go and meet Saidah and Jake. Oh, and I think David wants to see you in his office … don't look so worried … he's not going to fire you on your first day!

**3** Ask students to read the questions before they listen to 1:03 again. With lower-level classes, you could pause the recording at appropriate places to allow students to answer the questions one by one.

**ANSWERS:**

1 Because Warndar is a small company.
2 Because Warndar is growing fast, so it's going to change as they hire new staff.
3 Because right now they don't have an HR department as such.
4 The COO runs the business on a day-to-day basis. The CEO deals with strategy and she's on the board of the parent company.
5 Irysis is Warndar's parent company. They took Warndar over a couple of years ago.
6 He resigned when he was appointed Head of IT at a big consultancy firm, but was fired after three months.
7 Research and Development, Engineering, and Marketing.
8 Doug Pearson coordinates development programmes; he liaises with Marketing and Engineering.

**4** Set a time limit for students to do the exercise, then ask them to check their answers with a partner. Make a list of the key words and phrases on the board: *report to, look after, work under, run (something) on, deal with, take care of, responsible for, in charge of, my role is to …, liaise with*.

**ANSWERS:**

| | | | | |
|---|---|---|---|---|
| 1 c) | 2 e) | 3 d) | 4 a) | 5 b) |
| 6 i) | 7 h) | 8 j) | 9 f) | 10 g) |

**FURTHER PRACTICE 1**

Working with a partner, students take turns to make true / false statements about the organigram in exercise 2, using the words and phrases they have practised, e.g.:
*Herb Monroe is responsible for two software engineers.* (True) *Monica Overstreet is in charge of two salesmen.* (False) This could also be done in small groups or as a whole-class activity.

**FURTHER PRACTICE 2**

Prepare some sentences about the organigram using the words and phrases in exercise 4. Read them aloud or write them on the board and ask students to correct them, e.g.:
*Three accountants report to the Office Manager.* (Two, not three accountants report to the Office Manager.)
*The R&D Manager manages seven technical writers.* (He manages seven research scientists, not seven technical writers.)
*The IT Manager is in charge of one support engineer…,* etc.

Students could also prepare their own sentences.

## Prepositions

**5** This exercise focuses on the use of various prepositions with *to work*. When students have completed the exercise, these phrases can be added to the list compiled in exercise 4. Students can then refer to this list when they are doing exercise 6.

**ANSWERS:**

| | | | | | |
|---|---|---|---|---|---|
| 1 alongside | 2 under | 3 as | 4 at | 5 in | 6 on |

**EXTENSION ACTIVITY**

To personalize the activity in exercise 5, ask students to make sentences about their own company or job (or a company or job they know), using words and phrases from exercises 1–5, e.g.:
*I report to the Product Development Manager. My role is to research new products for the over-50s market.*
Or: *My sister is a research scientist. She is in charge of a project team with five engineers working under her. She reports to the R&D manager.*
Students could also bring in organigrams for their own companies or companies they know for comparison and discussion.

## Discussion and presentation

**6** To introduce the topic, ask if any students have ever had music lessons at a music school. If any have, get the other students to ask questions about the music school. If not, ask students to brainstorm (see page 7) what they think a music school might be like and what might happen there, e.g. they provide lessons in singing and playing instruments; you can get qualifications in music; they put on concerts, etc.

Check that students know the vocabulary in the box. Explain or give examples, if necessary.

**7** Circulate while students are speaking. Without interrupting the activity, make a list of any mistakes in the target language for remedial work later. For example, note down the exact words that were used wrongly and write them on the board, but without identifying the student who said them. Get the class to correct the mistakes.

When students have finished their presentations, display the organigrams on a table or wall so that students can see the similarities and differences. Get students to explain why they chose the structure they did.

## Defining words

**8** This crossword activity focuses on the vocabulary of employment: *demotion, transfer, fire, hire, dismiss, promotion, retire, join, resign, appoint.*

With lower-level classes, you could model one or two simple ways of defining words, perhaps by using some words from exercise 7, and get them to guess the word:
*this means the same as buying* (purchasing)
*when you pay someone money for working you give them this* (salary), etc.

**EXTENSION ACTIVITY**

When students have completed and checked their answers, focus on the meaning and use of these words. For example, ask students the following questions:
*Which pairs of words have the same or similar meanings?*
(hire, appoint; fire, dismiss; resign, join)
*Which pairs of words have opposite meanings?*
(promotion, demotion; hire, fire)
*What's the difference between resign and transfer?*
(*resign* – you leave the company completely; *transfer* – you move to another department or branch)
*What's the difference between resign and fire?*
(*resign* – it is your choice to leave the company; *fire* – you are forced to leave the company)
*What's the difference between resign and join?*
(*resign* – you leave a job; *join* – you start a job)
*What's the difference between appoint and retire?*
(*appoint* – you employ someone; *retire* – an employee leaves a job at the end of their working life, usually at 60 or 65 years old)

# 1.3 Grammar

## Past tenses and advice structures

This module focuses on the use of the past simple, past continuous and past perfect. It also introduces a set of advice structures. Students use this language to tell stories and give advice.

### Internet research

An Internet search will reveal that present tenses are commonly used to tell jokes. This helps to give the joke immediacy. This search can be done before the lesson and used as a lead in to exercise 5.

## Test yourself: Past tenses

**1** Start by reading the *Refresh your memory box* with students. If students seem unsure of the difference between the three tenses, work through exercises 1 and 2 in the *Grammar and practice* section (page 118 in the Student's Book, answers on page 116 in this book) with them.

Before they complete the anecdote, check that students know the meaning of:
*predecessor* (a person who had your job or position before you)
*successor* (the opposite of the person who has your job or position after you)
*to despair* (to lose hope).

Ask students to work alone, and then compare their answers with a partner. Take whole-class feedback. Elicit from students or explain why each answer is correct.

**ANSWERS:**

| | | |
|---|---|---|
| 1 told | 2 had fallen | 3 was beginning / had begun |
| 4 had given | 5 called | 6 had improved 7 had learnt |
| 8 had closed | 9 were rising | 10 closed |

### FURTHER PRACTICE

To focus on the meaning of the text and consolidate the use of the three past tenses, ask students the following questions (the answers are given in brackets):
*What was the first thing to go wrong?* (Sales fell by 10%.)
*How did the CEO feel?* (He began to despair.)
Ask students to complete this sentence:
*The CEO called a press conference after he ...* (had read / had opened the first envelope / read the first message).
Note that the past simple would also be possible here.
*What was the second thing to go wrong?* (The company had serious production problems.)
Ask students to complete this sentence:
*After the CEO had read the second message, he ...* (reorganized the company).
*What was the third thing to go wrong?* (Costs rose.)
Ask students to complete this sentence:
*Before he opened the third envelope, the CEO ... (had gone to his office and had closed the door)*. Note that the past simple would also be possible here.

For further practice of past tenses, get students to do exercises 3–7 in the *Grammar and practice* section (page 118 in the Student's Book, answers on page 116 in this book).

## Test yourself: Advice structures

**2** Ask students to complete the sentences with a partner. Check answers with the whole class.

**ANSWERS:**

| | | | | | |
|---|---|---|---|---|---|
| 1 ask | 2 asking | 3 asking | 4 to ask | 5 asking | 6 ask |
| 7 to ask | 8 ask | 9 to ask | 10 to ask | 11 asking | |
| 12 to ask | | | | | |

### EXTENSION ACTIVITY

Get students to group the advice structures under these three headings:
infinitive without *to* (*you should ..., you could ..., why don't you ...*)
infinitive with *to* (*it's a good idea ..., it's wise ..., you ought ..., you might want ... it's important ...*)
*-ing* form (*have you considered ..., how about ..., have you thought of ..., have you tried ...*)

Working with a partner, students decide which phrases are strong recommendations and which phrases are careful or friendly suggestions. Check answers with the whole class.

**ANSWERS:**

Strong recommendations: 1, 4, 7, 9, 12
Careful or friendly suggestions: 2, 3, 5, 6, 8, 10, 11

### EXTENSION ACTIVITY

Ask students to discuss other situations when they might use strong recommendations (e.g. with a subordinate) and when they might use careful or friendly suggestions (e.g. with a colleague or a boss). Ask them to think of examples, e.g.:
*You ought to get to work on time.* (to a subordinate)
*You might want to ask the other managers what they are doing about this problem.* (to a boss)

## Listening for detail

**3** 🔊 1:04 Check that students know the meaning of *CFO* (Chief Financial Officer). Ask the students to listen to the whole story once and answer the question: *Why did the CFO jump in?* (He didn't jump in, he was pushed in.)
Then ask individual students to read the sentences aloud. Check pronunciation and explain any new vocabulary, e.g. *to do very well for yourself* (to be successful). The meaning of *crocodiles* will be clear from the photograph!

Play the recording and get students to identify the event that happened first in each pair of sentences. For lower-level classes, you could pause the recording at appropriate moments to allow them to answer the questions one by one. Check answers with the whole class.

**ANSWERS:**

1 The CEO did very well for himself.
2 He showed the executives the pool.
3 Everyone followed the CEO to the barbecue.
4 The CFO swam for his life.
5 The crocodiles tried to catch him.
6 The CFO climbed out of the pool.

## RECORDING SCRIPT

🔊 1:04

Do you know the one about the CFO and the crocodiles? Well, there was this CEO, who was giving a party for his executive team. Over the years, the boss had done very well for himself, so he was proudly showing the executives around his luxurious country house. Anyway, at the back of the house, he had built the largest swimming pool any of them had ever seen. Absolutely huge, you know? But the pool was full of very hungry crocodiles. So, the CEO said to his executives, 'The most important quality for an executive is courage. Without it, you will never become a CEO like me. So, this is my challenge to each of you: if anyone can dive into the pool, swim through those crocodiles and reach the other side, I will give them anything they want. My job, my money, my house, anything!' Well, of course, everyone laughed at the challenge and nobody took it very seriously. Anyway, they had just started to follow the CEO towards the barbecue when suddenly there was a loud splash. Everyone turned around and ran back to the pool where the Chief Financial Officer was swimming for his life. The crocodiles had almost caught him when he reached the edge of the pool. He had just managed to climb out of the pool when he heard the mouth of the biggest crocodile close shut – snap – behind him. Well, the CEO shook the CFO's hand and said, 'I'm really impressed. Until you dived into that pool, I never imagined you had such courage. You accepted my challenge and now anything I own is yours. Tell me what I can do for you.' The CFO was still recovering from the swim. He looked up at the CEO and said, 'You can start by telling me who the hell pushed me into the pool!'

**4** Ask students to try to complete the sentences with a partner. Remind them that they should choose one of the past tenses practised in this module – the past simple, the past continuous, or the past perfect.

Play 🔊 1:04 again, pausing after each sentence to allow students time to check or write in their answers. Check answers by getting students to read the completed sentences aloud.

**ANSWERS:**

1  had done; was proudly showing
2  had built
3  had just started; was
4  turned around; ran back; was swimming
5  had almost caught; reached
6  had / 'd just managed; heard

## Telling a story

**5** Before students do this activity, you could work through exercises 8–12 in the *Grammar and practice* section (page 118 in the Student's Book, answers on page 116 in this book). This will provide students with some useful phrases to use when they are telling their stories.

Give students a few minutes to work out the sequence of their stories. Circulate and assist with pronunciation or any new vocabulary, or allow students to consult their dictionaries.

While students are exchanging stories, circulate and monitor. Listen for correct use of the past tenses and make a list of any common mistakes for remedial teaching at a later stage.

**ANSWERS:**

**Student A:**

1 c) Two engineers had recently been promoted, so they decided to celebrate with a flight in a balloon.
2 e) After a while the wind became stronger and the balloon went out of control.
3 d) By the time they had managed to regain control, they realized they were lost.
4 i) A man was walking along the road below them so they called down to him:
5 b) 'Excuse me, sir, we're lost. Can you tell us where we are?'
6 h) After he had thought for a while the man looked down, looked up again and then shouted:
7 a) 'You're in a balloon!' and walked away down the road.
8 g) As the man was walking away, one engineer said to the other: 'That man must be a manager.'
9 j) 'Why?' asked the other engineer.
10 f) 'Three reasons. First he took a long time to answer. Second, he was perfectly correct. Third, his answer was perfectly useless!'

**Student B:**

1 c) A young business student was interviewing a rich old businessman, and asked how he had made his money.
2 d) The old guy replied, 'Well son, times were hard, and I had spent everything except my last nickel.'
3 a) 'I invested that nickel in an apple, and I started to polish it.'
4 b) 'When I had polished that apple all day, I sold it for ten cents.'
5 h) 'The next day, after I had invested those ten cents in two apples, I spent the entire day polishing them and sold them at five o'clock for 20 cents.'
6 g) 'I continued this system for a month by the end of which I'd accumulated a fortune of $1.37.'
7 e) 'And that's how you built an empire?' the boy asked.
8 f) 'Heavens, no!' the man replied. 'Then my wife's father died and left us two million dollars.'

## Giving advice

**6** Ask students to match the sentences halves individually. Then get them to read aloud the correct, complete sentences.

**ANSWERS:**

| 1 b) | 2 d) | 3 e) | 4 c) | 5 a) |
|------|------|------|------|------|
| 6 g) | 7 i) or h) | 8 j) | 9 f) | 10 h) or i) |

### FURTHER PRACTICE

Working with a partner, get students to add one or two extra pieces of advice for new employees, perhaps referring back to earlier parts of the module, e.g.:
*You should be punctual.*
*It's important to adapt to the culture of the company.*
*You ought to ask permission if you need to go to the doctor or dentist in working hours.*
*It's a good idea to be professional at all times.*

**7** Give students a few minutes to read their roleplay notes. Help with any new vocabulary, e.g. Student A, *black looks* (expressions of anger or disapproval); Student B, *sombre* (serious). Tell students not to read the sentences aloud, but to put the situation into their own words. Ask students to add ideas of their own to make it more interesting.

Circulate while students are speaking and assist if necessary. Make a note of any mistakes you hear for remedial work at a later stage.

For further practice of advice structures, get students to do exercises 13–16 in the *Grammar and practice* section (page 119 in the Student's Book, answers on page 116 in this book).

## 1.4 Speaking

### Meetings – one-to-one

This module focuses on the ways of using diplomatic language to deal with difficult meetings.

### Internet research

A search for the key words "*learn English*" will generate a wide range of possible resources for learning English. You could ask students to investigate one or two of them, and report back to the class on their usefulness. This search task can be done at any point: during, before or after this module.

### Discussion

**1** The questionnaire focuses on personal relationships and behaviour at work. Read through the statements with students before they answer them.

#### SUGGESTED ANSWERS:

Answers depend on local and work cultures.
1  In most English-speaking cultures, this is the norm, with the notable exception of Africa, where superiors, and frequently peers, are addressed by their surname. Use of the first name is also unusual in much of Asia, and in Germany.
2  Some cultures, like France, make a clear distinction between business and personal life. Others, like the Swedish furniture company Ikea, organize regular social events where all levels of staff are expected to mix freely.
3  In most Latin cultures, managers will expect subordinates to perform tasks like making coffee. Some staff in Nordic cultures may be shocked and even insulted by such a request.
4  This usually depends more on the type of work involved than on local or work culture. Personal calls for staff in production may be very unwelcome, whereas in departments like sales or marketing there is usually no particular problem.
5  This is the case in many English-speaking and Nordic cultures, especially in the USA. In Latin and Asian countries, the opposite is often true, with a certain kudos or even machismo associated with working late.
6  This probably depends on the organization as much as on the culture: in large scientific meetings, for example, the majority of attendees will not be expected to speak.
7  Some organizations welcome and even encourage junior staff to suggest improvements; this is usually less well accepted in smaller companies, where the management feel more personally involved and responsible for the way things are done.
8  Some companies have a policy of not hiring couples and will more or less actively dissuade staff from entering romantic relationships. Other companies accept that relationships will occur, but when they do, will move the partners to separate parts of the organization. In extreme cases, one member of the couple may be asked to resign.

### Listening for detail

**2**  1:05 and 1:06  Check that students understand the adjectives. Remind them to use the *Wordlist* on page 148 in their books or explain any unfamiliar vocabulary, e.g.:
*diplomatic* (being skilful or tactful)
*frank* (honest, direct).
You could also get students to pick out the adjectives with negative connotations, e.g.: *impatient, dogmatic, threatening, insincere, weak*.

Remind students that they should listen not only to what Simon says, but also how he says it. Play both versions of the conversation. Get students to compare their initial impressions about Simon's behaviour with a partner and then play the recording again.

#### ANSWERS:

Version 1: impatient, firm, authoritarian, threatening, frank and possibly objective and dogmatic
Version 2: objective, a good listener, diplomatic, friendly, understanding, insincere and possibly weak

### RECORDING SCRIPT

🔊 1:05
Version 1
A: Morning, Tifany. Good weekend?
B: Oh, yes, it was cool. And you?
A: No, not really. Listen, Tifany, come into my office, I need to talk to you.
B: Oh no, what now?
A: Look, I hear you had a problem with Maureen on Friday.
B: Oh that. Yeah. That idiot refused to help me! Who does she think she is?!
A: You mustn't talk about your colleagues like that. Maureen is a very experienced assistant and a valuable member of the team.
B: Maybe, but she still refused to help me.
A: Yes, but she had a good reason to refuse. Maureen was very busy on Friday and you didn't ask for help: you demanded her immediate attention. As a future manager, you should show respect to all the staff.
B: But I was just trying to finish the job.
A: Well, you won't get results from people like Maureen if you're rude.
B: Look, I was tired. I had a difficult week, OK?
A: Tifany, everyone gets tired, and I'm getting tired of your attitude. You apologize, or there'll be trouble. Do you understand?
B: Me? Apologize to some stupid little secretary? No way!

🔊 1:06
Version 2
A: Morning, Tifany. Good weekend?
B: Oh yes, it was cool and you?
A: Yeah I had a good weekend too – apart from having to finish off this report. How about you? What did you do?
B: I went to the swimming pool yesterday. Gorgeous weather.
A: Mm, sounds good. Er, Tiffany, have you got a minute?
B: Sure.
A: Come in. I just wanted to have a quick word. I hear you had a problem with Maureen on Friday.
B: Oh that. Yeah. That idiot refused to help me! Who does she think she is?!
A: Well, Tifany, I think perhaps you should be more careful about how you talk about your colleagues. Maureen is a very experienced assistant and a valuable member of the team.
B: OK, but she still refused to help me.
A: Well, you might want to think about why she couldn't help you. Maureen was very busy on Friday, and I understand you didn't really ask for help so much as demand her immediate attention. We try hard to respect all our staff here. As a future manager, I think you ought to do the same.
B: But I was just trying to finish the job.
A: Well, I understand that, and I appreciate that you work hard and that you expect other people to show the same commitment. But, don't you think you might get better results from people like Maureen by being a little more diplomatic?
B: Yeah, OK. I'm sorry, you're right. I was tired. I didn't mean to be rude.

A: OK. It can happen to anyone. Why don't you ask Maureen to have a coffee with you, and just clear the air? OK?

B: OK. Thanks, Simon.

**3** Elicit from students the main differences between Simon's language in the two versions of the conversation. Point out that the tone of voice he uses is also different. In Version 1 it sounds abrupt and slightly aggressive; in Version 2 it is firm but not aggressive.

**ANSWER:**

In Version 1, Simon's language is direct, with short, simple sentences; in Version 2, it is diplomatic, with longer, more complex phrases.

**4** This exercise focuses on specific examples of Simon's language in the two versions of the conversation. Ask students to try to complete the sentences before they listen. Then play 🔊 1:05 and 1:06 again.

When they have completed the sentences correctly, get students to practise saying them to a partner using the appropriate intonation.

**ANSWERS:**

Version 1:
1  You mustn't talk about your colleagues like that.
2  Yes, but she had a good reason to refuse.
3  You won't get results from people like Maureen if you're rude.
4  You apologize, or there'll be trouble.

Version 2:
1  I think perhaps you should be more careful about how you talk about your colleagues.
2  You might want to think about why she couldn't help you.
3  Don't you think you might get better results from people like Maureen by being a little more diplomatic?
4  Why don't you ask Maureen to have a coffee with you, and just clear the air?

To draw attention to the effects of these two different approaches, ask students how Tifany's response to Simon at the end of Version 2 differed from her response at the end of Version 1. (At the end of Version 1 she was angry and confrontational; at the end of Version 2 she apologized for her behaviour.)

## Diplomatic advice

**5** Before they do this exercise, ask students to give you examples from Version 2 of:

modal verbs (*might, should, ought*)

introductory phrases (*Have you got a minute?*; *I just wanted to have a quick word ...*, *I think perhaps ...*; *I understand that, but ...*)

negative questions: (*But don't you think ...?*; *Why don't you ...?*)

To do this, students could refer to exercise 4, listen to 🔊 1:06 again, or read the recording script at the back of the Student's Book.

Then, ask students to add the phrases to the correct category in the table.

**ANSWER:**

Modals *would*, *could* and *might*:
  You might want to ...
  Wouldn't you agree that ...?
  You could maybe ...
  Wouldn't it be better to ...?
  You'd do better to ...

Introductory phrases:
  I think perhaps ...
  It seems to me that ...
  Actually, I think ...
  You could maybe ...

Negative questions:
  Don't you think ...?
  Wouldn't you agree that ...?
  Wouldn't it be better to ...?
  Why don't you ...?

**6** Students could work with a partner to make these comments more diplomatic. Point out that more than one answer is possible and encourage them to try two or three options in each case.

When they have finished, ask students to read their revised comments aloud, paying attention to intonation.

**SUGGESTED ANSWERS:**

1  Wouldn't it be better not to disturb your co-workers?
2  It seems to me that you need to prioritize if you want to meet deadlines.
3  You might want to delegate more if you want to finish the job.
4  I think perhaps you shouldn't eat at your desk.
5  You'd do better not to make personal calls at work.
6  Actually, I think if you ignore your colleagues, you can't expect them to help.
7  Wouldn't you agree that you should take care of your life-work balance if you don't want to get ill?

**FURTHER PRACTICE**

Give students a few more prompts and get them to create diplomatic statements, e.g.:
*Don't take three-hour lunch breaks.*
*You shouldn't arrive late every morning.*
*You won't make a good impression if you fall asleep at meetings.*
*If you work too hard, you'll get stressed.*

## Pronunciation

**7** Get students to underline the stressed keywords or syllables and then practice saying the sentences with the correct stress.

**ANSWERS:**

1  I hear you had a problem.
2  Perhaps you should be more careful.
3  You ought to do the same.
4  I appreciate that you work hard.
5  I didn't mean to be rude.
6  It can happen to anyone

**8** 🔊 1:07  Play the recording so that students can check their answers. Circulate while students are practising the sentences to check that they are putting the stress in the correct places.

## RECORDING SCRIPT

🎧 1:07

1  I hear you had a problem.
2  Perhaps you should be more careful.
3  You ought to do the same.
4  I appreciate that you work hard.
5  I didn't mean to be rude.
6  It can happen to anyone.

**9** Read the instructions aloud and get students to repeat the examples in italics. Play 🎧 1:07 again. First students should just listen for the regular rhythm; then play the recording again and get students to repeat the sentences as they listen.

### FURTHER PRACTICE

Get students to close their books and repeat each sentence after you, paying attention to the appropriate stress and rhythm.

### EXTENSION ACTIVITY

Get students to put the sentences in exercise 7 into the context of a short conversation. They do this by adding one or more sentences before or after the sentence, e.g.:
Sentence 3
A: *My team leader leaves at 3.30pm on Fridays.*
B: *You ought to do the same!*
Sentence 5
A: *I think I've upset Susie, but I didn't mean to be rude.*
B: *Why don't you explain the situation? I'm sure she'll understand.*

Students work with a partner to prepare the conversations and then present them to the class. Remind them to pay particular attention to stress and rhythm.

## Roleplay

**10** These roleplays review the language practised in this module and allow students the opportunity to develop their own skills in problem-solving.

Remind students to use the diplomatic language they practised in exercises 5–9.

Discuss the best kind of directive language to use, if they feel it is necessary. This is more likely to be the advice structures practised in module 1.3, exercises 2 and 6, than the language used by Simon in exercises 2–4. Remind students of the phrases they learnt to express strong recommendations, i.e. *you should ..., it's wise to ..., you ought to ..., it's important to ....*

Give students time to read roleplay 1 and think about what they want to say. Tell them to put the situation into their own words, adding ideas of their own to make it more interesting.

While students are speaking, circulate and assist where necessary. Make a note of any common mistakes in the target language for remedial teaching at a later stage.

When students have finished, choose or ask one or two pairs to present their roleplay to the class. Write these two headings on the board:
*Things I liked:*
*Things that could be improved:*
While the rest of the class is listening to the roleplay, they should make notes under these headings for a feedback discussion at the end.

Ask students to work with a new partner to do roleplay 2. Repeat the procedure.

## 1.5 Writing
## A placement report

This module focuses on writing reports and the language and style used in them.

**Internet research**

An Internet search for *find internships* will generate a wide range of websites which will undertake to match applicants to meaningful work placements. Internships are available in a number of industries, including retail, finance, banking, etc. The websites also offer guidance on how to make a successful application.

### Discussion

**1** Elicit ideas from students about what Henry's placement report might contain and the style it might be written in. Don't worry at this stage if the ideas are incomplete – the exercises that follow will draw out the important points that need to be made.

**SUGGESTED ANSWER:**
It will contain information about his work experience, colleagues and managers, the company, the department(s) he worked in and what he learned while he was at the company. It will be written in a formal style.

### Skim reading

**2** Ask students to cover the report extracts and just read the section headings. Ask them what kind of things they would expect to find in each section. Suggested answers in brackets.

*Observations about the company* (details about the company and the department he worked in); *Appendix* (extra information which may be of interest, but is not required in the main body of the report); *Introduction* (some background information answering some or all of the questions *who, what, when, why, how*); *Professional* achievements (the skills and experience he gained); *Experience during work placement* (the tasks Henry performed).

Remind students what skim reading is (see page 7). Get them to skim the report and do the matching task with a partner. Check answers with the whole class.

**ANSWERS:**
[3] Observations about the company
[5] Appendix
[1] Introduction
[4] Professional achievements
[2] Experience from work placement

### Reading for detail

**3** Students to work with a partner. Check answers with the whole class. Get students to explain the reasons for their choices.

**ANSWERS:**
[4] Conclusions
[2] Analysis of successes and failures
[1] Objectives of the internship
[2] Details of your responsibilities
[4] Analysis of what you learned
[3] Evaluation of the company as a potential employer
[4] Suggestions for the future
[1] Description of the company and how it is organized
[1] Practical details about the placement
[3] Description of the company's culture and policies

**4** You could do this as a whole-class activity, getting students to call out the formal phrases in the report as they find them.

**ANSWERS:**
1. under the supervision of Mr Geoffrey Thomson
2. customers were contacted by telephone
3. it became clear that
4. The order of the items was therefore modified …
5. To obtain a similar result through media campaigns would cost millions.
6. most impressive
7. was a major challenge.
8. Fortunately, I was able to apply the knowledge I had acquired in marketing in year two of my degree …
9. the results of my study were extremely well received

### EXTENSION ACTIVITY

Get students to work in small groups to summarize some key differences between the informal language of the phrases in exercise 4 and the formal language of the corresponding phrases in the report in exercise 2.
In formal language:
- colloquial words and phrases are not used, e.g. *guy, cool, worth a fortune*
- passive tenses are used more often, e.g. *were contacted, was modified, were well received*
- sentences are longer and more complex
- things are expressed in a positive way, e.g. *a major challenge* not *difficult and exhausting*
- exclamation marks are not used.

## Listening and note-taking

**5**  1:08 Ask students what things they think Jason might tell Alex about his placement. Use the headings in exercise 2 as prompts. Students listen and take notes individually, then compare their notes with a partner. Play the recording two or three times, if necessary.

Make sure students keep these notes for use in exercise 6. Check answers with the whole class.

**SUGGESTED ANSWERS:**
- three months near Birmingham at a place called Diftco – they export construction equipment
- It was all right
- a bit crazy there – people worked really hard, sometimes from eight in the morning to nine or ten in the evening
- in charge of preparing shipping documents
- did international trade last semester – it helped a lot to understand what was going on
- boss very strict but, OK – she didn't scream at me when I did something wrong.
- once sent a container to Austria instead of Australia
- really strong accent – I didn't understand half of what he said
- sophisticated automatic system
- can't ever completely eliminate human error
- good placement for first-years, but second-years should have more management responsibility
- was hoping to get some management experience, but I mostly worked alone
- learned quite a lot in three months
- wouldn't like to work there

## RECORDING SCRIPT

1:08

A: Hi, Jason!
B: Oh hi, Alex.
A: Do you fancy going out tonight? They're showing the new Will Smith movie at the Astoria!
B: Oh yeah. Look, I'd love to, but I've got this essay to finish, and then I've got to write my placement report.
A: Placement? Oh, that's interesting, I didn't know you did a placement. What did you do?
B: I spent three months near Birmingham at a place called Diftco. They export construction equipment.
A: Oh yeah, good job was it?
B: It was all right. They're a bit crazy there. People worked really hard, sometimes from eight in the morning to nine or ten in the evening.
A: Hm. Sounds like school!
B: Yeah! Anyway, I was in charge of preparing shipping documents. Good job we did international trade last semester. It really helped me understand what was going on.
A: Preparing shipping documents, eh? Sounds boring. Didn't like international trade much myself. Did you get on well with your boss?
B: Oh, she was very strict. But, OK, I suppose. She didn't scream at me or anything when I did something wrong.
A: Why, did you mess up a lot?
B: Nah. Only once when I sent a container to Austria instead of Australia.
A: You're joking!
B: Well, it wasn't my fault. This guy on the phone had a really strong accent. I didn't understand half of what he said.
A: So you sent a container to Austria? What an idiot!
B: Well, I bet you wouldn't do any better. Anyway, it was interesting, 'cos they had this really sophisticated automatic system, but you can't ever completely eliminate human error.
A: Yeah, Jason, the guys at IBM didn't expect you to be using their systems, otherwise they would've spent another ten years making it completely idiot-proof!
B: OK, OK … Now, if you've finished taking the mickey, I've got an essay to write.
A: No, come on. I'm just joking. I'm really interested in Diftco. I need to find a placement for next summer.
B: Well, it's a good placement for first-years, but I think second-years should have more management responsibility. I was hoping to get some management experience, but I mostly worked alone, so it wasn't that great.
A: You wouldn't recommend it, then?
B: No. I learned quite a lot in three months, but I certainly wouldn't like to work there.
A: Mm, I see what you mean.
B: Listen, now I've told you all about it, you couldn't help me with the report, could you? If we finish by nine, we can still make it in time for the movie. Look, I've already made these notes. You just have to write them up for me …

## Ordering and writing

**6** With lower-level classes, you could again do this as a whole-class activity. Write down the headings from exercise 2 on the board: *Introduction*, *Experience druing work placement*, *Observations about the company*, *Professional achievements* and *Appendix*.
Write up these notes and the notes from exercise 5 under the headings.

If you don't have time in class to write the whole placement report, you could write the introduction or the first sentence of each paragraph as a whole-class activity to get students started. Students then finish the report for homework.

## MODEL ANSWER:

I was employed for three months at Diftco, near Birmingham, under the supervision of Ms Witten. The objective of the internship was to gain management experience in an industrial environment. Diftco exports construction equipment and is one of the most profitable firms in the region.

I worked in the Export Office most of time, where I was in charge of preparing shipping documents. I was also responsible for checking containers in the warehouse, where the equipment is assembled and packed. I successfully learnt to use the automatic bar code system used in the warehouse. This is a sophisticated automatic system, which assigns a code and a position to every component in the warehouse. However, it was interesting to discover that even such a sophisticated tool can never completely eliminate human error. Perhaps the most valuable lesson I learnt was to double-check information. The importance of careful checking was emphasized when I unfortunately sent a container to Austria instead of Australia, because I had misunderstood my correspondent on the telephone.

The company is successful and well organized, with a very motivated, hard-working and dedicated staff. However, I feel I would be more effective in an environment with more variety and less routine paperwork. One area of the company's activity leaves room for improvement, and that is the problem of waste in the warehouse. A more systematic policy of recycling would help to solve this problem.

The course module in international trade studied last semester was extremely valuable in understanding how a company like Diftco works. Thanks to this preparation, I was able to establish a good rapport with the export staff. On the other hand, communication with the warehousemen was much more difficult, mainly because many of them do not speak English.

Overall, the internship was a positive experience, which allowed me to gain significant experience in three months. However, I mostly worked alone and therefore did not achieve the goal of acquiring management experience. A placement at Diftco would be most valuable for first-year students; second-year students would benefit from a position with greater management responsibility.

Appendix: A Daily journal, B Copies of letters to and from Ms Witten, supervisor

---

### EXTENSION ACTIVITY 1

Ask students to bring in some examples of reports they have received or written themselves. Compare them with the examples in this module – can they find the same elements? How would they change or improve their reports?

---

### EXTENSION ACTIVITY 2

As a whole-class activity, get students to brainstorm a list of guidelines entitled 'Tips on writing effective reports'. This might include the points below.
- Use a clear structure.
- Use informative headings.
- Write in a formal style.
- Use a clear layout, e.g. bullet points, numbers, etc.
- Send it to the right people.
- Don't write too much – if it's too long, people may not read it.
- If the report is long, write a summary.
- Check it carefully for typing and factual mistakes.
- Get a colleague to read it for you before you send it.

---

## 1.6 Case study
### Counselling

This module focuses on living and working abroad and the use of counselling skills and counselling language to discuss problems.

### Internet research

An Internet search about living and working in Japan, the UK or the USA will reveal numerous websites dealing with culture shock in general terms and the difficulties of adjusting to a new cultural environment. Many of them offer advice on how to tackle this problem. They also offer background information into the history of the country and practical information about everyday concerns such as work, study, accommodation, shopping, healthcare, banking, taxes, etc.

Students' investigations could be focused in various ways, e.g. they could research culture shock – what it is and what to do about it – or they could look into one or two topics in some detail.

Students could do this search before the lesson as preparation for the activity in exercise 7.

### Discussion

**1** Give students a few minutes to brainstorm with a partner. Then, collect ideas and make a list on the board. Keep this list of ideas – it will be useful for exercise 7.

#### SUGGESTED ANSWERS:

culture shock in general, language problems, homesickness, food, climate, housing, schools, family members don't make the adjustment, cultural differences at work and outside work

---

#### EXTENSION ACTIVITY

If any students have already worked abroad, ask them to share their experiences with the class.

---

### Listening for detail

**2** 🔊 1:09 Read through the handout with students before they listen. Working with a partner, get them to predict which words might fill the blanks and which skills are needed. Then play the recording. Check answers with the whole class.

#### ANSWERS:

Counselling = helping someone <u>manage</u> a personal problem using their own <u>resources</u>
Counselling skills = listening, talking, helping, assisting, exploring problems
The three phases of counselling = Phase one = <u>Talk</u>; Phase two = <u>Think</u>; Phase three = <u>Act</u>

#### RECORDING SCRIPT

🔊 1:09

Does that answer your question? Now, before we go on, I'll just summarize the three points we've already discussed. Firstly, the goal of counselling is to help another person manage a personal problem using their own resources. Secondly, counselling is about listening, not about telling. It's about talking to someone and helping, not about persuading or manipulating. And, counselling is about assisting and exploring problems. It's not about reassuring someone or solving their problems for them. Thirdly, the three phases of counselling. Phase one, talk. This is where you encourage the problem holder to talk about the problem, and to start to understand how they feel about the problem and why they feel that way.

Phase two, think. This is where you encourage them to think about the problem and reassess it. You help them to see their situation from a new perspective, so that they can consider the different options for dealing with the situation. And phase three, act. This is where you help them to choose their own solution and to establish an action plan to manage the problem. OK, are there any questions? OK, I now want to say a few words about some of the skills that counsellors need. I'm going to pass out another handout. As you can see, there are a number of …

To consolidate understanding, get students to complete these sentences: *Counselling is about …* and *Counselling is not about ….* You could also elicit more details about the three phases of counselling.

**3** Be aware that some students may not wish to discuss personal problems so point out that they could talk about less personal issues. Circulate while students are talking and assist where necessary.

Take whole-class feedback, drawing out the similarities and differences between students' own experiences and what was said in the lecture. Some possible differences might be:
*you helped someone with a problem*: you didn't know what to say or do; they asked you to come up with solutions; they talked for ages and you got bored; etc.
*someone helped you with a problem*: they didn't really listen to you; they didn't ask how you felt; they tried to tell you what to do; etc.

## Counselling language

**4** This handout gives a comprehensive list of important counselling skills. Read it through with students so that they get the overall idea of what is involved. You could then do the matching task as a whole-class activity.

| ANSWERS: |
| --- |
| 1   How did you feel? |
| 2   So you're saying that …? |
| 4   Right. |
| 5   You were *surprised*? |
| 6   So, to sum up, … |
| 7   What are the options? |
| 8   What would happen if (+ *past tense*)? |
| 9   What's your first priority? |
| 10   Why not start by -*ing* …? |

**5** Ask students to work with a partner to add more phrases to the counselling skills. Then take whole-class feedback, making a list of all the phrases students suggest. Keep this as it will be useful for exercise 6.

| SUGGESTED ANSWERS: |
| --- |
| 1   What did you do? |
| 2   So what you mean is … |
| 4   That's interesting. |
| 5   Really? You actually (said) …? |
| 6   So, basically, … |
| 7   What alternatives can you see? |
| 8   Would that get the result you want? |
| 9   Where do you think you need to start? |
| 10   Before you do anything else, why don't you …? |

## Roleplay

**6** These roleplays review the language practised in this module and allow students the opportunity to develop their own counselling skills.

Give students who are going to play *Problem holder A* time to read the notes and think about what they want to say. Remind them to put the situation into their own words, adding ideas of their own where possible. While they are doing this, the *Counsellor* can review the counselling skills language practised in exercises 4 and 5. The *Observer* should also review the handout in exercise 4.

While students are speaking, circulate and assist where necessary. Make a note of any common mistakes in the target language for remedial teaching at a later stage.
When students have finished, take some whole-class feedback on how the roleplay went – what was easy, what was difficult, what they might do differently next time, etc.

Then, repeat the procedure with problems B and C.

## Writing

**7** Remind students about the discussion they had in exercise 1. If it's appropriate, get them to refer to the results of their Internet research. Read through the phrases in the box and check that students understand them.

Give students a few minutes to write their emails. With lower-level classes, or if time is limited, the emails could be quite short, mentioning just one problem. Then get students to exchange emails and write their responses. Remind them to use as many of the phrases in the box as possible.

With higher-level classes, students could give their problem email to two or more students. The responses should be written on separate pieces of paper. The writer of the problem could then choose which response helps them the most.

If there is time, or for homework, get students to write a second email to the person who responded to the problem. In this email, they could thank them for the advice and say what they plan to do next.

## Subject background

The phrase 'customer service' refers to pre-sales (enquiries), sales itself (including order processing) and post-sales (returns, complaints, etc.). The phrase 'customer support' is usually limited to post-sales only.

Customer support is important because:
- in an age when many competing goods and services don't differ greatly from each other, the quality of customer support can make all the difference.
- good customer support leads to repeat business.
- a 'silent complainer' tells all their friends.
- customers have expectations of good service set by other companies.

Customer support staff are usually given pre-defined 'performance standards' which serve as guidelines in their day-to-day work. Here are some typical examples of such standards.
- Get it right first time.
- Only make promises that are realistic.
- When you 'inherit' an error from elsewhere in the organization, do not pass it on again (instead refer it to your supervisor if you cannot deal with it).
- Make all written work clear and simple (use standard formats where available).
- Treat customers with the maximum courtesy and helpfulness at all times.
- Leave all records and files in a state that they can be easily dealt with by someone who does not normally handle them.
- Answer all telephone calls within three rings, then give a name and a friendly greeting.
- Direct the conversation so that you identify the needs of the customer as soon as possible, then provide that information at the time it is needed.

Most customers are satisfied if their complaint is dealt with quickly and helpfully. They only get irritated or angry when their attempts to complain lead them nowhere.

Many modern companies see complaints as an opportunity. They are an excellent way of discovering problems, and once the cause of the complaint has been eliminated it should never happen again. So an efficient complaints procedure leads directly to constantly improving quality.

In addition, customers whose complaints have been resolved satisfactorily tend to become strong, long-term customers. The reason is simple: they are impressed with the care and attention given to their complaint – and how that contrasts with the indifference they have met in other companies.

A key skill for customer support staff is active listening. This means:
- let the customer fully explain the problem with no interruptions (except for clarification questions). Only move to the problem-solving part of the conversation when they have 'let off steam'.
- pay full attention while the customer is speaking. From time to time give a brief summary of what they have been saying. This shows that you are listening and are on common ground.
- resist the urge to argue, defend or excuse. Apologize sincerely and acknowledge any inconvenience caused.
- use the other person's name.
- make written notes of key points.
- if the conversation is face-to-face, then maintain frequent eye contact and an open body posture leaning slightly towards the other person.
- as the conversation progresses, focus on positive action for the future.

## Useful websites

The UK's professional body for customer service has a website:
http://www.instituteofcustomerservice.com
Follow the links for 'Information Centre' and then 'Glossary of terms' for useful teaching material.
These two sites have useful background information:
http://en.wikipedia.org/wiki/Customer_service
http://money.howstuffworks.com/customer-service.htm

## 2.1 About business

### Call centres

This module examines the use of call centres in India by a wide range of companies and the global impact on employment practices.

### Internet research

An Internet search for *call centre racist abuse* will yield articles on the abuse experienced by Indian call-centre employees from their customers in the UK and USA. They often experience shouting, swearing, and racist comments from angry customers. Some customers resort to this kind of abuse when they are not happy with the service, but some are also angry because the call centre jobs have been outsourced and employment has been lost in their own countries. Call-centre employees are taught to remain calm and polite and not to respond to the abuse, but some are leaving their jobs because they find the abuse difficult to take.

Possible solutions for combating this type of abuse: allow staff to warn customers that this behaviour is not acceptable; allow them to hang up on abusive customers.

You could ask students to do this search as preparation for the first exercise in this module or as a follow-up to the lesson.

---

### LEAD-IN ACTIVITY

Establish that students know what a call centre is (a call centre provides customer service by telephone, e.g. for water, gas and electricity companies; mail order shopping; airlines; insurance companies, etc.).

Get students to talk about their own experiences of call centres, if they have any, and what impressions they got of them. Prompt with questions like:
*How long did you have to wait for a response?*
*Was the operator pleasant and helpful?*
*Was your problem solved?*
*How long did it take?*
*Did your experience influence your opinion of the company?*, etc.

---

### Discussion

**1** Get students to discuss the reasons why someone would or would not want to work in a call centre. Take whole-class feedback and make two lists on the board. Refer back to the lists once students have done exercises 1–7 to see how their views match those presented in the article and the interview.

#### SUGGESTED ANSWERS:

Postive aspects:
a satisfying job with fun people; physically undemanding; clean, modern environment; flexible hours; promotion prospects; steady income
Negative aspects:
a boring, dead-end job; stressful, humiliating sweatshops; inhuman conditions; unsociable hours; staff are under-trained and overworked; poorly-paid

### Summarizing

**2** Read the introduction and the first paragraph aloud with the whole class. Elicit from students:
a) the reason Sir Keith Whitson gives for using call centres in India (workers in India are smart, enthusiastic, efficient and well educated)
b) and the reason given by the writer of the article (wages in India are much lower).

Ask students which opinion they agree with or if they think there is truth in both.

Then give students a few minutes to read the first five paragraphs of the article silently and match the correct headings to the paragraphs. Remind them to use the *Wordlist* on page 149 in their books. Check answers with the whole class.

#### ANSWERS:

Paragraph A: Smarter Indians
Paragraph B: Call of the East
Paragraph C: UK jobs leak
Paragraph D: Unions strike back
Paragraph E: More Britons concerned

**3** Students could do this exercise with a partner, and then compare their answers with another pair.
With lower-level classes you could first get students to read each paragraph in turn and tell you in one or two words what each one is about, e.g. paragraph F (call centre employees and their training), paragraph G (experiences / feelings of call centre employees), paragraph H (protection of call centre employees wherever they are). Students then use these prompts to help them write the summarizing sentences.

Get two or three pairs to tell you their sentences and write them on the board. Look at the strengths and weaknesses of each one.

#### SUGGESTED ANSWERS:

Paragraph F: It's not as easy for Indians to get a job in a British call centre in India as one might think.
Paragraph G: Coming into contact with the wealthy Western world is a hard learning experience for Indian employees.
Paragraph H: Call centre employees need to be protected from redundancy and exploitation wherever they are.

**4** Students could do this exercise with a partner. Get students to give you their reason for rejecting the wrong answers.

#### ANSWER:

3  Trade unions are worried about job losses, poor working conditions and exploitation of workers worldwide in a growing industry where work is stressful.

### Discussion

**5** Get students to scan the article for references to the trade union viewpoint (paragraphs C, D, and H) and discuss the pros and cons of the trade union argument (i.e. betrayal of workers in the UK; strike action; exploitation of workers, wherever they are located).

Give students time to explore their ideas, then take whole-class feedback.

## Predicting and listening

**6** 🔊 1:10  Read the topic headings with the whole class. Remind them to use the *Wordlist* on page 149 in their books and explain any other vocabulary that might be new to them, e.g.:

*employee profile* (a description of the kind of person who works somewhere)
*prospects* (opportunities).

Play the recording and allow students to check their predictions.

### RECORDING SCRIPT

🔊 1:10

Host: Good evening, and welcome back to Career Choices. Tonight's programme looks at one of the fastest growing businesses in India today – customer care.
Call Delta Airlines, American Express, Citibank or IBM from almost anywhere in the world, and there's a good chance you'll be talking to an Indian. With more than a million English-speaking college graduates entering the job market each year, India is the ideal location for American call centres: low labour costs for highly competent staff mean savings of around 50% over the equivalent operation in the States. Attracted by good money, comfortable working conditions and genuine promotion prospects, Indian graduates are queuing up for jobs in call centres. Only five applicants out of every 100 are accepted. Nevertheless, staff turnover in many call centres is high and critics talk about dead-end jobs in sweatshops where staff are routinely monitored and humiliated. So before you rush out to join the queues for jobs in customer care, Career Choices has invited two experts to give us the facts about call centres. With me in the studio are Lavanya Fernandes, who is a Customer Relationship Management expert with a New Delhi consultancy, and Tashar Mahendra, a Call Centre Manager from Mumbai. Lavanya, call centres have had a lot of bad publicity recently: how much truth is there in the sweatshop stories?
Lavanya: Well, first of all, I think it's important to say that call centres have now largely been replaced by contact centres. Customers' problems and queries are no longer handled just by telephone, but also by email, SMS, online chat and even browser sharing – this is where the operator actually takes control of the customer's computer and shows them how to resolve their problem. This means that the operator's job has become more complex and, at the same time, more satisfying. Now, it is certainly true that in the past there were cases of abuse, you know, where employees were closely monitored, and so on …
H: Yes, only three seconds between each call and being timed when they went to the toilets!
L: Yes. Of course this kind of intimidation can still happen. But, on the whole, contact centres now realize that forcing operators to deal with customers as quickly as possible is not in their interest. One long conversation which solves the customer's problem is obviously much better than several short calls which leave the customer feeling dissatisfied. So in fact most centres are trying very hard to respect their staff and make their lives more pleasant.
H: Yes, I see. Tashar, I've heard that you pay for taxis to bring your staff to work?
Tashar: Yes that's right. More than 60% of our customer care executives are young women between 20 and 35 years old, many of them working part-time. As in Mumbai we are almost 11 hours ahead of New York, most of the work is at night. Taking a taxi to and from work means their husbands or their families don't have to worry about them.
H: Yes, I see. Tell us about some of the other ways you look after your staff. I believe you also supply drinks and cakes?
T: Yes, that's right. Our customer care executives spend about 80% of their time communicating with customers. We want them to be energetic and happy because we know that happy staff make satisfied customers. So, for the rest of the time, they can enjoy fresh fruit, drinks, cakes, subsidized meals, on-site massage, air conditioning, competitions, meetings at the beach …
H: At the beach?!
T: Yes, that's right. We have a meeting area with real sand, deckchairs, parasols and the sounds of the seaside. It feels just like being on the beach!
H: Wow, that sounds great! Lavanya, we know that salaries are six to ten times the average wage, so it's not surprising that these jobs are so popular. But what sort of profile are the call centres, sorry, the contact centres, looking for?
L: Well, the most important thing is very good English. And then computer literacy, good typing speed, marketing skills … these are all a plus. But, basically, good communication and listening skills are essential. You need to be patient, polite, good-natured and reasonably intelligent. In some jobs, persuasion skills are needed when you have to collect debts from customers or encourage them to use your client's products.
H: And Tashar, I suppose you give your new staff special training?
T: Yes, that's right. Usually between two weeks and three months, depending on the project. This training includes accent training and neutralization, listening skills, slang training, telephone etiquette, telesales etiquette and customer relationship management skills, and call centre terminology.
H: And I believe your staff all have American names, Tashar, is that right?
T: Yes, that's right. For our customers it's easier to talk to Sharon, Julia or Alison than to Jayashree, Suhaila or Kanjri, and it helps our customer care executives to slip into an American identity.
H: And what about promotion prospects?
T: Yes, that's r… Oh, yes, after about three or four years, depending on your skills and results, you can become a supervisor, and then eventually a manager. And, if you decide to work in another sector, experience in a contact centre is very valuable, especially in sales, insurance or other customer relations jobs.

## Listening for detail

**7** Play 🔊 1:10 again. With lower-level classes you could pause the recording after the host's introduction and then after each speaker's turn to allow students more time to write their notes.

When they have finished, you could check students' understanding of the main ideas of the radio discussion by asking them quick questions on the topics covered, e.g.:

1  *Why are Indian graduates queuing up to join call centres?* (They offer good money, comfortable working conditions, and genuine promotion prospects.)
2  *In what way is work in call centres more interesting than it used to be?* (Operators can use a variety of means to help customers solve their problems; they can spend more time with each customer.)
3  *Why are the operators now allowed to spend more time on each phone call?* (Because the outcome is more satisfying for customer and employee.)
4  *Why are taxis provided to bring staff to work?* (Because most of the staff are women and they work late at night – this makes them feel safer.)
5  *What are some of the perks provided for workers?* (Fruit, drinks, cakes, subsidized meals, on-site massage; air conditioning; competitions and a 'beach' area.)

6 *What is the employee profile of people working at call centres?* (Good English, computer literate, good typing speed, marketing skills, good communication skills, polite, good natured and intelligent.)

7 *What kind of special training and instructions do they get?* (Accent training, listening skills telephone etiquette, telesales etiquette, customer care, etc.)

8 *What other sectors could call centre operators work in?* (Sales, insurance and other customer relations jobs.)

### SUGGESTED ANSWERS:

Why India?

1 ... one million English-speaking college graduates enter job market every year.

2 Low labour costs for highly competent staff.

Changes to call centres:

1 New technology: email, SMS, online chat, browser sharing.

2 The operator's job has become more complex and more satisfying.

3 Centres are trying hard to respect their staff.

Perks of the job:

1 Transport: by taxi to and from work.

2 Good working conditions with fruit, drinks, cakes, subsidized meals, massage, air conditioning, competitions, the beach.

Employee profile and training:

1 Good communication skills: English, listening, patience, persuasion.

2 Technical skills: computer literacy, good typing speed, marketing skills.

3 Special training: 2 weeks – 3 months, accent, listening, slang, etiquette, telesales, CRM, terminology.

Promotion prospects:

1 Can become a supervisor after 3 or 4 years, and eventually a manager.

2 Experience in a contact centre is valuable in other jobs.

### EXTENSION ACTIVITY

Point out that the interviewees do not really address the less positive aspects of working at a call centre. Given what they now know from the article and the interview, get students to brainstorm aspects of the job that might make it unattractive or unappealing to Indian graduates in the long term, e.g. the work is monotonous and repetitive; the abuse from customers is too much to tolerate; always working at night becomes unacceptable, etc.

## Debate

**8** Give students time to read the information in their roleplay and prepare their arguments. Circulate and assist where necessary. Remind students to look back at the article and the notes they made in exercise 7.

You could use the following procedure to structure the debate:

1 You open the debate by briefly introducing the topic and explaining the procedure.

2 One speaker from each group gives the opening speech, without interruption. This should take around 3–4 minutes.

3 A different speaker responds to the opposing side's argument – around 1–2 minutes.

4 The discussion is open to the whole group, with individuals making comments as they wish.

5 You summarize the discussion briefly.

6 The whole class votes for or against.

## 2.2 Vocabulary
## Customer service and telephoning

This module explores a range of vocabulary and expressions for describing problems and dealing with customer service.

### Internet research

An Internet search for *"golden rules of customer service"* will reveal a number of listings. After students have done exercise 10, they can carry out their Internet search and look for ideas to add to their own.

## Adjectives

**1** Give students a few minutes to read the adjectives in the box and check that they know the meanings. Allow them to use their dictionaries to look up any new words. Students' answers to this exercise may vary from those given below – in that case, accept any answers that students can justify.

### SUGGESTED ANSWERS:

abusive (C), annoyed (B), appreciative (C), cheerful (H), competent (H), difficult (C), frustrated (B), grateful (C), helpful (H), irritated (B), knowledgeable (H), patient (H), persuasive (H), pleasant (H), reassuring (H), rude (C), satisfied (C), sympathetic (H), understanding (H), upset (C)

**2** You could do this as a whole-class activity. Write the words on the board. Point to each one in turn and get students to tell you where the stress lies in each case. Then circle the ones with the stress on the first syllable and underline the ones with the stress on the third syllable.

### ANSWERS:

Stress not on first syllable: abusive, annoyed, appreciative, frustrated, persuasive, reassuring, sympathetic, understanding, upset

Stress on third syllable: reassuring, sympathetic, understanding

To explore the meanings of the adjectives further, get students to divide them into two groups:

positive emotions: *appreciative, cheerful, competent, grateful, helpful, knowledgeable, patient, persuasive, pleasant, reassuring, satisfied, sympathetic, understanding*

negative emotions: *abusive, annoyed, difficult, frustrated, irritated, rude, upset.*

This will also help students to prepare for exercise 3.

## Listening for attitude

**3** 1:11–1:20 Play the extracts one by one and have students identify the appropriate adjectives or play all the extracts and check answers at the end. Point out that there is usually more than one possible answer in each case. When you check the answers, ensure that students are putting the stress in the correct place in each word.

### SUGGESTED ANSWERS:

1 reassuring, pleasant, sympathetic, understanding

2 abusive, frustrated, annoyed, irritated, rude, upset

3 knowledgeable, competent, helpful

4 appreciative, grateful, satisfied

5 frustrated, annoyed, irritated, upset

6 sympathetic, understanding, patient

7 persuasive, pleasant

8 upset, frustrated, grateful, appreciative

9 cheerful, helpful, pleasant

10 difficult, irritated

## RECORDING SCRIPT

🔊 1:11–1:20

1 Operator: Now, don't worry, Madam. This is just a minor problem that a few customers experience at first. It will only take a few minutes to resolve.

2 … or if you would like more information about our products, please press four.
Customer: All I want is to speak to a human being, not a stupid, condescending, brainless piece of … silicon!

3 Operator: All right sir. Yes, it is an unusual problem, and it's a little complicated, but you'll be pleased to know there is a solution.

4 Customer: Oh, that's wonderful. You're so clever! Thank you so much!

5 Customer: It's just so annoying. I thought your product would solve all my problems, but it just seems to be creating new ones!

6 Operator: I fully understand your position, sir, and I would feel exactly the same way myself.

7 Operator: Alternatively, the simplest solution is to upgrade to the professional version of the software. The extra cost is only around one euro per month. I think you'd agree that that's excellent value, wouldn't you?

8 Customer: Oh, thank you so much. You're so patient. I bet nobody else has these problems. I just feel so stupid!

9 Operator: A very good morning to you, and thank you for calling the helpline. How I can help you today?

10 Customer: Well, that's all very well. You say you've sorted out the problem and it's working now, but how can I be sure it won't break down again tomorrow?

## Describing problems

**4** Students work with a partner to match these ten sentences to the appropriate devices. Check answers.

### SUGGESTED ANSWERS:

1 When I switch it on, nothing happens. (fax, photocopier, PC, mobile phone)
2 It broke down on the way to work. (car)
3 It keeps crashing. (PC)
4 There's something stuck inside. (fax, photocopier)
5 I can't switch it off. (photocopier, PC, mobile phone)
6 It's not working properly. (car, fax, photocopier, PC, mobile phone)
7 It won't start. (car, PC)
8 It's out of order. (fax, photocopier, PC)
9 I think it's a complete write-off. (car, fax, photocopier, PC, mobile phone)
10 The battery's dead. (car, PC, mobile phone)

### FURTHER PRACTICE

Give students a few minutes to look at the sentences again. Then get them to close their books and reconstruct the sentences from one-word prompts that you give them:
*stuck* (There's something stuck inside.)
*order* (It's out of order.), etc.

## Collocations, Antonyms and Phrasal verbs

**5**, **6**, **7** and **8** Exercises 5–8 bring together a number of useful words and phrases for talking about customer service problems. Students could complete these exercises individually or with a partner. Circulate while they are working and assist where necessary. Check answers with the whole class.

When students have finished, get them to pick out any words or phrases which are new to them or that they are unsure of, and review their meaning and use.

### ANSWERS:

Exercise 5
1 identify the symptoms
2 diagnose the fault
3 sort out a problem
4 talk the customer through the process
5 escalate the problem to the supervisor
6 arrange a visit from our technician
7 exchange the product
8 give a full refund
Exercise 6
1 a)   2 d/e)   3 c)   4 b)   5 d/e)   6 g)   7 f)
Exercise 7
1 switch off   2 disconnect   3 unscrew   4 remove
5 release   6 Lift out   7 insert   8 push into
9 Fasten   10 Replace   11 screw in   12 turn on
Exercise 8
1 Could you <u>hold</u> on a moment, please? = b) I'm in the middle of an interesting conversation.
2 We tried to contact you, but we couldn't <u>get</u> through. = c) We lost your phone number.
3 I'm going to <u>put</u> you through to my supervisor. = d) Heh, heh, let's see how *she* likes your ridiculous questions.
4 Could you <u>hang</u> up, and I'll call / ring you back? = a) Maybe. If I have nothing else to do.
5 I'll just <u>take</u> down your details. = f) I'll pretend to do something useful.
6 I can't hear you very well. Could you <u>speak</u> up please? = g) They're playing my favourite song on the radio.
7 We'll <u>get</u> back to you as soon as we solve the problem. = h) We might ring next week if we remember.
8 The engineer is out at the moment. Please call / ring back later. = e) We don't know what you're talking about.

## Listening for detail

**9** 🔊 1:21   Read the words and expressions in the box. Remind students that they have already have met some of them in previous exercises in this module.

Before students listen for the words and expressions, ask them to listen to the conversation and answer the following questions:

*What complaints does the woman have about customer service today?* (You can't speak to a human being; you can't get your problems sorted out; they don't call you back; you are put on hold.)
*How do you think the interviewer feels?* (Frustrated, irritated.)
*What might the interviewer have done to improve this interview?* (Possibly nothing! Or he could have tried to interrupt her or pick up on one of the points she was making.)

Then play the recording again so that students can listen for the word or expression that is not spoken. Check answers with the whole class.

### ANSWER:

It doesn't work.

## RECORDING SCRIPT

🔊 1:21

Interviewer: Excuse me, madam, I see you've just been to the bank. We're doing a survey about customer service, and …
Old Lady: Ooh, don't talk to me about service! Now, in the old days, the customer was always right! You could telephone the bank and there was always a pleasant young man or woman, you know, who would listen to your problems, and they used to provide a solution in no time. Nowadays, you're lucky if you even get to speak to a human being, let

alone get your problems sorted out.

I: Yes, now, could I just ask you …

OL: And if you want to actually see someone, you can't just walk in, oh no, you have to phone the bank to make an appointment. And they have these machines now, you know, if you want this, please press one, if you want that, please press two, if it's the second Thursday in January, please press three … dear, oh dear. I just get so annoyed!

I: Yes, of course, but …

OL: So, then you have to wait for ages and when you do finally speak to someone, either they say they'll call you back and then you never hear from them again, or they tell you they'll have to escalate the problem to their supervisor. Huh! 'Escalate the problem!' They're supposed to be so competent and knowledgeable and all that, but really they just don't want to take any responsibility these days.

I: Yes, but could I …

OL: So, then they tell you to hold on again and you get another machine playing the same twenty seconds of Vivaldi again and again, and then finally you go back to the beginning again … 'If you would like to speak to an adviser, please press four.' What is the world coming to, I ask you?

I: Well, yes, I see what you …

OL: And now they want me to use that interweb thingy with all those viruses, as if we didn't have enough trouble already! Anyway, I haven't got time to stand here and talk. I must be getting on. Goodbye!

## Discussion

**10** Set students a time limit to write down as many rules as they can. Then get students to call out their ideas and write them on the board or flip chart, until you have a comprehensive list of ideas. Get students to expand on what they mean by each statement, if necessary. Keep this list for reference in the modules that follow.

### SUGGESTED ANSWERS:
The customer is always right.
Make the customer feel valued and important.
Be courteous and friendly at all times.
Give customers what they want.
Always deliver what you promise.
Pay attention to detail.
Deal with problems quickly and efficiently.
Choose the right people to do the job.
Train your customer service staff to the highest standards.
Don't stand still – keep reviewing what you do and how you do it.

### EXTENSION ACTIVITY

Students work in groups. They are a team of consultants with the task of improving customer relations in the following businesses:
- a beauty salon
- a dry-cleaning service
- a coffee shop
- a car repair shop.

They should think of ideas for each business that will attract and keep new customers.

Give students a time limit and circulate and assist where necessary. When students have finished, get each group to present their ideas, explaining why they think they will work.

## 2.3 Grammar
## Asking questions and giving instructions

This module focuses on different ways of asking questions, making requests and giving instructions.

### Internet research

An Internet search for *FAQ learning English* reveals that the most frequently asked questions are usually about how to improve the four skills (reading, writing, listening, speaking), grammar and vocabulary. Other questions refer to studying abroad, examinations, learning English for work purposes, and how to study online.

Students could be asked to choose one question that particularly interests them and search for the answer to it on several different websites.

## Test yourself: Asking questions and giving instructions

**1** Start by reading the *Refresh your memory* box with students. Write a few examples on the board and get students to match them to the rules given in the box:
*Are you listening*? (auxiliary verb + subject + main verb)
*When will he arrive*? (question word + auxiliary word + subject + main verb)
*Who telephoned?* (*who* is the subject so no auxiliary verb is needed)

Check answers with the whole class. Accept all correct answers.

### ANSWERS:
1 can I / may I   2 Is it / Is that   3 would you mind
4 do I / can I / will I   5 Did you   6 was it   7 have you
8 Do I   9 you don't   10 could you / can you / would you
11 can you / could you / will you
12 Will I have / Do I have / Do I need
13 You needn't / You don't have to / You don't / You won't
14 you might have / you might need / you may have / you may need / you'll have / you'll need / you have / you need

### FURTHER PRACTICE

Ask students to comment on the tone of the conversation, using some of the adjectives they practised in 2.2, exercise 2. Possible answers are: *appreciative, reassuring, patient, pleasant, helpful*. Get students to practise the conversation with a partner using an appropriate tone.
If you think students need more practice of questions before they continue, work through the exercises in the *Grammar and practice* (page 120 and 121 in the Student's Book, answers on page 116 in this book).

## Listening

**2** 🔊 1:22 Play the recording, pause at the beep, and ask students to summarize the features of the product (it's found in every office; it's small enough to put in your pocket; it uses electricity; it is connected with computers, but you don't use it to speak to people. It isn't expensive; it has replaced the floppy disk). Accept all guesses about what the mystery product might be, but don't confirm the correct answer yet.

Play to the end of the game so that students can check the answer.

### ANSWER:
a USB memory stick

## RECORDING SCRIPT

 1:22

A: Welcome back to *Guess the Product*. Our next mystery product is a very clever and very practical piece of technology. Panel, you've just ten questions to help you 'guess the product'!

B: OK. Is it advertised on TV?

A: No, it isn't.

C: Do you use it for work?

A: Yes, you do.

D: Would you find one in every office?

A: Yes, you would.

C: Can you put it in your pocket?

A: Yes, you can.

D: Did it exist ten years ago?

A: No, it didn't.

C: Does it use electricity?

A: Yes, it does.

B: Do you use it to speak to people?

A: No, you don't.

C: Is there a connection with computers?

A: Yes, there is.

B: Does it cost more than $30?

A: No, it doesn't.

D: Has it replaced the floppy disk?

A: Yes it has.

[beep]

A: All right, that's ten questions. Now, have you 'guessed the product'?

D: We think it's a USB memory stick.

A: Yeesss! Well done! You have correctly 'guessed the product'!

**3** Get students to try to complete the questions before they listen again. Then play 1:22 again so that they can check or complete the answers. Draw attention to the formation of questions using auxiliary verbs.

### ANSWERS:

1  Is it advertised on TV?
2  Do you use it for work?
3  Would you find one in every office?
4  Can you put it in your pocket?
5  Did it exist ten years ago?
6  Does it use electricity?
7  Do you use it to speak to people?
8  Is there a connection with computers?
9  Does it cost more than $30?
10 Has it replaced the floppy disk?

**4** To help students with this activity, you could bring in some pictures of products or simply write the name of some products on cards. You could match the products to students' areas of interest or the work they are involved with.

## Making requests

**5** Give students a few minutes to complete the sentences and put them in order. Then elicit which words need to be followed by the *-ing* form of the verb (in sentence 2 *mind* is followed by the *-ing* form; in sentence 6 *to* is used as a preposition so needs to be followed by the *-ing* form).

Ask students what features the most direct sentences have (they're shorter and less complex) and what features the most polite sentences have (they're longer, with introductory phrases leading up to the request).

### ANSWERS:

Ordered from most direct to most polite:
4  Fax me the details, will you?
1  Can you fax me the details?
5  Could you fax me the details, please?
2  Would you mind faxing me the details?
3  Do you think you could possibly fax me the details, please?
6  I was wondering if you would have any objection to faxing me the details?

**6** With a partner, students say each request aloud and reply with the responses given here. They should be able to hear what works and what doesn't work and identify the inappropriate ones.

### ANSWERS:

e)  No, no problem.
The negative is appropriate for 2 and 6, but not for the others.

## Roleplay

**7** Read the list of requests with students and get them to comment on how 'big' each one is, i.e. how much trouble will it cause the person you are asking? Is the request fairly simple / undemanding or is it more substantial? Point out that this will influence how direct or indirect the request will be. Remind students about appropriate tone of voice – the more demanding the request, the more tentative their tone might need to be.

Circulate while students are speaking and assist where necessary. When they have finished, ask some pairs to present their requests and responses.

If students need more practice with making requests, work through the exercises in *Grammar and practice* (page 121 in the Student's Book, answers on page 116 in this book).

## Giving instructions

**8** If students are uncertain about the six modal verbs here, work through exercises 13 and 14 which provide simple definitions of each one in *Grammar and practice* (page 121 in the Student's Book, answers on page 116 in this book).

Students could work alone to complete Steve's side of the conversation, then compare their answers with a partner. Check answers with the whole class, referring to the definitions given on page 121 in the Student's Book.

### ANSWERS:

1  don't    2  'll have to / 'll need to
3  needn't / don't have to    4  Don't    5  might have to
6  'll need to / 'll have to    7  don't
8  needn't / don't have to    9  don't
10  needn't / don't have to

**9**  1:23  With a partner, get students to try to complete Pete's side of the conversation. You might want to point out that not all of his lines are questions. Ask students to note down what he says. Then play the recording. Get students to dictate their lines to you and write them on the board. Take whole-class feedback on the versions they wrote themselves – some of them may be perfectly acceptable.

### RECORDING SCRIPT

1:23

Steve: OK, Pete. First of all, you open the printer. No, wait a minute, don't just open it, select 'change cartridge' from the menu.

Pete: From the menu? Do I have to switch the printer on?

S: Er, yes, of course you have to switch it on, otherwise you can't use the menu!

P: Oh, right. What about the computer?

S: No, that's all right, you needn't switch the PC on, just the printer.

P: All right. So, the printer's on, select 'change cartridge', OK, and open the printer. What now?

S: So now you gently remove the old cartridge. Don't force it. If it's difficult, you might have to pull it back first, then upwards.

P: Backwards, then upwards. All right, I've got it.

S: OK, so now you can install the new cartridge. You'll need to remove the adhesive tape first, but be careful you don't touch the printed circuits – they're very fragile.

P: You needn't worry. I'm being very careful. OK, that's it.

S: Right. *It*'ll ask you if you want to align the new cartridge, but you needn't bother. Usually it's fine as it is.

P: OK; what about the old one? Can I just throw it in the bin?

S: Oh no, don't throw the old cartridge away. You can recycle them.

P: Oh yes, right. Listen, that's great. I really appreciate your help. Is there anything I can do for *you*?

S: No, that's all right, Pete. You needn't worry. Just buy me a beer some time!

**10** Read through the list of topics with students. Give them a few minutes to come up with at least two ideas of their own, if necessary. Remind students to start by making a request – refer them back to the language in exercise 5. They should also try to use the modal verbs and reformulate their answers to show understanding, if they can.

Conversations should begin something like this:

A: *Would you mind explaining how to change the oil in a car?*

B: *No, no problem.*

---

**FURTHER PRACTICE**

Give students a list of answers and get them to write the questions. Do the first one with the whole class. Then ask students to work with a partner and write questions. Some of the examples below are deliberately quite open-ended, and there are many possible answers.

*Yes, that's fine.* (Possible questions: *Could I call you tomorrow? / Can I leave early today? / I was wondering if I could borrow your laptop?*)

*I'll finish the report tomorrow.*

*I'm sorry, but I'm not in the office on Wednesday.*

*I never work on Sundays.*

*I'm afraid I can't do that.*

*She's not here at the moment. Could you call back later?*

*I'll do it straight away.*

*I'd be happy to help.*

*Yes, we can deliver on Friday.*

---

**EXTENSION ACTIVITY**

Get students to write three requests on three separate slips of paper, using the phrases practised in the unit, e.g.:

*Can you …*

*Would you mind …*

*I was wondering if you could …*

The requests could be work-related or on a general topic; the request could be to a colleague, customer, friend, etc. They may need to write an extra sentence to set the context for the request, e.g.:

*I forgot to go to the bank today. I was wondering if you could lend me some money for lunch?*

*You haven't got the printer I want. Can you sell me the next model up for the same price?*

Students circulate, making their requests and responding to each other. The responses could be positive or negative.

---

This module deals with appropriate language and intonation for a telephone helpline conversation, and focuses on explaining problems, diagnosing causes, giving instructions, and promising help.

**Internet research**

The BBC World Service radio programmes typically include news, business, science and nature, health, technology, entertainment, sports, etc. so students should be able to find something to interest them. Lower-level students might prefer to choose a short programme.

Remind students that they are listening to get the general meaning of the programme and to pick out three interesting points. They may need to listen to the programme two or three times to do this. Students could make a note of any new vocabulary they learn connected with the topic.

## Giving instructions

**1** To prepare students for this task, ask them to draw a 3x3-square grid like this and to number it as shown.

| 1 | 2 | 3 |
|---|---|---|
| 4 | 5 | 6 |
| 7 | 8 | 9 |

Ask them to do the following without letting anyone else see:

*Draw a small circle in the middle of square 1, and a slightly bigger circle in the middle of square 9.*

*Join the circles with a straight line that goes diagonally through square 5.*

*Draw small crosses in the middle of squares 3 and 7.*

*Join the crosses with a curved line that goes through squares 4 and 2 and which touches the top left-hand corner of square 5.*

Ask students to compare their drawings with each other. Tell them they are now going to give similar instructions to their partner so that their partner can draw the sign they are describing. The signs are typical signs that you might see on public transport or on road signs.

Before they begin, you could check that students know the following words that may be useful: *square, triangle, semicircle, corners, curved, straight, along (the line), the middle of, diagonal, vertical, horizontal.*

**ANSWERS:**

Student A will describe a 'no mobile phones allowed' / 'switch off mobile phones' sign.

Student B will describe a 'disabled access' / 'disabled toilets' sign.

## Listening

**2** 🔘 1:24 Read the questions and get students to predict the kind of things that might be said, given that this is a telephone conversation on a software helpline.

Play the recording and check answers with the whole class. Ask students:

*Did the helpline operator handle the call well?*

*Was the customer satisfied?*

**ANSWERS:**

1 The customer can't import spreadsheets into a Superword document.

2 The operator promises to ask the spreadsheet specialist to call back in a few minutes.

---

## RECORDING SCRIPT

 1:24

Helpline: Thank you for calling the Superword hotline. Please hold the line.

Dean: Good morning. Dean speaking. How can I help you?

Customer: Oh, good morning. Yes, I'm afraid your programme isn't working properly.

D: Oh, I'm sorry to hear that. What exactly seems to be the problem?

C: Well, the thing is, I can't put those automatic table thingies in my documents.

D: I'm sorry, it's not a very good line. Could you speak up a little?

C: Yes, sorry. I'm on my mobile. Is that better?

D: Yes, that's much better, thank you.

C: All right. Anyway, I was just saying, I can't insert those tables.

D: Oh, I see. You're having trouble importing spreadsheets into a Superword document?

C: Yes, that's right.

D: All right, I'll put you through to our spreadsheet specialist.

C: Thank you.

D: Hello?

C: Yes?

D: I'm sorry, the number's engaged. Could I ask her to get back to you in a few minutes?

C: Yes, that's fine.

D: OK, then. So, you're on 0680 425232?

C: That's right.

D: And could I have your name please?

C: Wyndham. Delia Wyndham.

D: Is that Wyndham with a 'y'?

C: That's right. W-Y-N-D-H-A-M.

D: Thank you, Ms Wyndham. I'm sure we'll be able to sort it out.

C: Thank you very much.

D: Not at all. Goodbye.

**3** Play  1:24 again. Pause from time to time to allow students to write down the expressions they hear. Check answers with the whole class.

### ANSWERS:

| | |
|---|---|
| 1 | Please hold the line. |
| 2 | Dean speaking. |
| 3 | How can I help you? |
| 4 | What exactly seems to be the problem? |
| 5 | It's not a very good line. |
| 6 | Could you speak up a little? |
| 7 | I'll put you through to ... |
| 8 | The number's engaged. |
| 9 | Could I ask her to get back to you? |
| 10 | So, you're on ... |
| 11 | Could I have your name please? |
| 12 | Not at all. |

## Improving a conversation

**4** You could get a student to read the part of the customer, while you read the part of the helpline operator so that you can exaggerate the negative tone of the operator. Ask the rest of the class:
*How does the helpline operator sound?* (e.g. rude and aggressive)
*How would you feel if a helpline operator spoke to you in this way?* (e.g. annoyed).

With lower-level classes, get students to first tell you how they could improve the conversation (make the sentences less direct / longer; use a more polite tone of voice).

During the activity, circulate and assist where necessary. Choose one or two pairs to present their conversations to the class.

Get students to turn to the second conversation on page 112 in the Student's Book. This time get two students to read the conversation aloud. Ask students:
*How does the hotline operator sound?* (e.g. bored / uninterested).
Repeat the rest of the procedure as above.

### SUGGESTED ANSWER:

**Conversation 1**

Helpline: Superword helpline. Hold the line, please ... Thank you for holding. May I help you?

Customer: Yes, I'm afraid I'm having a problem with your program.

Helpline: I'm sorry to hear that. Let me sort that out for you.

Customer: Yes, I'd appreciate that.

Helpline: All right. What sort of problems are you having?

Customer: Well, I can't print PDF files.

Helpline: Sorry? I'm afraid it's not a very good line. Could you speak up a bit?

Customer: Oh sorry, yes. Is this better? I was just saying that I can't print PDF files.

Helpline: I see. In that case, I think it would be best to speak to our PDF expert.

Customer: All right, can you put me through?

Helpline: Well, I'm afraid he's not available at the moment, but I can ask him to call you back. When would be convenient for you?

Customer: Tomorrow morning?

Helpline: That would be fine. On this number, Ms, er,...?

Customer: Gearhirt. Jamila Gearhirt.

Helpline: Could you spell that please?

Customer: Yes, of course. That's G-E-A-R-H-I-R-T.

Helpline: All right, Ms Gearhirt. Tomorrow morning at about 9 o'clock, then?

Customer: Yes, that's perfect. Thank you very much.

Helpline: You're welcome. Goodbye.

**Conversation 2**

Helpline: Good afternoon. May I help you?

Customer: Oh, hello. Is that Autosales?

Helpline: Yes, sir. Pamela speaking. How can I help you?

Customer: Oh, good. Well, I'm calling about the new car I bought last week. It won't start.

Helpline: Oh, I'm very sorry to hear that. It must be very annoying for you.

Customer: Well, can you do something about it?

Helpline: I'm afraid the mechanics are all out to lunch right now, sir.

Customer: Well, can I leave a message?

Helpline: Yes of course. Could I have your name please?

Customer: It's McCready. Alistair McCready.

Helpline: Ah, yes, Mr McCready. All right, I'll make sure someone calls you back first thing after lunch.

Customer: All right. Well, I'll be expecting your call. Goodbye.

Helpline: Goodbye, Mr McCready.

## Handling problems

**5** 1:25  Read the questions with the students and then play the recording. You could pause the recording after the customer's question, *What do I tell them?*, and see if students can predict what the operator says, before playing through to the end.

> **ANSWERS:**
>
> 1  The customer can't use WordPerfect because there is a power outage.
> 2  The operator tells the customer to take his computer back to the store because he is too stupid to own a computer.

## RECORDING SCRIPT

1:25

Operator: Customer support. May I help you?
Customer: Yes, well, I'm having trouble with WordPerfect.
O:  Well, let me sort that out for you. What exactly seems to be the problem?
C:  It doesn't work. It won't accept anything when I type.
O:  I see. How long have you been having this problem?
C:  Well, about ten minutes.
O:  And was it working properly before that?
C:  Sure. I was just typing away, and all of a sudden the words went away.
O:  You mean they just disappeared?
C:  Yes. Just like that.
O:  Hm. So what does your screen look like now?
C:  Nothing.
O:  Nothing?
C:  It's a blank. Like I said, it won't accept anything when I type.
O:  Uh-huh. Have you tried hitting 'Escape'?
C:  Yes. Nothing happens.
O:  OK. Did you quit WordPerfect?
C:  I don't know. How do I tell if I quit?
O:  Can you see the toolbar on the screen?
C:  What's a toolbar?
O:  OK, never mind. Can you move the cursor around on the screen?
C:  There isn't any cursor. I told you, I can't type anything.
O:  I see. Does your monitor have a power indicator?
C:  What's a monitor?
O:  It's the thing with the screen on it that looks like a TV. Does it have a little light that tells you when it's on?
C:  I don't know.
O:  Well, could you look on the back of the monitor and find where the power cord goes into it? Can you see that?
C:  Yes, I think so.
O:  Great. Now you just have to follow the cord to the plug, and tell me if it's plugged into the wall.
C:  Er, yes, it is.
O:  All right. Now, when you were behind the monitor, did you notice that there were two cables plugged into the back of it, not just one?
C:  No.
O:  Well, there are. I need you to look back there again and find the other cable.
C:  … OK, here it is.
O:  Good. Could you tell me if it's plugged securely into the back of your computer?
C:  I can't reach.
O:  Uh-huh. Well, you don't have to touch it. Can you just see if it's plugged in?
C:  No. It's too dark.
O:  So, you mean the lights are off?
C:  Yes.
O:  Well, couldn't you just turn on the light?
C:  I can't.
O:  No? Why not?
C:  Because there's a power outage.

O:  A power … A power outage? Ah, OK. I can handle this now. Listen, for the power outage, I'll have someone call the electricity company. For your WordPerfect problem, do you still have the boxes and manuals and packing stuff your computer came in?
C:  Well, yes. I keep them in the closet.
O:  Good. I'd like you to go and get them, to unplug your system and to pack it up just like it was when you got it. Then I want you to take it back to the store you bought it from.
C:  Really? Is it that bad?
O:  Yes, I'm afraid it is.
C:  Well, all right then, I suppose. What do I tell them?
O:  Tell them you're too stupid to own a computer.

**6**  Play 1:25 again, pausing at appropriate places to allow students time to complete the expressions. Get students to read the expressions aloud and check for pronunciation.

> **ANSWERS:**
>
> A  Explaining the problem
>    I'm having <u>trouble</u> with WordPerfect.
>    It doesn't <u>work</u>.
>    <u>It won't</u> accept anything when I type.
>    Nothing <u>happens</u>.
>    <u>I can't</u> type anything.
> B  Diagnosing the causes
>    Was it <u>working properly</u> before that?
>    What does your screen <u>look like</u> now?
>    Have you <u>tried hitting</u> 'Escape'?
>    <u>Did you</u> quit WordPerfect?
>    <u>Can you</u> move the cursor around?
>    <u>Does your monitor have</u> a power indicator?
> C  Giving instructions
>    <u>Could you look</u> on the back of the monitor?
>    Now <u>you just have to</u> follow the cord to the plug.
>    <u>I need you to</u> look back there again.
>    <u>I'd like you to</u> go and get them.
>    Then <u>I want you to</u> take it back to the store.
> D  Promising help
>    <u>I'll have someone call</u> the electricity company.

**7**  Get individual students to read the expressions aloud one by one. Ask the rest of the class to say which category they belong to.

> **ANSWERS:**
>
> [B] Have you installed any new software?
> [D] I'll get our technical expert to help you.
> [A] I'm having difficulty connecting to the Internet.
> [A] It keeps crashing.
> [C] You'll have to adjust the settings in the control panel.
> [D] We'll get back to you in a couple of hours.
> [B] What happens if you press 'Control' – 'Alt' – 'Delete'?
> [D] I'll have a technician call as soon as possible.

## Pronunciation

**8** 1:26  Play the recording and ask students to note down whether the intonation rises or falls at the end of each question. Ask if they can see the pattern, i.e. intonation falls at the end of the *wh-* questions and rises at the end of the *yes / no* questions.

While students are practising reading the questions with a partner, circulate and check intonation.

> **ANSWERS:**
>
> 1  a) down    b) down    c) up    d) up    e) up
>    f)  down

## RECORDING SCRIPT

🔊 1:26

a) What does your screen look like now?
b) What's a toolbar?
c) Did you quit WordPerfect?
d) Does your monitor have a power indicator?
e) Can you see the toolbar on the screen?
f) What do I tell them?

## FURTHER PRACTICE

Ask students to provide answers to the questions, to turn them into simple exchanges.

## Roleplay

**9** Read through the instructions with students. Make sure they understand all the technical problems listed. For their own ideas, students could use a real problem that they have experienced themselves. Remind students to use the language they practised in exercises 6–8 and to use the appropriate intonation.

With lower-level classes you may like to construct a conversation using one of the problems as a whole-class activity.

To consolidate the language work, get students to write down one or two of the conversations for homework.

## EXTENSION ACTIVITY

Finishing a telephone call can often be difficult to do. Brainstorm the kinds of things that students might need to do at the end of a call, and suggest some useful phrases or expressions for each one, e.g.:

- Signal that you would like to end the call
  *Well, it's been good talking to you.*
  *Is there anything else we need to discuss?*
  *I'm afraid I have to go – I have a meeting in five minutes.*
- Confirming action
  *Can we just go over what we've agreed to do?*
  *Could you put that in an email for me?*
  *I'll put that in writing and send it to you later today.*
- Promising action
  *I'll take care of that.*
  *I'll get back to you about that.*
- Closing statements
  *It's been very nice talking to you.*
  *See you at the meeting next week.*
  *Have a good weekend.*
  *Well, I really must go now.*

Students should practise saying these expressions with the appropriate intonation. Then, with a partner, they use them in the closing stages of some telephone conversations, e.g.:

A: *That's been a very helpful conversation. We've covered a lot today. Thanks a lot.*
B: *You're welcome.*
A: (Finish the call.)

A: *I think that's everything I wanted to ask you. Do you have any more questions?*
B: *Not right now, no.*
A: (Finish the call.)

A: *I really appreciate your help with the sales report. I've made a lot of notes about what we've discussed.*
B: *That's great. I'm glad I could help.*
A: (Finish the call.)

## 2.5 Writing
### Formal and informal correspondence

This module explores aspects of formal and informal style in different kinds of business correspondence.

### Internet research

*Email risk policy* refers to the range of issues that companies need to be concerned about in their use of email. It covers, for example, privacy issues, sexual harassment, bullying, online libel, theft of confidential information, etc. This can lead to losses in productivity, financial loss, and damage to a company's reputation. Companies may find themselves involved in costly legal proceedings as a result of email misuse or abuse. Companies should have a clear policy in place to cover these eventualities.

Students could also be asked to search news or business websites for items about the misuse or abuse of email, and report back to the class on any interesting stories they find which illustrate the risks involved.

### Discussion

**1** Remind students to think about grammar, vocabulary, style, opening, closing, etc. when they are discussing the differences between formal and informal correspondence.

Give pairs a few minutes to discuss and note down their answers, then take feedback from the whole class. Make a list on the board of all the points they raise. Keep this list, and add to it throughout the lesson as other points come up.

> **SUGGESTED ANSWER:**
>
> Depending on the language, typical features which distinguish formal from informal or neutral styles are: use of titles or specific form of address; use of polite / familiar 2nd person pronoun; absence / use of 1st person pronoun; absence / use of conventional polite expressions; use of indirect / direct style; use of formal / informal vocabulary; absence / use of contractions; use of references; reference to previous correspondence; length of sentences; layout constraints.

### Skim reading

**2** Remind students what skim reading is (see page 7). Question 1: Ask students to skim read the emails quickly to identify who the emails are from.

> **ANSWERS:**
>
> 4 a customer service department
> 3 a senior colleague
> 1 a junior colleague
> 2 a customer

Question 2: Students can work with a partner to decide which two emails are formal and which two are neutral / informal. Ask them to give reasons for their answers.

> **ANSWERS:**
>
> Formal messages: 1, 2
> Neutral / informal messages: 3, 4

## Reading for detail

**3** Students should re-read the emails in exercise 2 more closely to complete the grid.

With lower-level classes, you could do the first email as a whole-class activity. When the grid has been completed, elicit from students the differences between the two columns, i.e. in the formal column, the expressions are usually longer and more complex; in the informal column, they are shorter; unimportant words are omitted; vocabulary is less formal/more colloquial, etc.

**ANSWERS:**

| | Formal | Neutral / Informal |
|---|---|---|
| Greeting | Dear Ms Reckett, | Hi James, |
| | Dear Sir or Madam, | Dear Miss Roebotham, |
| Opening | I am writing with regard to ... | Thanks for your mail. |
| | I am writing to enquire about ... | Re your email ... |
| Requests | I was wondering if you could ...? | Give me a ring ... |
| | I would be very grateful if you could ... | Can you just ... ? |
| Closing | I would very much appreciate any help. | Hope this helps. |
| | Thank you for your help. | Don't hesitate to get back to me. |
| Salutation | Yours sincerely, | Cheers, |
| | Yours faithfully, | Regards, |

## Skim reading

**4** Get students to read each pair of emails and refer back to the emails in exercise 2 to decide which two writers have changed style and why.

Point out that it is usually good practice to write a first email to someone in a fairly formal style, and then to adjust (or retain) this style according to the response that you receive.

**ANSWERS / SUGGESTED ANSWERS:**

Question 1
James has adapted to Margaret's informal style after confirming that she remembers him from the party.
Max has switched to Miss Roebotham's formal style after discovering that she is not in fact an old friend.

Question 2
Email 5
Thanks → Thank you ...
Cheers → Yours sincerely
Email 6
I would be very grateful if you could → Can you ...
I would like to express my gratitude for → Thanks for ...
Email 7
I've attached ... → Please find attached ...
Hope this helps. → Do not hesitate to contact us again if you need any further information.
Email 8
I was wondering if you would mind coming ... → Could you come / Why don't you come ...?
Yours sincerely → Best wishes

## Writing

**5** Before students start this activity, explain the context to the whole class, i.e. Students A and B work for Relopharma, a pharmaceuticals company. Student A works in the Accounts Department and Student B in the Information Systems Department. Student C works for Nakisoft, a software company specializing in accountancy software, and one of Relopharma's suppliers. The task is for students to write and reply to a number of emails.

Get students to predict the kinds of things they might be asked to write about. It doesn't matter if they don't get the right answers – the idea is simply to get them thinking about the topic.

To help students focus on the task, ask them to tell you the style they will use (this will depend to some extent on the contents of the emails, but as they are all colleagues a fairly neutral style would be most appropriate). Remind them that the emails should be fairly short and to the point, but still polite.

Give students time to read the instructions and circulate to assist with understanding them, where necessary. Remind students that they have already practised much of the language needed to do the task in earlier parts of the unit, i.e. explaining the problem giving instructions, making requests, etc. Once students are sure what to do, get them to start writing. Higher-level students could be asked to write within a time limit.

To simulate reality, students should not ask their partners to clarify or explain anything in the email – if something is unclear, they should 'email' back for clarification.

While students are writing, circulate and assist where necessary. When they have finished the task, ask groups of students to read a string of emails aloud. Get the rest of the class to comment on the following questions:
*Is the correspondence effective?*
*Is the style appropriate? If not, can you* (either the person who wrote it or a classmate) *suggest ways of improving it?*

### EXTENSION ACTIVITY

Use this matching exercise to extend students' formal vocabulary. For lower-level classes, give both the informal and formal words. You could dictate the words or write them on the board. With higher-level classes, you could give just the informal words, and get them to work out the formal words for themselves, possibly with the help of a dictionary. (The informal / formal words are presented in the correct order. You will need to mix up one list of words so that students have to match them to the correct equivalent.)

| *Informal* | *Formal* |
|---|---|
| *to say sorry* | *to apologize* |
| *enough* | *sufficient* |
| *secret* | *confidential* |
| *quickly* | *promptly* |
| *to tell* | *to inform* |
| *late* | *overdue* |
| *to get in touch* | *to contact* |
| *to move* | *to relocate* |
| *to ask* | *to enquire* |
| *help* | *co-operation* |

## 2.6 Case study
## Cybertartan Software

This case study examines the problems faced by a contact centre – customer dissatisfaction, staff recruitment and retention, rising costs – and how they might be tackled.

### Internet research

*FLSA* stands for *Fair Labor Standards Act*. This is a law in the USA which deals with employment issues, including minimum wage, overtime pay, record-keeping, and working conditions for children. It covers full-time and part-time workers in the public and private sector. Employers who violate the Act may be fined or prosecuted.

The FLSA does not require employers to give employees meal or rest breaks, but if they do, they should usually be paid for short breaks (up to about 20 minutes), but not for longer breaks (usually lasting at least 30 minutes).

According to the FLSA, employees should be given bathroom breaks, but there are no federal laws that refer to the number and duration of bathroom breaks. This is covered by regulations issued by the Occupational Safety and Health Administration (OSHA) in the USA.

Students can research these issues in the employment laws of their own countries and report back to the class. Possible discussion questions are:
*Did they find out anything that surprises them?*
*What effect do they think these laws might have on productivity and morale among workers?*
*Do you disagree with any of the regulations?*
*What would you change?*

### Discussion

**1** Read the list of customer problems with the whole class and ask them to give you some real-world examples of each one. This could be things they've experienced themselves or things they've heard about.

With lower-level classes you could give one or two examples of your own to get them started, e.g. you got poorly translated instructions with an electronic product you bought; you were put on hold for a long time by a bank or insurance company and the call cost you a lot of money; the waiter / waitress in a coffee shop was very unfriendly and the service was slow, etc.

With a partner, get students to pick the three things that annoy them most. Take whole-class feedback, asking students to raise their hands for each problem listed in the box. Ask individual students to say why the problem annoys them.

Give students a few minutes to discuss what a customer could do about these problems. The solutions could be realistic or imaginary, i.e. what would you really like to do, even though it might be very difficult or impossible to achieve, but would be very satisfying!

### SUGGESTED ANSWERS:
Customers can make a complaint; send a product back to the manufacturer; refuse to buy specific products or use specific shops, etc.

### Scan reading

**2** Remind students what scan reading is (see page 7).
Question 1: Get students to read the email silently and look for the four problems. Ask individual students to tell you what the problems are.
Question 2: Answer this as a whole-class activity. Ask individual students to explain the links in their own words.

### ANSWER:
Question 1
customer satisfaction, recruitment problems, high staff turnover, need to reduce costs
Question 2
Customers are dissatisfied because there aren't enough advisers and because they are kept on hold to increase call charges; more money rather than less is required to recruit and keep good staff.

### Reading for detail

**3** Ask students to read the statements silently. Then read the email aloud. Get students to raise their hands when they hear the answer to the statements. Tell them that they will need to look at the email and the pie charts to find the answers. Ask them to give the words from the email which match the true statements, correct the false statements, and explain the 'it depends' statements.

### ANSWERS:
1 T
2 F (employees and customers are dissatisfied)
3 F (average call 12 minutes @ £0.50 / minute = £6: cost of call = £4.50)
4 D (it depends – perhaps not if hold time is reduced)
5 T
6 F (only 'very dissatisfied' tripled)
7 T

### Listening for detail

**4** 🔊 1:27 Play the first two lines of the interview – the interviewer's question and Laurie McAllister's response – and elicit the answer to the question. Ask:
*What other problem does she mention?* (salaries)
*How does the problem with salaries affect the contact centre?* (The salaries haven't kept pace with the cost of living and the company can't attract workers to the area.)

Get students to discuss briefly why they think working conditions and job satisfaction are more important to the workers than salary. Do they feel the same way about their own jobs?

### ANSWER:
The shift system

### RECORDING SCRIPT
🔊 1:27
Interviewer: So, Laurie, these recruitment and turnover problems we're having — is it just a question of money?
Laurie McAllister: Well of course salaries are not terribly attractive these days. They were quite good a few years ago when the centre opened, but they haven't really increased with the cost of living, especially now house prices are so expensive here, so we're finding it more difficult to attract people from outside the area. But, actually, salaries are not the biggest problem. Basically there are two reasons why our turnover is high: working conditions and job satisfaction.
I: I see. What's the matter with working conditions? We give them free coffee, don't we?
LM: Well, things are very different now from when we started. In the past, the volume of calls was much lower, so things were more relaxed. Advisers had time to chat or have a cigarette between two calls. Now, the workload is much heavier, and the supervisors have to be very strict about breaks. Two bathroom breaks per day, and twenty minutes for lunch. There's a lot of unhappiness about that. And

punctuality, well, the bus service here is totally inadequate. A lot of advisers can't afford a car, so transport is a real problem, especially at night.

I: Yes, I can see why that's a problem.

LM: And there are little things, you know, like having your own personal space. When you share your desk with your colleagues on the other shifts, you can't really personalize anything.

I: Hm. Maybe there are things that can be improved there. What's the problem with job satisfaction?

LM: Time, mostly. Our software products have become so complex that customers need more and more help. There are more calls than we can answer, so advisers have to keep them as short as possible. That's frustrating because there isn't time to build a relationship with the customer; sometimes there isn't even time to explain the solution properly. And then of course they say if they can't spend longer on the phone, they would like to send out instructions by email.

I: Yes, well, the customers would like that too, but we can't charge them for it like we can phone calls!

LM: Exactly. And we really need to give the advisers more training, especially the new people, but there just isn't time. They often have to read out instructions from the manual; it's not much fun answering questions when you don't really understand the answers yourself!

I: No. I can see that.

LM: Of course the thing they really don't like is the shift system. They work one week in the morning, from 6am to 2pm, one week in the afternoon from 2pm to 10pm, and one week nights, 10pm to 6am. I mean, it's OK for young, single people, but it's impossible for women with children, so that's a whole category of the population we have virtually no chance of employing. And some people actually like working nights, so they would happily swap their day shifts with other colleagues who don't want to work nights — but the company won't let them. It's company policy, but it's too rigid, it's just not realistic … Anyway, perhaps you should talk to the advisers themselves – get it straight from the horse's mouth, as they say.

**5** Read the statements aloud or get students to read them aloud and predict what effects they might have on the workers at the contact centre. Then play 🔘 1:27 again. Pause the recording after the answer to each statement and allow students a few minutes to make notes. Check answers with the whole class.

**ANSWERS:**
1 This leads to high staff turnover.
2 Supervisers have to be strict about punctuality and breaks.
3 Punctuality is a problem.
4 Advisers can't personalize their work space.
5 Customers need more help; there are more calls than the centre can answer, so advisers have to make calls as short as possible.
6 Advisers have to read out instructions from the manual; explaining things they don't understand themselves is not satisfying.
7 There is no chance of employing women with children.

## Solving problems

**6** Read through the instructions and the agenda with the whole class. As a reminder, you could get students to list the problems experienced at the Kirkcaldy contact centre. Students then use this list to prepare their presentations. Then in groups, students should brainstorm solutions and make recommendations.

## Writing presentation slides

**7** Before students prepare their slides, brainstorm what makes an effective slide (use only short phrases or sentences; use headings and bullet points to make the text easier to read and remember, etc.). Don't go into too much detail at this stage as Unit 7 deals with this in more depth.

Remind students that the slides are just about their recommendations, and each recommendation should have three parts – what it is, why it's a good idea, and what the expected results will be.

Circulate while students are working on their slides and assist where necessary.

## Presentations

**8** To help students with their presentations, you could give them a list of useful phrases, e.g.:
*First of all, I'd like to …*
*Let's look at the problem of …*
*That's all I have to say on …*
*Now let's move on to …*
*That brings me to the end of my presentation.*
*Are there any questions?*

The presentation should be fairly short and concise. One student in each group could be nominated to give the presentation, or each student could present one recommendation.

### FURTHER PRACTICE

Get students to write a short report from the consultants to Hamish Hamilton, consisting of a summary of the situation and the recommendations they have made in their presentations.

### EXTENSION ACTIVITY

Students rank these factors related to job satisfaction from most important to least important. They could do this individually first, and then discuss their answers in small groups.

- *good interpersonal relationships with colleagues*
- *job security*
- *promotion prospects*
- *interesting, challenging work*
- *a good salary and bonuses*
- *independence / autonomy to act*
- *good communications and information flow within the organization*
- *opportunities for personal growth and development*
- *a good manager*
- *benefits package (healthcare, gym membership, etc.)*
- *company pension scheme*

# Review 1 and 2 answers

## Review 1

(page 30 in the Student's Book)

### 1 Corporate culture

**1**

1 Incorporate b)
2 Enhance e)
3 Relate a)
4 Be assessed c)
5 Be supervised d)
6 Offer f)

**2**

1 deadline
2 insight
3 appraisal
4 workload
5 commitment
6 etiquette
7 overview
8 predecessor
9 outcome
10 threaten

**3**

1 of
2 in
3 for
4 with
5 under
6 with
7 after
8 to
9 on
10 of

**4**

1 in charge of
2 responsible for
3 deals with
4 looks after
5 takes care of

**5**

1 F
2 T (mostly, but can depend on hierarchy in a company)
3 F
4 F (Chief Operations Officer)
5 T
6 T
7 F (Research and Development)
8 F (subsidiaries)
9 T
10 F (organigram)

**6**

1 was working / started / had never thought
2 had already been / spoke / was parking

**7**

1 Actually
2 seems
3 might
4 could
5 Don't
6 Wouldn't

**8**

1 analysis
2 description
3 evaluation
4 observation
5 suggestion

## Review 2

(page 31 of the Student's Book)

### 2 Customer support

**1**

1 clean environment
2 satisfied customer
3 high staff turnover
4 subsidized meals

5 heavy workload
6 hourly rate
7 competent staff
8 dead-end job

**2**

1 annoyed (also: annoying)
2 competent
3 frustrated (also: frustrating)
4 grateful
5 helpful
6 knowledgeable
7 persuasive
8 reassuring (also: reassured)
9 satisfied (also: satisfying)
10 rude

**3**

1 push in
2 replace
3 offer
4 escalate
5 call
6 replace

**4**

Helpline operator: Before I can sort out the problem, I first need to locate exactly where the fault is.
Customer: OK, no problem, we can do that. But if it's still not working properly, can you replace the product, or at least give me a refund?
Helpline operator: Yes, that's possible, but I'm not authorized to do it. I would first have to escalate the problem to my supervisor.

**5**

I'll look into it, sort it out, and get back to you tomorrow.

**6**

1 through
2 down
3 in
4 on
5 through
6 down
7 into
8 on
9 up
10 up

**7**

1 monitor
2 toolbar
3 crash
4 upgrade
5 cartridge
6 plug in
7 attach
8 customer
9 supplier
10 guarantee

**8**

1 regard
2 would
3 grateful
4 could
5 attached
6 hesitate
7 get back to
8 further
9 appreciate
10 urgently

**9**

1 need
2 Q4
3 threat
4 linked
5 suggest
6 counting (could also be *depending*)

**P**roduct is one of the famous '4 Ps' of marketing (the others being *Price*, *Place* (i.e. distribution) and *Promotion*. In the past, when business people talked about 'products and services' the term *product* referred only to manufactured goods. Nowadays the distinction between a product and a service is increasingly blurred, so that a bank can offer 'financial products' and a manufacturing company can offer a service (e.g. customizing their products).

When developing a new product, a company needs to take into account a wide range of factors:

- the origin of any new product ideas: customers? sales staff?
- the fit with the existing product line
- manufacturing questions like: 'How easy will it be to make this new product with our existing equipment?'
- pricing, distribution and promotion of the new product.

The feasibility of new products depends very much on production and operations as well as marketing. If a product cannot be manufactured for a reasonable price then it cannot be sold for one.

Designing and developing a new product involves a number of different stages.

1 Research: Market research to find out customers' needs; technical and scientific research and development of a more fundamental nature (R&D); prioritizing research into different projects; lead time between starting a project and the product coming to market;
2 Design: Deciding the specifications to include in the design brief (features, size, weight, materials, etc.); screening out poor designs and choosing the final design; limitations in the production technology available; designing for manufacture (an easy process will lower production costs and mean fewer defects); designing for ease of disposal at the end of the product's life.
3 Prototype: Deciding how many working models to build; coordination between marketing and production when evaluating the prototype; which to prioritize: speed to market or more time for a better product?
4 Consumer tests: Choosing the target group for the test; deciding what to measure and how to measure it; modifying the prototype on the basis of the test results.
5 Full production: Set-up of machines and machine tools; supply of materials and parts; run time (time taken for a batch of products to go through the process); estimating consumer demand.

When the finished product is finally on the market, sales staff will need to know:

- its functions (what it does)
- its features (selling points)
- its customer benefits (how the features and functions make the customer's life easier)
- improvements that have been made (in what ways it's better than previous models)
- possibilities for customization
- how it compares with competitors' products.

Packaging is of course a key issue in the product mix, and its importance is often underestimated. Amongst other things, it a) attracts the buyer's attention, b) advertises the benefits of the product inside, c) lists the contents of the product inside, d) protects the product during handling and e) contributes to convenience and ease-of-use.

## Useful websites

In terms of Internet resources for further study, this is a good online magazine with free access to some articles and a sign-up newsletter:
http://www.designnews.com
The following site has a 'body of knowledge' (BOK) for new product development, including a link to a glossary:
http://www.npd-solutions.com/bok.html

## 3.1 About business
## Packaging

This module examines the packaging of products from the point of view of manufacturer and consumer.

### Internet research

*Universal design* refers to the design and delivery of products and services that can be used by everyone, regardless of age, ability, or situation, with the aim of promoting equal access for all. In packaging, this would mean that the packaging used must be accessible to a wide range of people, including the elderly, infirm, disabled, etc.

Students could research some examples of universal design in packaging and present the products to the class. For example, a liquid soap dispenser for children which is designed with a broad base and easy-action pump so that it is accessible to small hands; easy-open packaging of hearing aids, consumers of which are likely to be elderly people with little strength in their hands; easy-open ring-pulls on drinks so anyone can open them, etc.

It would be useful for students to do this search before the module as it will provide them with a good base of background knowledge about the subject of packaging. Or, students can use it as a follow-up activity to the lesson.

---

#### LEAD-IN ACTIVITY

Get student to write down every product they have bought or used in the last 24 hours which has been packaged in some way. Give them a few examples of your own to get them started, e.g. a doughnut in a paper bag; sandwiches in a plastic container; a notebook which a sales assistant put in a plastic carrier bag; a CD, etc. Ask students to put a tick next to each item of packaging that was essential and a cross next to the packaging which was not essential. Get students to estimate what percentage of the packaging used was non-essential.

---

### Discussion

**1** Bring in examples of pre-packaged goods, e.g. items of food and drink, stationery, batteries, a bottle, a carton, etc. Teach any new vocabulary, e.g. *cellophane*, *blister pack*, *child-proof top*, *cardboard*, *container*, etc. Students can also look at photographs and identify the types of packaging they see in them.

Hold the items up so that everyone can see them or pass them around so that students can handle them.

Discuss the topics listed in the Student's Book and make a list on the board of the points made.

### Listening for gist

**2**  1:28 Read the questions with students and play the whole interview through. Get them to compare their answers with a partner. Then take whole-class feedback.

As a follow-up, discuss the these questions:
*Do you agree with Charlie Wang's view that packaging is the best way to communicate the differences between products? Does packaging influence your choice of purchase, or are there other factors?*

Check that students understand the meaning of 'cross-functional task force' (a group of people with different backgrounds or expertise working towards a common goal. It could include people from finance, production, marketing, human resources and might involve employees from all levels. Some members of the group might also come from outside the organization, e.g. suppliers, customers). Do not develop this theme yet, as it comes up in more detail in exercise 4.

### RECORDING SCRIPT

1:28

**Interviewer:** Mr. Wang, you often say that packaging is the manufacturer's last chance to seduce the customer. Why is that?

**Wang:** Yes. Today's marketplace is highly competitive; many products are almost identical, at least from the consumer's point of view. Branding is not enough: unless you are the number one brand on the market, you start from the same level as everyone else. That's especially true here in Asia where there may be literally hundreds of competitors making the same product in the same city. In order to persuade the customer to buy your product rather than your competitor's, you have to differentiate, that is to say, to create and, above all, to communicate the difference which makes your product the better choice. In his book *Differentiate or Die*, the American business guru Jack Trout says, 'Every aspect of your communications should reflect your difference. The bottom line is: You can't overcommunicate your difference.'

**I:** So, packaging is the best way to communicate your difference?

**W:** Exactly. 75% of purchasing decisions are made at the point of sale. Today, nine times out of ten that purchase will be made in a self-service context. Your product is alone on the shelf, surrounded by its competitors. According to Wal-Mart, the world's largest retailer, your product has to pitch its promise to the customer in three seconds or less, from up to fifteen feet away. If your packaging is not attractive, effective and distinctive, how are you going to communicate its difference? That's why I say that packaging is the last chance to seduce the customer.

**I:** Yes, I see. Now, if packaging is so critical, with millions of dollars poured into design, graphics and efficient use of limited shelf space, why is it that there are so many failures?

**W:** The principal problem is a lack of communication between the different partners involved in the design and development process. Typically there'll be several different groups of experts, all working in their own specialized field: market research people who know nothing about design, designers who know nothing about manufacturing, and production people who know nothing about consumer needs. Traditionally, the design team has always been kept well away from business and manufacturing constraints so as not to limit their creativity. The result is inevitably a compromise. What starts out as an original, creative idea turns out to be impractical, for reasons of cost or technical limitations. So, it gets watered down, simplified, adapted – until, in the end, you are left with a package which is easy to make, easy to transport and within budget, so production, logistics and finance are happy, but it's no longer what the consumer wanted! So, you get focus groups where consumers don't really like any of the concepts that are presented. That means, in the best case, you go back to the drawing board and start all over again or, in the worst case, you have to choose the least unpopular option!

I: So, how do you avoid this problem at New China Packaging?

W: Well, basically, what we do is to build what we call a 'task force'. This a cross-functional team with players from all the stakeholders in the project. We literally lock them up in a hotel together, we provide all the tools they need to produce mockups and prototypes, and we don't let them out until they produce something that everybody is enthusiastic about.

I: And do you include consumers in the task force?

W: Yes, indeed. We need the end user's input right from the beginning. Everything is consumer-led. And, because we know that what consumers say they need and what they really need are frequently two different things, we also observe them using the product. Frequently, we can detect behaviours and needs that the consumer is not even conscious of.

I: Really? Uh-huh. So, who else is involved?

W: Corporate Marketing, because we need to work within the constraints of brand strategy, funding and schedules; manufacturing, so that we deal with technical issues as and when they arise; and, of course, our own designers and consultants, who contribute creative ideas, technical know-how and marketing expertise.

I: And how long does the process take?

W: Traditionally, months or sometimes years. Today, our task forces can usually deliver an optimal solution in one week, sometimes less. And remember, when they deliver, it means that every aspect of the package is consumer validated, is realistic and practically feasible, and respects business limitations. So, this extremely short turn-around means that the manufacturer can react very, very quickly to changes in the market, almost in real time.

I: Yes, I see, and …

## Listening for detail

**3** Read the statements aloud or get students to read them aloud and see if they can respond to any before they listen again. Then play 1:28 again. Check answers with the whole class. Get students to correct the false statements.

| ANSWERS | | | | |
|---|---|---|---|---|
| 1 T | 2 F | 3 F | 4 T | 5 T |
| 6 F | 7 T | 8 T | 9 F | 10 T |

## Discussion

**4** Get students to do this with a partner. Take whole-class feedback on the arguments for and against cross-functional task forces from the point of view of different departments.

**ANSWERS / SUGGESTED ANSWERS:**

1 a) HR (for)    b) Sales (against)
2 R&D: 'The benefits are similar to those in packaging design: knowing customer needs, production constraints and financial priorities helps engineers produce better products.' (for)
Training: 'They might perhaps be useful in designing programmes, but not in delivering them; attendees prefer to have a single contact.' (against)
IT: 'They're very useful in determining the exact needs of users and administrators at all levels, as well as the financial and technical constraints.' (for)

### EXTENSION ACTIVITY

Get students to comment on how they think cross-functional task forces would work in their jobs / company, or if they have any personal experience of them.

## Scan reading

**5** Get students to look at the photo. Ask: *What is the man doing? Is he trying to eat this product? Look at his face – how do you think he feels?* Read the caption '60,000 people a year are injured in Britain' and ask: *How do you think these people are injured?*

Read the questions with your students. Ask if they can predict the answers to the questions before they read. If necessary, explain *triggers* (causes).

Give students a few minutes to read the text silently, underlining the words that help them with the answers to the questions as they read. Remind them what scan reading is (see page 7). Remind students to use the *Wordlist* in their books on page 151. Check answers with the whole class.

**ANSWERS:**

1 'Wrap rage' is a new term used to describe the irritation and loss of self-control experienced when struggling to open wrapping / product packaging.
2 It's especially prevalent amongst seniors: 70% of over 50s experience wrap rage-related injuries.
3 It's triggered by sterile food packs, child- or pilfer-proof packaging, ring-pull cans, price tags and overpackaging.
4 There is pressure on manufacturers to meet stringent protection standards at low cost.

## Paraphrasing

**6** Students could do this exercise with a partner. Allow them to use dictionaries. Remind them to re-read the sentence in which the phrase occurs so that they can see it in its full context. Check answers with the whole class.

**SUGGESTED ANSWERS:**

1 to decrease the amount of stock that disappears from shops because it is stolen by customers or staff
2 the factors which most often cause people to become frustrated and irritated with packaging
3 people can even lose their temper trying to remove labels with prices from some products
4 something which enrages people who feel strongly about ecology
5 after a long period of discouragement there are signs of hope
6 Basically, unless they respond, they'll lose customers.

## EXTENSION ACTIVITY

Ask students to share any similar experiences of their own with packaging. Ask them if they can they identify one item of packaging which they find particularly difficult or annoying?

## Discussion

**7** Read the instructions with the whole class.

With lower-level classes, brainstorm answers to the questions to help them get started, and write any useful vocabulary on the board. Students could also refer to the results of their Internet research on universal design and packaging.

Get each group to present their packaging solution using the questions in the Student's Book to provide a structure for their presentation. Groups should also be prepared to take questions from the rest of the class.

### SUGGESTED ANSWERS:

1 Most commonly used materials are plastic and cardboard or paperboard. Paperboard is cheap, recyclable, easy to print on, plastic is more versatile and more secure. Other materials such as metal, glass and wood are unlikely to be used for this type of product.

2 and 3 Anything is possible, but preferably not a standard, rectangular box with pale or dark colours and small photos and print.

## EXTENSION ACTIVITY

As a follow-up, get students to evaluate the packaging solution using the criteria in the discussion activity on page 32, i.e. protection, identification, transport, storage, display, security. Alternatively, they could discuss the pros and cons of each packaging solution using the points mentioned by Charlie Wang in the listening activity on page 32, i.e. Is the design attractive, effective and distinctive? Does the packaging help to communicate the difference between this product and other products? Will this packaging help to persuade consumers to buy the product?

## 3.2 Vocabulary
## Specifications and features

This module practices describing products and outlining their main features in a product presentation.

### Internet research

Two common ways of recording vocabulary are to use vocabulary notebooks or word cards. In a vocabulary notebook students might record, for example, individual words, pronunciation, useful phrases or chunks of language, word families, collocations, or lexical sets. They could also use mind maps or make their own dictionaries.

Encourage students to find and try out as many different techniques as possible so that they can find the ones that suit them best.

## Discussion

**1** Give students a few minutes to put the stages of product development in the right order. Check answers with the whole class by calling on students to read the sentences aloud.

### ANSWERS:

The most likely chronological order:

6 Beta test the product by users in typical situations.

5 Conduct market studies to test the concept.

8 Launch the product.

4 Draw sketches and build mockups.

7 Go into production.

3 Draw up specifications for the product.

1 Generate new ideas in focus groups and brainstorming meetings.

2 Screen out unfeasible or unprofitable ideas.

## FURTHER PRACTICE

To provide further practice of the collocations, get students to close their books and give you the correct verb in each case, e.g. *to ____ ideas, to ____ ____ unprofitable ideas*, or the noun, e.g. *to test the ____, to launch the ____*.

## Reading for detail

**2** When students have completed the sentences, get them to read them aloud. This is an opportunity to check that students can say numbers with decimal points, e.g. *thirty-one point four*, and the abbreviations *g* (grams), *cm* (centimetres), *kg* (kilograms).

If students are unsure of the words, write them in two columns on the board under *adjectives* and *nouns*.

| | |
|---|---|
| *high* | *height* |
| *wide* | *width* |
| *long* | *length* |

You could also check that students know how to say the three dimensions shown in the picture, e.g. '45.4 by 31.4 by 7.6'.

### ANSWERS:

1 The large FedEx Box is 31.4 cm wide and 45.4 cm long. It is 7.6 cm high. When empty, the box weighs 400 g; it can be used to ship small parts or computer printouts up to 9 kg in weight.

2 The FedEx Tube is 96.5 cm in length and 15.2 cm in height and width. With a weight of 450 g when empty, it can be used to ship plans, posters, blueprints etc. weighing up to 9 kg.

## Describing products

**3** Students could put a range of items from their pockets and bags on the desk in front of them to do this activity. Without naming it or pointing to it, each student in turn describes an object while the other students guess which one it is. Circulate and check that students are using the target language correctly.

## Collocations

**4** Read through the words in the box and the compound adjectives with the class. Draw students' attention to the meanings of some of the adjectives, e.g. *eye-catching* and *attention-grabbing* have similar meanings; *waterproof* (does not let water through) is different from *water-resistant* (offers only some protection from water damage).

**ANSWERS:**

1 energy-saving / labour-saving devices
2 fire-retardant / water-resistant materials
3 waterproof / shockproof personal stereos
4 child-resistant / tamper-resistant packaging
5 future-proof / foolproof technology
6 eye-catching / attention-grabbing design

Elicit from students any other compound adjectives they might know, and some possible collocations, e.g. *heat-resistant (materials), stain-resistant (materials, clothing), time-saving (device), rainproof (jacket), soundproof (room), bullet-proof (car, vest)*.

## Listening for gist

**5**  1:29–1:34 Play the six conversations and allow students to choose the correct collocations individually before checking answers with the whole class. Get students to pick out the words or phrases they heard which helped them arrive at the answer.

**ANSWERS:**

1 shockproof personal stereos
2 a labour-saving device
3 eye-catching / attention-grabbing design
4 child-resistant packaging
5 water-resistant materials
6 foolproof technology

### RECORDING SCRIPT

 1:29–1:34

**1**
A: I want to listen to English while I go jogging. Is that possible?
B: Oh, yeah. Jogging, cycling, skiing … whatever you like. Nothing can stop it. I even dropped mine down two flights of stairs, and when I picked it up, it was still working.

**2**
C: I hear you bought one of those new robots. What do you think of it?
D: It's fantastic! I used to spend hours cleaning the flat. Now I can just program the robot and sit back and watch it work.
A: That's incredible! I must get one …

**3**
E: I really like the colour. It's a beautiful car!
F: Yes, and it's an interesting shape too. Quite unusual. Very different from other cars in this category, isn't it?

**4**
G: Mum, what's in this bottle? I can't open it!
H: Give that to me, dear. You mustn't touch that. It's for cleaning the kitchen, and it's dangerous. Fortunately, they put it in a special bottle that children can't open …

**5**
I: Quick, it's starting to rain and there's a pallet of those electronic toys outside!
J: OK, I'll move it straight away. But don't worry – the boxes are made of special paperboard. A little rain won't do any damage.

**6**
K: Are you sure I'll be able to record TV programmes? I mean, I'm not very good at anything technical.
L: Oh, yes. No worries. My five-year-old can operate this model. It's dead easy.

For further practice, students could work with a partner to produce similar short conversations using more of the collocations in exercise 4 and/or the additional ones listed above.

**6**  1:35 Ask students to listen to the start of the presentation and tell you what the Maptech i3 is (an integrated nautical information system). Play the first two paragraphs of the recording and then pause so that students can give you the answer. Ask them to brainstorm what kinds of features it might have.

Then play the rest of the presentation, pausing, if necessary, to allow students to make notes about the three main features of the Maptech i3. Ask students to note down the name of each feature and a brief description of it in their own words. Check answers with the whole class.

**ANSWERS:**

one-finger navigation, underwater radar and fishfinder, communications functions

### RECORDING SCRIPT

 1:35

Good afternoon everybody. Imagine you're on a fishing trip. It's the middle of the night. It's dark, it's foggy, you can't see a thing, and you're sailing your boat between small islands and dangerous rocks. Are you afraid? Not at all. You are supremely confident, checking and adjusting your route with just a touch of a finger on a screen. How do you do it?

Well, I'm here today to tell you about the Maptech i3, an extraordinary, integrated nautical information system, where a touch-controlled screen enables you to enjoy single finger operation of several different navigation functions.

Let's start with Touch Screen Command. 'Let your finger do the navigation' is our slogan. Just by touching the screen, you can view and change charts, calculate distances, create a route and a lot more. The large colour display screen automatically shows you a bird's-eye view of where you are and where you're heading. Let me show you an example of what I mean. As you can see, it's a little like floating about 1,000 feet above the boat and watching as you progress up the channel.

Moving on to what's below the water, thanks to the radar overlay, you see exactly what the fish are seeing. Some of you here today may think fishing is boring, but I can assure you that it's a lot more exciting when you know where the fish are – and with the Touch Screen 3D Fishfinder, that's exactly what you can do!

Now, can I just turn to communications? The Maptech i3 can send fax, email and voice messages. You can even send a message showing your boat's location on a real chart. You can request and receive weather reports based on your actual GPS position. And you can even automatically monitor vital onboard systems when you're away from your boat.

So, I'll just sum up the Maptech i3's main benefits. Let's just go back to our midnight fishing trip. First, Touch Screen Command lets you navigate between the rocks with just one finger and a bird's-eye view. Secondly, the underwater radar and fishfinder shows you where the rocks are, and where the fish are hiding.

Finally, the communications functions mean you can receive and send important data on the weather, your location and your boat at any moment.

I'd like to finish by inviting you to try the Maptech i3 for yourself. Our website has an incredibly realistic simulation that you can try out without ever getting your feet wet. Thank you very much.

## Listening for detail

**7** Get students to try to complete the expressions before they listen again. Then play 🔘 1:35 again so that they can check their answers.

**ANSWERS:**

| 1 about | 2 with | 3 of | 4 on |
|---|---|---|---|
| 5 to | 6 up | 7 back | 8 by |

**8** Do this matching exercise with the whole class. Play the recording again. This time, get students to focus on the structure of the presentation and the five stages identified here. They can also practise repeating the expressions aloud.

**ANSWERS:**

a) Beginning the presentation (1, 2)
b) Moving to a new point (4, 5)
c) Developing an idea (3)
d) Returning to a point made earlier (7)
e) Ending the presentation (6, 8)

## Presentation

**9** Give students a few minutes to choose an electronic product that they want to present. They can use the products in the photos or their own ideas. Remind them of the work they have done on product specifications and features, the nouns and compound adjectives they have practised, and the structure of the presentation they listened to.

Students could make some notes about their product and the points they want to make so that the structure is clear. Each student in the group could then be asked to prepare one or more parts of the presentation, depending on the size of the group. Circulate and assist where necessary.

You could ask groups to do their presentation for the whole class. The rest of the class could listen and check that it follows an appropriate structure and provides clear information. While students are making their presentations, make a note of any common mistakes in the target language for remedial teaching.

# 3.3 Grammar
## Articles, relative clauses and noun combinations

This module practises articles, relative clauses and noun combinations in the context of expanding notes and defining words.

### Internet research

Searching an online dictionary for the noun 'information' will reveal that it is an uncountable noun. Its informal form is *info*. It is used with *about* and *on*. Some typical collocations are: *information technology, information retrieval, information overload*; some typical constructions are: *a piece of information* and *a mine of information*.

In addition to providing definitions, phonetic transcriptions, and example sentences, online dictionaries allow students to hear audio pronunciations and find links to other useful websites. When they are browsing different online dictionaries, get students to conduct searches for the same word(s) in two or more dictionaries. This will allow them to do a more accurate comparison between them.

### Test yourself: Articles

**1** Start by reading the *Refresh your memory* box on articles with students. If students seem unsure of how to use them, work through some or all of exercises 1–4 in the *Grammar and practice* section (page 122 in the Student's Book, answers on page 117 in this book) before they do the exercise.

Students could work with a partner to insert the missing articles. Check answers with the whole class, getting students to explain the reason for their choice.

**ANSWERS:**

In 1485, Leonardo da Vinci made detailed sketches of parachutes. He also sketched studies for a/the helicopter, a/the tank and retractable landing gear. The first helicopter that could carry a person was flown by Paul Cornu at the beginning of the twentieth century. During the first World War, tanks were first used in France in 1917. An airplane with retractable landing gear was built in the United States in 1933.
Bar codes were invented by Silver and Woodland in 1948. They used light to read a set of concentric circles, but it was two decades before the advent of computers and lasers made the system practical. However, the bar code system in use today is the Universal Product Code, introduced by IBM in 1973. The first bar coded items sold were packs of chewing-gum in 1974.
The computer was launched in 1943, more than 100 years after Charles Babbage designed the first programmable device. In 1998, the Science Museum in London built a working replica of the Babbage machine using (the) materials and (the) work methods available in Babbage's time. It worked just as Babbage had intended.

### Test yourself: Relative clauses

**2** Get students to complete the exercise and check answers with the whole class. If students need further information or practice, turn to the *Grammar and practice* section (page 122 in the Student's Book, answers on page 117 in this book). Students could simply read the tinted explanation boxes to help them understand any answers they got wrong or they could do the exercises too, either in class or for homework.

**ANSWERS:**

| 1 which | 2 that / which | 3 that / which / no pronoun |
|---|---|---|
| 4 who | 5 who | 6 that / which / no pronoun |

## Test yourself: Noun combinations

**3** Lower-level classes could work through the exercises in the *Grammar and practice* section (page 123 in the Student's Book, answers on page 117 in this book) before they do the exercise, as they involve a more progressive build-up from shorter to longer combinations.

**ANSWERS:**
1. ever-shorter product development cycles
2. increasingly complex technical support requirements
3. Web-based customer feedback programs
4. real-world pre-market product feedback
5. cross-functional product development team

## Expanding notes

**4**  1:36 This exercise and exercise 5 allow students to do further practice on articles within a real-world context of expanding notes. Write the notes on the board before playing the recording. Once they have listened, get students to come to the board to insert the missing words. Or, elicit the missing words from students and write them on the board yourself. Make a list of the words which have been omitted: *the*, *this*, *it's*, *I*, *it*, *there are*, *be*, *have*, etc.

### RECORDING SCRIPT

🔘 1:36

Message: Please record your product review and your rating out of five after the beep. Thank you for your feedback.
Customer 1: This is easily the best phone I've had so far. It's the perfect phone for the basic user. I have already bumped it and dropped it a few times but it's still going strong. The battery life is incredible. Overall, it's a real workhorse – there are no frills, but it does what a cellphone needs to do. I rate it five out of five.

**5** 🔘 1:37–1:38 Circulate while students are discussing how to expand the notes. Refer them to the list of omitted words on the board. Get students to read their sentences aloud and compare versions before listening to the recording.

### RECORDING SCRIPT

🔘 1:37–1:38

1
Message: Please record your product review and your rating out of five after the beep. Thank you for your feedback.
Customer 2: I hate this phone. It's too small – I can't open the flip cover with one hand. There's no screen on the outside to see the caller identity. The reception is horrible. It drops calls probably 30% of the time. There is a very long key delay, which is incredibly annoying. I am anxiously awaiting the day I can upgrade and get rid of this monstrosity. I rate it zero out of five.

2
Message: Please record your product review and your rating out of five after the beep. Thank you for your feedback.
Customer 3: I've had the phone for about three weeks. I like the size and the design. The features are good too. It's easy enough to use, and it has survived a couple of drops. However, the alarm clock won't work anymore. I'm not too sure about the internal antenna. I hate having a full signal when making a call, only to have a dramatic drop when I put the phone to my head. Everybody says it's the telecom company's fault, not the phone, or maybe I just got a bad one. We'll see. I'm going to try the 9200 next. I would give it a rating of three out of five.

## Defining words

**6** and **7** Get students to work with a partner to do these exercises. Check answers with the whole class.

Some students may be concerned that some of the sentences end with a preposition, even when this is grammatically correct. This is acceptable in conversation and in much professional writing. To avoid putting the preposition at the end would often make the sentence sound more formal than is required for the context. However, in more formal writing, it may be better to avoid putting the preposition at the end.

**ANSWERS / SUGGESTED ANSWERS:**

Exercise 6
1 c)    2 a)    3 d)    4 b)

Exercise 7
1. Focus groups are groups <u>which / that</u> companies get product feedback <u>from</u>.
2. Consumer empowerment is an approach <u>which / that</u> gives consumers <u>power</u>.
3. A ring-pull can is a can <u>which / that</u> has a ring to open it <u>with</u>.
4. Complex text layout languages are languages <u>whose</u> text layout is <u>complex</u>.
5. Child-proof packaging is packaging <u>which / that children</u> can't open.
6. An award-winning design is a design <u>which / that</u> a jury has given an award <u>to</u>.
7. Portable document format (PDF) is a standard format <u>whose</u> code can be read by all computers.
8. Household-cleaning products are products <u>which / that</u> you clean the house <u>with</u>.

## Definitions game

**8** Give students a few minutes to read the instructions and look up any new words in their dictionaries. Remind them to use what they practised in exercises 6 and 7 to help them prepare their definitions. However, they should start their definitions: *This is …* or *These are …* to avoid giving the answer, e.g. from Student B: *This is a container that is economical with material.*

## 3.4 Speaking
## Presentations – structure

This module focuses on how to organize and deliver an effective product presentation.

### Internet research

This research will be particularly helpful for exercise 8, so ask students to do the search before they do that task. Students will find a range of websites offering a wealth of tips on how to make effective presentations. After individual research, get students to compare and exchange their answers to the questions.

You could also use this information as the basis for a poster or handout providing a detailed list of presentation tips for future reference.

## Brainstorming

**1** If students need help getting started on this brainstorming activity, give them a list of topics to think about, e.g. structure of the lesson, lecture or presentation, content, delivery, teacher / speaker, visuals, pace, timing / length. At this point, students should simply note down key words and phrases. Take whole-class feedback and make a list on the board. Get students to expand on their basic points by giving examples to clarify what they mean or anecdotes about real situations they have experienced.

### SUGGESTED ANSWERS:

well-structured, well-researched, well-prepared, well-targeted, well-paced, entertaining, sense of humour, varied, interactive, interesting voice, good eye-contact, smart appearance, clear and attractive visuals, not too long

## Listening for gist

**2**  1:39  Play the first part of the recording, up to '… enormous potential for this product'* and ask students: *What is wrong with the opening of this presentation? How does it compare with the points in the checklist in exercise 1?*

Then play the rest of the presentation and get students to check what they hear against the list of qualities of a good presentation. Check answers with the whole class, getting students to make complete sentences, e.g.:
*The speaker is very hesitant. It makes him/her sound uncertain.*
*The information isn't well-structured, which makes it a bit confusing.*

### RECORDING SCRIPT

 1:39

Version 1
Um, shall I start then? OK, I know, erm, I know you're going to be very excited by the Pingman, like me! So, I'm sure you'll have lots of questions. And, perhaps we'll take questions after the demonstration.
OK, er, we've done lots of tests, which have all been very positive, and, er, there are lots of different markets for the Pingman, children, adults, dogs, businesses, and so on. We think there's an enormous potential for this product. *Until now, GPS tracking systems have been too bulky, too heavy and too unreliable indoors to be used as personal tracking devices. Our Pingman weighs only 75g, and, well, we'll show you how it works in a few minutes… on the, er, Internet. So, you know, you can connect to the Internet from anywhere in the world, and just ping your user to know exactly where they are. Within

one metre … er. Nobody else has a product like this on the market, so we want you to approve the investment, because there's a huge market. Ping? Oh, yes, on the Internet, you tell a satellite to send a signal to the device, and the device answers the signal, and then the satellite can calculate the device's exact location.
Anyway, it only weighs 75g, did I say that already? Yes, er, 75g, it's five centimetres in length and about three point five centimetres wide, so, about half the size of a cellphone, and there are different models for children or adults. Tests were really positive, and our sales forecasts are excellent. There's also a model for animals; it's built in to a collar so, if you lose your dog, for example, you just ping it from the Internet to know where it is.
So, er, unless you want to ask questions, I think we'd better have the demonstration. Oh, I forgot to mention profitability. We think it will, er, will be profitable. Very profitable. OK, are there any questions? No? No questions? Um, OK then, let's have the demonstration. It's, er, at the back of the room. Yes. Er, …

**3** With lower-level classes you could give some sentence stems to help students formulate their suggestions for improvement: *The speaker should / could …; Instead of …(-ing* verb), *the speaker should / could …*, etc. Take whole-class feedback.

### SUGGESTED ANSWERS:

Aspects to improve: structure, voice, pace, stress and intonation, hesitations.

## Listening for detail

**4**  1:40  Play Version 2 of the presentation and get students to raise their hands when they hear each item on the checklist.

Get students to work with a partner to decide what other aspects of the presentation have improved. Refer students back to the list compiled in exercise 1.

### ANSWERS:

All items on the checklist should be ticked.
Suggested answers for improvements in presentation technique in Version 2:
- The presentation is better prepared with fewer hesitations.
- The speaker addresses the audience's interests and gets them involved.
- The voice is firmer, clearer, more audible, more confident and persuasive.
- The pace is more appropriate.
- Stress and intonation give variety and interest and convey the speaker's enthusiasm.

### RECORDING SCRIPT

 1:40

Version 2
Good morning everybody. How would you like to know at all times exactly where your young child or teenager is? How comforting would it be to know that your elderly mother is safely back home from the shops? Did you know that, on average, sales representatives spend less than 20% of their time actually with customers? How much would it be worth to know precisely where your sales reps or technicians were? And how much time would you save if you knew where, to the nearest metre, your dog was hiding?
Well, now you can. I'm here this morning to present the Pingman, a revolutionary new personal GPS tracking device – an eye in the sky which will bring peace of mind to parents, carers, businesses, animal lovers and many, many other potential customers. As you know, the reason I'm here today is

to demonstrate our prototype and to ask you, members of the Board, to approve the investment needed to start production. Now, I know you're going to be very excited by the Pingman, so I'm going to give you a quick overview of the product and the market in about fifteen minutes. After that, there'll be a hands-on demonstration, and I've allowed about 45 minutes for questions and discussion after that. But if you have questions that can't wait, feel free to interrupt me. OK?

I've divided my presentation into three sections. First of all, I'm going to remind you of the background to this project and the current offer on the market. After that, I'll be talking about the prototype, the specifications and the data we've collected from tests, focus groups and market studies. Finally, I'd like to present a business plan; this will show you why we expect a return on investment that is without precedent for our company. Is everybody happy with that agenda? OK, so, let's start with the background. Now, GPS tracking systems are not new. We've been able to install them in vehicles and containers for some time, but until now they've been too bulky, too heavy, and too unreliable indoors to be used as a personal tracking device. What's new about the Pingman is that for the first time we can build it into a wrist strap or collar small and light enough to be worn comfortably by a small child or a dog. For the first time, it will be possible to locate the wearer via the Internet, anywhere in the world, indoors or out, 24 hours a day and up to every ten seconds …

… does that answer your question? OK, so, I'd like to wrap up the presentation and move on to the demonstration. Let me just summarize what I've already told you. Firstly, I explained why there is a huge market just waiting for this product, and why the competition are still months behind us. Secondly, I presented the different specifications for the child, adult and animal versions we intend to launch, and the overwhelmingly positive reactions we've had during trials. Last, but not least, I have given you the strongest possible reasons why you should approve this investment: extraordinary sales forecasts, strong cash flow and unprecedented profitability.

So, ladies and gentlemen, these are the reasons why I am asking you to give this project the green light. I believe we cannot afford to miss this opportunity.

Now, if you'd like to move to the back of the room, our R&D staff are ready to start the demonstration and to answer your questions. Thank you very much for your attention.

**5**  1:40  Read through the language in the table with the students. Then play Version 2 again, pausing at appropriate places, while students complete the expressions.

**ANSWERS:**

Hook
1  How <u>would you like</u> to know …?
2  Did <u>you know</u> that, on <u>average</u>, …?
Objective
3  <u>I'm here</u> this morning <u>to present</u> the Pingman …
4  The reason <u>I'm here today</u> is …
Agenda
5  <u>Feel free</u> to interrupt me.
6  I've divided my presentation <u>into three sections</u>.
7  <u>First of all</u>, I'm going to …
8  <u>After that</u>, I'll be talking about …
9  <u>Finally</u>, I'd like to present …
Summary
10  I'd like to <u>wrap up</u> the presentation.
11  <u>Firstly</u>, I explained why …
12  <u>Secondly</u>, I presented the different specifications …
13  <u>Last</u>, but not <u>least</u>, I have given you …
Call for action
14  These are <u>the reasons why</u> I am asking you to …
Close
15  Thank you very much <u>for your attention</u>.

## FURTHER PRACTICE

Get students to substitute the phrases in column 2 of the table for the actual words they heard on the recording, e.g. instead of: *Did you know that on average sales representatives …* use the phrase: *Somebody once said*, i.e. *Somebody once said that on average sales representatives…*, etc.

## EXTENSION ACTIVITY

Put students into groups to discuss solutions for the following 'presentations problems'. What would they suggest that the speaker does in each case to change or improve their approach?

a) *Norman is very nervous about giving presentations. He is an expert in his field so the content of his presentations is good, but gets very nervous and forgets what he wants to say.*
b) *Olivia always overruns when she gives a presentation. She finds it difficult to be concise and never finishes on time.*
c) *Dieter doesn't speak clearly and never looks at his audience when he gives a presentation. He plays with the keys or loose coins in his pocket. His audience often becomes bored and restless.*
d) *Marie's presentations are usually very boring. She prepares detailed handouts and usually reads aloud what is written on them, adding comments as she goes.*

Students can refer to the work they have done in this module to help them or they can use their own ideas. Take whole-class feedback.

As a follow-up, ask students if they have experienced any of these problems. If they have experienced any other problems, they could share them and the rest of the class could suggest ways of dealing with them.

## Pronunciation

**6**  1:41  Students could do this exercise on pausing and intonation with a partner. Encourage them to say the words aloud so that they can hear what they sound like. When they have finished, ask a couple of students to read their paragraphs aloud and get the rest of the class to comment. Then play the recording and have students check their answers. See answers for exercise 7 on the next page.

## RECORDING SCRIPT

 1:41

I've divided my presentation into three sections. First of all, I'm going to remind you of the background to this project and the current offer on the market. After that, I'll be talking about the prototype, the specifications and the data we've collected from tests, focus groups and market studies. Finally, I'd like to present a business plan; this will show you why we expect a return on investment that is without precedent for our company. Is everybody happy with that agenda?

## FURTHER PRACTICE

Play  1:41 again. Stop at each pause so that students can repeat it quietly to themselves, either with their eyes closed or by reading the words from the book.

**7** ⏺ **1:41** Follow the same procedure as for exercise 6 for this exercise on stress and linking.

Finally, get individual students to read the paragraph aloud, bringing intonation, stress, and linking together in a naturalistic way.

For homework, students could record themselves reading the paragraph. They could then play it back and assess their own delivery.

**ANSWERS:**

I've divided my presentation into three sections. ↘ |First of all, ↗ I'm going to remind you of the background to this project ↗ | and the current offer on the market. ↘ |After that, ↗ |I'll be talking about the prototype, ↗ |the specifications ↗ |and the data we've collected from tests, focus groups and market studies. ↘ |Finally, I'd like to present a business plan; ↘ |this will show you why we expect a return on investment that is without precedent for our company. ↘ |Is everybody happy with that agenda? ↗

## Presentation

**8** This activity may require two lessons, with part of it done for homework. Read the instructions with the students. First, get students to decide which product they are going to present and what they want to say about it. The decisions they make here will also feed into the content of the presentation.

Then get students to review the work they did in earlier exercises in this module. This will help when it comes to preparing what they are going to say.

Students can divide the presentation among two or more people, but should ensure that there is a smooth transition from one speaker to the next.

You could spend some time discussing the last question (*How can you avoid an embarrassing silence at the end of your presentation?*) as this hasn't been covered in the material so far. Possible answers to this question:

- Don't be afraid to let a minute or two go by before someone asks a question – people can be a little hesitant at first, but once one person has asked a question, others are likely to follow.
- Say: 'One question that people often ask is ....'. This approach will often relax your audience and encourages them to start asking questions.
- If there are no questions, invite audience members to speak to you afterwards or contact you by email if they have any questions.

**9** Once students have prepared their presentations and have had time to practise delivering them, get groups to present to the whole class. If you have time, students can assess each other in a supportive way by referring to the list of qualities for a good presentation in exercise 1 and the presentation tips they gathered as a result of their Internet search. They could also listen out for appropriate use of expressions, intonation, etc.

A quicker, alternative method of assessment would be simply to ask students to identify two things they liked about the presentation and two ways in which they think it could be improved.

## 3.5 Writing
## A product description

This module focuses on the features and benefits of consumer products and requires students to write their own production description.

**Internet research**

Students will find a range of news and business reports in response to a search for *MP3 player market China*. Remind students that that they should write a short summary in their own words, picking out the key information on the topic.

## Discussion

**1** Check that students understand the difference between a feature (a factual statement about a product) and a benefit (the value or advantage customers get from the product; a positive outcome or result that will make them want to buy it).

Read the vocabulary in the box and get student to pick out the four features and their corresponding benefits. Students can then discuss questions 1 and 2 with a partner or in small groups. Get them to make lists of one or two features and benefits for each product, to show that they have understood the difference.

Other products they might discuss are a digital camera, a bike, or a watch.

**ANSWERS:**

(feature, followed by benefit)
ABS – safe braking and cornering; alloy wheels – head-turning good looks; 3.0l V6 engine – power on demand; automatic climate control – air-conditioned comfort

## Scan reading

**2** Get individual students to read each section aloud and then call on other students to select the best section heading from the box.

Get students to try to differentiate the features and the benefits in the text. At this stage, accept all answers as this is dealt with in more detail in the next exercise.

**ANSWERS:**

3 compatibility 1 background 4 details of features and benefits 5 invitation 2 overview of benefits

## Reformulating

**3** When students have completed the task, focus on the language used to describe benefits and features as this will be useful for the writing task in exercise 5. This text, for example, uses:

- the present simple tense to give the effect of immediacy
- *will* to promise things, e.g. *you'll start to appreciate the extras*
- *can*, e.g. *you can create, you can integrate*
- the first conditional, e.g. *If you're used to using other office suites, you'll feel completely at home...*
- imperatives, e.g. *use ..., produce*
- a number of adjectives and adverbs to get the message across, e.g. *easily, impressive, dynamic, powerful, effective*
- comparatives to get the message across, e.g. *more compatible, more international, more accessible, more open.*

**ANSWERS:**

2   OpenOffice.org 1.1 gives you everything you'd expect in office software.

3   You can publish your work in Portable Document Format (PDF), and release your graphics in Flash (SWF) format – without needing any additional software.

4   If you're used to using other office suites – such as Microsoft Office – you'll be completely at home

5   You can of course continue to use your old Microsoft Office files without any problems

6   You can easily integrate images and charts in documents

7   Use built-in charting tools to generate impressive 2-D and 3-D charts.

8   produce everything from simple diagrams to dynamic 3-D illustrations and special effects.

**4**   Students could do this reformulation exercise in small groups. When they have finished, get groups to read their sentences aloud.

**SUGGESTED ANSWERS:**

2   You can download this amazing audio manager software – free!

3   Run Creole Audio Manager without problems on any Mac or PC.

4   You can search for music on the Internet, download it and organize your music files on your computer.

5   Listen to radio and watch TV online.

6   Creole lets you burn your favourite music onto CDs.

7   If you're used to using other audio players, you'll be completely at home; Creole Audio Manager is really easy to use.

8   You can even display song lyrics and sing along in karaoke mode!

## FURTHER PRACTICE

Write the following features on the board or dictate them to students:

*50-number speed dial*
*One-click business reports*
*Open 24 hours*
*Batteries included*

With a partner or in small groups, get students to note down what products each of these features could refer to and some benefits that users might get from them.

Give students a few minutes to exchange ideas and encourage them to be imaginative. Take feedback from the class.

Possible answers:
50-number speed dial: phone – fewer keystrokes; quick and easy to use; I won't waste time by misdialling
One-click business reports: website – you can see the latest news very quickly and easily; you can use the time you save to do other things.
Open 24 hours: supermarket you can shop whenever you want; if you feel like ice-cream late at night, you can get some.
Batteries included: child's toy – the product is ready to use; you don't have to spend more money on batteries; you don't have to make another shopping trip to buy batteries.

## EXTENSION ACTIVITY

Get students to think of the features and benefits of some everyday objects, e.g. a toothbrush, a cushion, a bar of chocolate.

## Writing

**5**   Read the notes with the whole class. They are structured in the same way as the text in exercise 2, which can act as a model for students' own writing.

Circulate while students are writing and help where necessary. Students should write a first draft, making sure they have several benefits. They could then exchange their texts with another student for feedback. When they are reading each other's texts, students should be able to easily identify the benefits and should also look for the appropriate use of language.

Students then revise their texts. Display the finished texts on a table or on the wall so that students can read them all. If you wish, get them to choose the best two or three texts, i.e. the ones which make them want to buy the product.

**MODEL ANSWER:**

The music lover's favourite player
Over 30 million people all over the world already use Earworm players. Now there's an even better way to listen to music: the Earworm2. It's smaller, lighter and even stronger than the original Earworm, and has more memory for more music. And, believe it or not, we've actually reduced the price!
Now better than ever
The Earworm2 gives you everything you ever wanted from a portable music player. It's so compact (no bigger than a credit card) that you can slide it into the smallest pocket or purse. An enormous 40GB of memory means that you can take your complete music collection everywhere you go – up to 20,000 songs!
Forget about compatibility problems
If you're used to downloading your music files on a PC, that's fine. If you prefer the Mac, there's no problem. You can play all your favourite music formats; whether they're from subscription services or P2P exchanges, the Earworm2 can handle them all!
What's new in Earworm2?
You'll love the attention-grabbing new design with its funky fluorescent colours. Shake it, rock it, rattle and roll it; with its shock-proof aluminium case, anywhere you can go, the Earworm2 will go too. It's even water-resistant for singing in the rain!
The Earworm2 gives you an enormous 40 gigabytes of storage space, so you can take all the music you'll ever need with you. Pack up to 20,000 songs into an amazingly small space; the Earworm2 is only 9 cm long by 5 cm wide and just 1 cm thick. And as it weighs only 245 g, it's so light you won't even notice it's in your pocket. With the latest battery technology, you can listen all day and all night for up to 30 hours non-stop.
When you want to hear something new, just switch on the built-in FM radio; if inspiration hits you while you're on the road, record your future number one with the Earworm2's built-in mic.
Playing and organizing your files has never been so easy; everything is displayed so clearly on the Earworm2's large 4 x 3 cm LCD screen, you'll be completely at home after just a few minutes. And the Earworm2 comes with a two year guarantee, giving you real peace of mind.
Try it today
We're so sure you'll love Earworm2 that we're offering a two week, no quibble, money back guarantee. Try the Earworm2 for two weeks; if you're not 100% satisfied, we promise to give you a full refund with no questions asked. What do you have to lose? Try the Earworm2 today!

## 3.6 Case study
## Big Jack's Pizza

This module draws together the work on product packaging and making an effective presentation by asking students to consider ways that a pizza company could strengthen its brand and improve its packaging.

### Internet research

An Internet search for *pizza box advertising* will reveal the ways in which companies use pizza boxes and other fast food containers to advertise their products and services.

It would be most useful if students could do this search before the final task in exercise 6.

## Discussion

**1** Before students start this exercise, get them to brainstorm the names of some fast food chains in their town or city, and write them on the board. At this point just write down the names and the kind of food they sell. Then give students a few more minutes to discuss with a partner or small groups how each of them tries to differentiate itself from its competitors. They might mention factors such as price, taste, service, quality, range of meals, special offers, etc.

## Scan reading

**2** You could do this as a whole-class activity by reading the first question aloud and giving students a few minutes to find the answer in the texts. They should then raise their hands when they have found the answer. Wait until most of the class have raised their hands and then call on a student to give you the answer. Continue in this way until students have answered all the questions.

### ANSWERS:
1 A pizza franchise with 23 restaurants in Hong Kong with takeout and home-delivery activities.
2 Three: Billie, Mick and Jack Jr.
3 The President & CEO (and presumably the son of the founder, Big Jack).
4 Value: large pizzas at low prices.
5 Less than one third.
6 Attracting new franchisees.
7 Loss of market share to international majors.
8 Convenience – proximity of stores and 24/7 delivery service.
9 The banal product.
10 A new range of pizzas, new promotional ideas, a new logo and colour scheme, a new box

## Listening for gist

**3**  1:42  Before students listen, go back to the texts in exercise 2 and re-read the four points on the agenda. Get students to predict what kinds of things might be discussed under these headings at the marketing meeting. Then play the recording. Remind students that they are listening only for definite decisions. For lower-level classes you might like to point out that they will hear the word 'agree' around the discussion of things that have definitely been decided.

### ANSWERS:
1 To introduce a new range of fusion cuisine pizzas.
2 To bring in brand-building and packaging consultants.

## RECORDING SCRIPT

1:42

**Jack Jr:** OK, so, we all agree on that then? A completely new range of pizzas for the 21st century, featuring fusion cuisine with the best of contemporary Chinese and Western influences? Great. We'll need at least five really new recipes, so see what you can come up with.

**Mick:** We'll need new names for each new pizza, then, Jack …

**Jack:** Of course, but we can come back to that later. OK, so, can we move on to point two – new promotional ideas? What suggestions do we have? Billie?

**Billie:** Well, obviously with the new pizza range we should do a relaunch. And what about doing specials at different times in the year? You know, New Year, National Day, Dragon Boat Festival …

**J:** Well, Billie, it's been done before, but I guess we could do that. Why not? Mick?

**M:** What about a BOGOF?

**J:** I'm sorry?

**M:** You know, B.O.G.O.F. – buy one, get one free. Two pizzas for the price of one. And another idea would be to have a two-pizza box. The pizzas stay hotter when you have two in a box.

**J:** Hm. I'm not sure that's a direction we really want to go in. The franchisees won't like it, and we want to get away from the idea that Big Jack's is just good for filling your stomach.

**M:** Well, what about a gourmet club? Customers get special privileges if they become members. Or feature different national cuisines each month – Indian in the first month, Thai in the second, and so on?

**B:** Yes, that's good, Mick. And don't forget the Internet – what if you could build your own pizza and order your take-out or delivery online?

**J:** Sounds like it might be expensive, Billie, but yeah, that's more the kind of thing I had in mind. Anyway, let's go on to points three and four on the agenda. I think we can take them together, because the box depends very much on the logo and the color scheme. Billie, I think you feel strongly about this?

**B:** Yes, Jack, I do. We've had our current logo ever since your dad started the business. The Big Jack logo was perfect thirty years ago, but a lot of things have changed since Big Jack's time. Apart from anything else, the symbolism is all wrong, and remember, people are very sensitive to that kind of thing here.

**J:** What do you mean, the symbolism is all wrong? Green and red are the colors of Italy, it's what pizza is all about!

**B:** Maybe, but the green chequered table-cloth on the round table – it symbolizes old-world values that people in Hong Kong just don't identify with. And it's well-known that green isn't a good colour for packaging for the Chinese.

**M:** Oh, really? Why's that?

**B:** Oh, you know, it's that thing about green hats – it means your wife is, you know, seeing another man …

**J:** Billie, this is all very interesting, but …

**M:** No, hang on, Jack. I think Billie's right. We have to take this kind of thing into account. And the box; the box is really important. It's easily the best way we have to communicate with our customers. Couldn't we have a more exciting box, as well as new colors and graphics? I mean, every baker in the city sells pizza in the same standard box as us. We need to differentiate! An octagonal box would be good, maybe with a window so you can see the delicious hot pizza you're carrying?

**J:** Well, as long as it doesn't complicate storage or delivery, I don't see why not. But it seems to me we need to get more advice on this. I trust you'll agree that we need to have some brand-building and packaging consultants work on this … we'll consider their proposals at our next meeting.

## Listening for inference

**4** Students could work with a partner to do this exercise. Play 🔊 1:42 again, two or more times if necessary, to allow students to get as many of the suggestions as possible. Make a list on the board. Then get students to choose the three best suggestions in their opinion. Ask them to give reasons for their answers. They could also say why they think some of the other ideas might not be successful.

**ANSWERS:**

1 new names
2 relaunch
3 specials
4 BOGOF
5 two-pizza box
6 gourmet club
7 feature national cuisines each month
8 compose and order by Internet
9 change logo and colours
10 more exciting box
Jack likes 2, 3, 6, 7, 8 and 10.

**5** Point out that the phrases on the left are from the listening in exercise 4. Give students a few minutes to do the matching task. Check answers with the whole class by getting one student to read out the phrase on the left and another student to read the corresponding phrase on the right.

**ANSWERS:**

1 b)  2 d)  3 a)  4 g)  5 c)
6 h)  7 e)  8 f)  9 j)  10 i)

You could then play the recording through so that students can hear the phrases again in context.

## Brainstorming and presentation

**6** Read the instructions through with the whole class. Remind them of the suggestions they heard at the marketing meeting in exercise 3 – they could take some of these ideas and expand them. They could also think of completely new ideas. The important thing is to have some concrete ideas to present. Students could be encouraged to use realia in their presentation, e.g. some pieces of card or paper with the names of the new pizzas written in large bold letters; a mockup of a new logo or new shape of pizza box, etc. Alternatively they could use Powerpoint for their presentations.

Before students start preparing for their presentation, remind them of the work they did earlier in the unit on how to structure a presentation and how to deliver it clearly. They could also look back at the work they did on describing specifications and features. All of this should feed into the presentations they are preparing now.

Give students a fixed time for their presentation, e.g. no more than 5–10 minutes. One student in each group could be nominated to give the presentation, or each student could present one recommendation.

While students are speaking, make a note of any common mistakes in the target language for remedial teaching.

After the presentations, get students to comment on their own performance – ask them what two things they liked and what two things they could have done better.

## Writing practice

Get students to write a short report on their recommendations to Big Jack's Pizza. This could be done for homework.

# 4 | Careers

## Subject background

This page gives a brief six-point job search plan aimed at students and other people early in their careers. You can photocopy this plan for your students if you think it will be a useful reference tool for them.

## Job search plan

**1 Decide on the 'big picture' issues.**

- Determine the job you want.
  If you have no idea, make a list of the things you like to do. If you have an idea of the general field (e.g. marketing), but nothing more specific, then investigate various job titles in your area of interest.
- Determine where you want to live. Are you open to relocating? If you have a specific location in mind, then identify the companies that have offices / plants / locations in those areas.
- Determine the best companies for you. You need to make some decisions about the types of companies that fit your needs, style, and personality.

**2 Determine your search strategy.**

On-campus recruiting? Career fairs? Networking through personal contacts and going to events such as conferences? Writing to specific companies with your résumé and a covering letter? Internet job sites? Company websites? Classified ads in newspapers and professional magazines? Local careers agencies?

**3 Write a résumé (CV) and covering letter.**

There are hundreds of Internet sites to help you write a résumé (CV in BrE) and a covering letter. Just type phrases like *résumé tips* or *CV tips* or *covering letter* into a search engine.

Obtain critiques of your résumé and covering letter from your family, friends, colleagues, professors, etc.

As well as any other ways you are thinking of using your résumé, post it on the Internet anyway.

**4 Prepare for interviews.**

Learn to research companies. One of the secrets of great interviewing is knowing something about the company where you are looking for a job.

Practise, practise, practise. For example, carry out mock interviews with other students / colleagues or a career counsellor. Also, if you are a student then have some on-campus interviews with companies who come to visit – just to gain confidence and experience.

Use an Internet search engine to research *Frequently Asked Interview Questions*.

**5 Gain experience.**

Employers value work experience as much as educational background.

- Internships – work part-time in your expected career field, either during one of the semesters or over the summer.
- Summer jobs – these jobs are not always in your field of interest, but having any kind of work experience is valuable and many offer transferable skills that carry over to other jobs.
- Self-employed jobs – a growing number of students start their own (very small) businesses in areas such as gardening or web design.
- Temporary work – do work for an agency while you are waiting for something better, and make sure to include any transferable skills on your résumé.
- Volunteer work – charity, community group, not-for-profit organization, etc.
- Campus activities – key positions on sports, social, cultural and other organizations.

**6 Follow up.**

Be proactive after an interview – don't just sit and wait for the phone to ring.

Write a brief 'thank you letter' restating why you would be the right person for the job.

Or make a follow-up call to ask how the decision process is going.

## Useful websites

Typing key terms like *CV* or *Job interview* into a search engine will produce many useful sites. Here are three good ones:

http://www.quintcareers.com/jobseeker_glossary.html
http://www.businessballs.com/curriculum.htm
http://www.alec.co.uk

## 4.1 About business
### Career choices

This module explores the ways in which working life has changed in recent years. It considers what motivates individuals in their choice of career and how to make more successful career decisions.

### Internet research

An Internet search for *"job sculpting"* will reveal details about the eight life interests (the 'business functions' referred to in the interview with career experts, James Waldroop and Timothy Butler from the Harvard School of Business in 🔊 2:01) that can be linked to good career decisions. They are:

- Application of technology (connected with engineering, production, operations, and the general use of technology to accomplish business goals)
- Quantitative analysis (problem-solving that relies on mathematical analysis)
- Theory development and conceptual thinking (involves broadly conceptual approaches to business problems)
- Creative production (for example, the development of new products or marketing concepts, the generation of new business ideas, etc.)
- Counselling and mentoring (involves developing relationships, such as coaching, training and mentoring)
- Managing people and relationships (developing relationships, such as coaching, training and mentoring)
- Enterprise control (decision-making authority for complete operations)
- Influence through language and ideas (exercising influence through the skilful use of written and spoken language).

*Job sculpting* is a means of matching people to jobs in which they can express their true life interests.

Students could conduct this research before class and use it as part of the discussion activity in exercise 5 on page 44 or after the scan reading and summarizing activities in exercises 6 and 7. Alternatively, they could use it as the basis for further discussion when they have completed this module.

> ### LEAD-IN ACTIVITY
>
> With a partner or in small groups have students tell or remind each other what their jobs are and why they chose that career. For pre-work learners, get them to say what kind of career they would like to have and why. Take whole-class feedback. Write the reasons for career choices on the board.

### Discussion

**1** Get students to read each pair of statements aloud. Explain any new vocabulary, e.g.:
*status* (position of somebody or something in relation to others)
*priorities* (things that are regarded as more important than others).

After students have discussed their answers with a partner, get them to raise their hands to indicate which end of the scale they occupy for each pair of statements. Ask some students to share their choices and the reasons for them.

### Predicting and listening

**2** 🔊 2:01 Discuss the two statements with the whole class, making a list of their predictions on the board.

Question 1: If pre-work students have difficulty with this question, ask them to think about the careers of family members and friends.

Question 2: If students are unsure of the meaning of *vocation*, give them some examples, e.g. nursing or teaching.

Play the first part of Part 1 of the recording and check answers. Ask students to explain the tree / surfboard metaphors used by James Waldroop in their own words.

Then play the second part of Part 1 and get students to note down the differences between *vocation*, *career* and *job*. Get them to compare their answers with a partner. Then take whole-class feedback.

**ANSWERS:**

1 Ten years ago, you specialized in one area and did the same job all your life. Companies were also more responsible for their employees. Nowadays, you tend to change jobs more often and you are responsible for creating your own career.
2 A vocation or calling is something that's right for you, something you have to listen out for.
A career is a line of work, and you can have several of these in your working life.
A job refers to whatever you are doing and whoever is employing you at the moment.

### RECORDING SCRIPT

🔊 2:01

**Interviewer:** Most people sense that choices in business today are different. When it comes to people and careers, what actually has changed?

**James Waldroop:** People in business simply have many more choices today than ever before. Just a decade ago, when you took a job, the company dictated the moves you made. When it came to your career, you had one area that you specialized in. That was all you did, and you more or less did it for your whole work life. Ten or twenty years ago, you'd join a company, put down roots, and stay put, like a tree. Today the image of the tree has been replaced by a surfer on a surfboard: you're always moving. You can expect to fall into the water any number of times, and you have to get back up to catch that next wave.

But the biggest change is in who is responsible for your career. Ten or fifteen years ago, a social contract went along with a job. Companies accepted certain responsibilities for their people. Today that contract is completely different. You are responsible for creating your own career within an organization – and even more important, between organizations.

**I:** It's frequently said that careers are over. Instead, you should expect to hold a series of jobs and to participate in a succession of projects. Timothy Butler, how do you see the evolution of the career?

**Timothy Butler:** There are three words that tend to be used interchangeably – and shouldn't be. They are 'vocation', 'career', and 'job'. Vocation is the most profound of the three, and it has to do with your calling. It's what you're doing in life that makes a difference for you, that builds meaning for you, that you can look back on in your later years to see the impact you've made on the world. A calling is something you have to listen for. You don't hear it once and then immediately recognize it. You've got to attune yourself to the message.

Career is the term you hear most often today. A career is a line of work. You can say that your career is to be a lawyer or a securities analyst – but usually it's not the same as your calling. You can have different careers at different points in your life. A job is the most specific and immediate of the three terms. It has to do with who's employing you at the moment and what your job description is for the next six months or so. These days, trying to describe what your job will be beyond twelve to eighteen months from now is very dicey.

## Listening for detail

**3** Read the questions with the students and play the whole of  2:01 again. Check answers with the whole class. Ask students if they agree with these statements about the nature of employment today – does this match their own experience or what they know of the workplace?

**ANSWERS:**

1  a) Ten or fifteen years ago, a social contract went along with a job. Companies accepted certain responsibilities for their people.
   b) Today that contract is completely different. You are responsible for creating your own career.
2  These days, trying to describe what your job will be beyond 12 to 18 months from now is very dicey (risky).

**4** 2:02 Read the statements aloud or get students to read them aloud and to predict whether they are true or false.

For lower-level classes explain the meaning of these words:
*tension* (a situation in which different forces or elements are in opposition to each other)
*geothermal* (originating from or produced by the internal heat of the earth)
*signature* (a distinctive quality or pattern).

Play Part 2. With lower-level classes, pause at appropriate points so that they can answer one question at a time. Play each section more than once, if necessary. Check answers with the whole class.

Students may be surprised that statements 1 and 3 are false. Get them to explain why the speaker thinks it is not a good idea to compromise between or ignore two competing needs (these strategies won't work – the needs won't disappear). Ask if they agree with the speaker.

Statement 3 is also false, but this is included in the *Discussion* activity below, so tell students they will discuss it in more detail later. At this point, simply draw attention to the fact that the speaker makes a distinction between being good at something and enjoying it or being interested in it.

At this point, refer back to the list of reasons for career choices that you made during the lead-in activity. Are any of them the same or similar to those mentioned in the interview?

**ANSWERS:**

| 1 F | 2 T | 3 F | 4 T |
|-----|-----|-----|-----|

## RECORDING SCRIPT

2:02

Part 2

Interviewer: What advice do you have for people facing a tough career choice, one that could permanently change the direction of their work life?

Butler: Everyone tries to do something that seems like the wise thing to do – but that you shouldn't do: compromise. You've got two competing needs or desires – say, independence and security – and you try to find the position that's halfway between them. Typically that doesn't work.
An equally bad approach is to jump radically from one pole to the other, to pretend that you can forget entirely about one need and recognize only the other. When you do that, the genuine need you're trying to deny simply goes underground and becomes stronger.

Waldroop: We have exercises where we ask people to choose among 13 different business reward values. An obvious one is financial gain. How important is it to you to make a lot of money? Another one is lifestyle. How important is it to you to work in a way where you're networking all the time? A third is power and influence. How important is it to you to

be a player?
It's not uncommon for an individual to have a high score on financial gain, a high score on lifestyle, and a high score on power and influence. You can try to jump from one to the other to the other, but when you choose one, the other two don't go away.
So, what's the answer? To be aware of and live with this tension. It's a dynamic part of your personality. And if you try to come up with an easy solution, you're only going to get into trouble. At different times in your life, you're going to shift more toward one pull than toward the others. But the tension is never going to go away. You can't balance them out, you can't take an average of them, you can't somehow live in the middle. Ultimately, what's required is to live with the tension – and to know that you have to live with it.

I: The biggest decision that people face in the world of work is which career to choose. What advice do you have for people who aren't sure what their career – or their vocation – should be?

W: Good career decisions have to be based not just on your aptitudes, but also on your 'deep' interests. The most common mistake that people make in their career decisions is to do something because they're 'good at it'. It's a story I hear all the time. Someone will say to me, 'I'm an engineer, but I don't like it.' Why did you become an engineer? 'I was good at science and math, so people told me I should be an engineer.' Did you ever like engineering? 'No, but it was easy.'
The real question is: Where are your deep interests? Think of your interests as a deep geothermal pool. Once you tap your interests, you can express them in any number of ways. You may have a particular aptitude – science and math, for instance – but without a deep interest in expressing that aptitude, you'll fail.

B: Identifying those deep interests has been the focus of our research for the past ten years. Once you recognize that those deep interests are the best predictor of job satisfaction, the next step is to get in touch with your interest patterns and connect them with the activities that go on in business. Human interests are quite difficult to measure until we reach our early twenties. At that point, they gel – we can measure and describe them. We each develop a unique signature of life interests. And that signature remains virtually constant over time. The pattern won't change.
Our research tries to tap into this deep structure of interests and translate them into the kinds of work that go on in business. There are eight core business functions – not functions like marketing, sales, and finance, but basic activities such as managing people, enterprise control, and influencing through language and ideas. If you look at your deep interests and think about how your interests can be expressed in specific business behaviours, then you'll have the elements of a good career decision.

## Discussion

**5** First students discuss what they think these statements mean. Then they should decide if they agree or disagree with them. Students might also want to consider other, related questions, e.g. Does everyone make a conscious career choice or does it happen by accident? How easy is it to combine your interests with your choice of career? Take whole-class feedback.

## Scan reading

**6** Before students start reading the text, explain any of the colloquial expressions which may be new to them, e.g.:
*light someone's fire* (make someone enthusiastic)
*passion* (a thing for which someone has great enthusiasm)
*pick someone's brains* (question someone who knows a lot about something in order to get information)
*up in the air* (uncertain, not yet decided)
*earth-shattering* (having a powerful effect).
Remind them to use the *Wordlist* on page 153 in their books.

With lower-level classes, you could break down the text into more manageable chunks to help them complete the task. First get students to simply read the headings for each section and predict what they think the section will be about. Then, get a student to read the two summarizing sentences aloud. Finally, read each section aloud and ask students to raise their hands if they think it matches the sentences they have just heard.

**ANSWERS:**

1   tip 4
2   tip 7

## Summarizing

**7** With lower-level classes, you could divide students into pairs or groups and get them to summarize just one or two tips.

Circulate while students are working and assist where necessary.

Get students to choose one or two tips that particularly impressed them.

**SUGGESTED ANSWERS:**

Tip 1   Take time to identify what motivates you.
Tip 2   Brainstorm ways to integrate what motivates you into your life.
Tip 3   Ask other people for advice about things you are interested in.
Tip 5   Identify your obstacles and the reasons why they prevent you from reaching your goals.
Tip 6   Surround yourself with people who can help and support you.
Tip 8   Make a practical, structured action plan.
Tip 9   Start taking action as soon as possible.
Tip 10 Make a visible commitment to achieving your goal.

## 4.2 Vocabulary
### Careers, personal skills and qualities

This module focuses on vocabulary and expressions which enable students to discuss activities and performance in the workplace and the effect it has on career development.

**Internet research**

A search for *mentoring* will reveal that a mentor is a person who guides and helps people in their careers. Mentoring can help people to explore their needs, motivation, desires, skills, and thought processes; it can help them to set goals, take action and make changes. Information from this search will be useful for exercises 8–10.

## Discussion

**1** Students could do this activity with a partner or in small groups. Take whole-class feedback. You could also ask students to rank the benefits from the viewpoint of different kinds of people, e.g. a 25-year-old recent employee; an employee in their 40s with three children; a 55-year-old.

**ANSWERS:**

Answers depend on personal values. Suggested answers in terms of probable financial value:
1   free accommodation
2   company car
3   pension plan
4   free medical insurance
5   luncheon vouchers
6   profit-sharing
7   stock options
8   Christmas bonus
9   sports and social facilities

---

**EXTENSION ACTIVITY**

To personalize the activity, ask in-work students if they receive any of these benefits from their employer. Can they describe them and explain the pros and cons, e.g. *We get free membership of a sports club. They have good facilities, but it's a long way from where I live.*

---

**2** Ask students to read through the sentences. Then, give them a few minutes to complete this activity with a partner. They could try to do this even if they don't know all of the words in bold. Check answers with the whole class.

**ANSWERS:**

1 Before graduating, Josef applied for jobs in twenty companies.
4 Josef was offered a position as a management trainee.
3 He attended a second interview conducted by a panel of managers.
7 He found a new job, but was dismissed after arguing with his boss.
5 Two years later he was appointed logistics manager.
2 He was short-listed for a second interview at Wilson Brothers.
8 While he was unemployed, Josef studied for a master's degree.
6 When Wilson's got into difficulties, Josef was made redundant.
10 In his early fifties he took a sabbatical to write a book.
12 He retired from business and now lives in the south of France.
9 Thanks to his enhanced CV, Josef was hired by a firm of consultants.
11 The book was a best-seller, and Josef resigned from the firm.

If necessary, explain *sabbatical* (a period of leave, paid or unpaid, to allow an employee to do something which may or may not be related to their work; e.g. a company might offer one month off on full pay every four years; other companies might offer one month's unpaid leave after six years of service, and so on). Ask students if their company offers its employees sabbaticals and what the arrangements are. If they don't know, they could find out and report back. Pre-work students could investigate which local companies offer sabbaticals.

Focus on the words in bold and guide students towards an understanding of them and how they are used. For example: Get students to pick out the expressions using the passive (*was offered a position, was dismissed, was appointed, was short-listed, was made redundant, was hired*). Ask students what the expressions have in common (they are all actions by a company towards an employee).
Ask students to pick out the expressions related to 'not being in work' (*dismissed, unemployed, made redundant, retired, resigned*).
Get students to pick out the verbs followed by *from* (*resign, retire*), by (*hire*) and for (*shortlist*).

**3** and **4** Ask students do these exercises individually or with a partner. Circulate and assist where necessary. Check answers with the whole class.

**ANSWERS:**

Exercise 3
1  Could you tell me exactly why you <u>were dismissed</u> from OQP?
2  Was that before or after you <u>were appointed</u> Quality Manager?
3  After the factory closed, was it difficult to <u>find a new job</u>?
4  Have you <u>applied for</u> jobs in other companies in the area?
5  Would you be available to <u>attend a second interview</u> next week?
6  How would you feel if we <u>offered you a position</u> as a product manager?

Exercise 4
| 1 | short-listed | 5 | resign |
|---|---|---|---|
| 2 | hired | 6 | made redundant |
| 3 | on sabbatical | 7 | unemployed |
| 4 | dismissed | 8 | retire |

---

**FURTHER PRACTICE**

To check that students have understood and can use the vocabulary correctly, get them to make sentences using the words in bold. The sentences could be about themselves or people they know or invent. They could do this orally and as a whole-class activity. Alternatively, they could work with a partner and write three sentences on a slip of paper. Students then exchange the slips of paper with another pair and check each other's sentences.

---

## Collocations

**5** Do this matching task as a whole-class activity. Explain any new vocabulary e.g.:
*initiative* (willingness and ability to realize what needs to be done without being told)
*negotiating skills* (ability to reach an agreement through discussion).

**ANSWERS:**

| 1 b) | 2 a) | 3 d) | 4 e) | 5 c) |
|---|---|---|---|---|
| 6 h) | 7 i) | 8 f) | 9 j) | 10 g) |

**6** and **7** Ask students to do these exercises with a partner. Check answers with the whole class. Then get students to discuss with their partner which of the four qualities mentioned in exercise 7 they think they already have and which ones they need to develop.

**ANSWERS:**

Exercise 6
1  I enjoy taking initiative, and I keep my promises; when I <u>make a commitment</u> to a project I always deliver.
2  I have a lot of experience in <u>working closely with</u> both product development and sales teams, and can adapt to their different working styles.
3  I have excellent organizational skills, and I hate being late – so I have no problem with <u>working to strict deadlines</u>.
4  I liaise with government officials: fortunately, I <u>possess strong negotiating skills</u>.
5  I'm used to <u>managing a busy workload</u>; I'm good at multitasking, and coping with pressure is no problem.
6  I often <u>take on ownership</u> of projects with multi-million dollar budgets.
7  I believe I can <u>make a valuable contribution to</u> any work group.
8  I'm <u>a good listener</u>, so I build good working relationships with colleagues.

Exercise 7
a)  Are you able to take responsibility? 1, 6
b)  Are you a good communicator? 4, 8
c)  Are you a good time manager? 3, 5
d)  Are you a good team worker? 2, 7

## Listening for gist

**8**  2:03 Elicit from students what they understand by *high-flier* (a person with great potential for achievement) and *concerns* (people whose performance is causing worry or concern) and what the criteria might be for assessing individuals as one or the other. Then, play the recording through once.

With lower-level classes pause after the discussion of each person or play each section more than once.

**ANSWERS:**

| Rachel Ratcliff + | Paul Stevens + |
|---|---|
| Michael Diegel - | Shane Garney - |

### RECORDING SCRIPT

🔊 2:03

B:  All right. So that brings us to Rachel Ratcliff. You've flagged her as a high-flier. She's certainly very committed to her work.
A:  Absolutely. Rachel is doing a terrific job for us. She's an excellent team-player, and she really enjoys taking initiative.
B:  Great, so what's the problem?
A:  Well, she's a very talented lady, but she's also very ambitious.
B:  Nothing wrong with being ambitious, is there?
A:  No, except we don't really have any way to satisfy her ambition for the moment. We planned to make her a department manager in a couple of years' time, but there are no openings right now. She's obviously had other offers, perhaps from a headhunter, and she's thinking about resigning.
B:  Hm. It would be a shame to lose her. Solutions?
A:  Well, we could offer her a two-year assignment in Germany. I know there's a vacancy over there for someone with her profile, and she'd certainly be able to make a valuable contribution. But I don't know whether she'd agree. She has a fiancé, so it may be difficult.

B: Hm. A two-year assignment in Germany? I'm not sure. But go on, I can see you have another idea.

A: Well, yes. I'd like to put her on the fast track. Send her on an MBA course, and start preparing her for senior management.

B: You really think she's that good? A potential MBA? Well, let me think about that one. I'll come back to you in a couple of days.

A: OK.

B: By the way, how is young Paul Stevens getting on? I believe he had a problem with his manager?

A: Yes, that's right. He was working to very strict deadlines, and just needed a break. I'm working closely with him now, and everything's fine. He's back on the high-fliers list. He has strong negotiating skills, and I think he'll be an excellent engineer.

B: Good. OK, then, let's move on to Michael Diegel. He's a new hire too, isn't he?

A: Yes. Michael's been with us almost a year now, and we've marked him as a concern because he's not really delivering the goods. He arrived with a fantastic CV, lots of skills and some good experience. We thought he'd be a real asset, but he's consistently underperformed, he just isn't able to manage the workload.

B: Hm. Any idea why?

A: Well, I'm not too sure. There are two views of Michael in the department. Some people feel that it's a problem of motivation; he doesn't like Seattle, and he wants to move east just as soon as he can. On the other hand, some of us feel that perhaps he just doesn't have the strengths that his CV claimed. He looked good in the interview process, but he isn't taking on ownership of his projects in the way we hoped he would. Maybe he has more weaknesses than strengths.

B: So, what do we do, give him an official warning? Tell him we'll fire him if he doesn't deliver?

A: Maybe. But we've already invested too much time and money to just dismiss him. Perhaps we should think about moving him East, if that's what will motivate him.

B: And pass the problem on to our colleagues in Chicago or Boston? I'm not sure they'll thank us for that.

A: Hm. How about offering him an easier position in Chicago? Something that won't be so difficult. If he realizes that the job here in Seattle is too much for him, perhaps he'd be more motivated to perform at his real level. Moving to Chicago would be a good way to save face.

B: Yes, that's not a bad idea. Could you liaise with his manager, and see what's available in Chicago or Boston, then come back to me?

A: OK.

B: Good. Now then, we come to our old friend Shane Garney. Mr Wannabe himself. Is he still on the high-fliers list?

A: Not really. He's more of a concern now. He certainly has the skills, but he's getting greedy. We gave him a big raise six months ago when he was promoted, but now he says it's not enough. He says he's had a much better offer from the competition.

B: Well, I think it's time we had a serious talk with Mr Garney. He needs to understand that, although we appreciate ambition, our corporate policy is to reward achievement, not potential.

A: The problem is, of course, that he's very well-connected. You remember that his father's a senator. Wouldn't it be easier to give Shane a small raise to keep him happy?

B: Yes, I'm fully aware of that, and I'm aware that government contracts are very important to this company. But if Shane is only interested in money, he should join his father in Washington. The answer is no. If he thinks he can get a better deal somewhere else, then fine, he can resign. We have a lot of good people like Rachel Ratcliff who would be happy to take his place.

## Taking notes

**9** Remind students they are listening for words and expressions that describe the qualities of each person which are causing problems. Play 2:03 again. Check answers with the whole class.

**ANSWERS:**

|  | Rachel Ratcliff | Michael Diegel | Shane Garney |
|---|---|---|---|
| problem | thinking about resigning | new hire; under-performing | wants more money; has a better offer |
| causes | ambitious, no opportunities | motivation, or doesn't have potential | getting greedy; over-ambitious; father is a senator |
| possible solutions | transfer her to Germany; send her on an MBA | warning; move him east to an easier job | give him a small raise; say no |

## Discussion

**10** Give students a few minutes to discuss their ideas. Remind them to use the vocabulary they have learnt in this module, and to consider the ideas explored in 4.1, to do with career choice and values.

Check answers with the whole class. Get students to give reasons for their solutions.

### EXTENSION ACTIVITY

Ask students to consider how mentoring might help Rachel, Paul, Michael and Shane in their careers. Remind them of the information they gathered on the Internet about mentoring. Students write a list of questions for each person to try to find out more about what their values and interests are. They then roleplay a mentor/mentee discussion using these questions.

Finish by asking students if they have any personal experience of mentoring. Ask if they found it useful? If they have no personal experience, ask if they would find it useful in their own careers?

## 4.3 Grammar
### Present tenses

This module focuses on the use of the present simple and continuous and on the present perfect simple and continuous. It also practises the past simple.

### Internet research

Students will find numerous websites offering grammar explanations if they search under *English grammar practice*. Before students do this task, agree with them a list of questions to use when assessing each website, e.g.:
*Are the grammar explanations clear and easy to understand?*
*Are the exercises useful?*
*Is the site easy to navigate?*
*Are the layout and presentation clear?*

Get students to choose one or two of the tenses practised in this unit and work through the explanations and exercises on two or three websites so that they can compare how each one performs on the same task.

Students then present one or more of the websites they found to the whole class, commenting on the best and worst aspects of each one. You may find that several students liked or disliked the same website.

Students could do this task before you start this module or afterwards, as a follow-up to the work done in the unit.

### Test yourself: Present tenses

**1** Start by reading the notes on the present simple and continuous in the *Refresh your memory* box with students. If they seem unsure of the two tenses, work through exercises 1–5 in *Grammar and practice* on page 124 in the Student's Book.

Do this exercise with the whole class. Elicit from students or explain to them why each answer is correct.

**ANSWERS:**

Jane Houseman <u>considers</u> herself a happy woman. Based in London, she <u>works</u> as a project manager for Arbol Oil, a South American oil company which <u>is expanding</u> rapidly, especially in Asia. Jane loves travelling; at the moment she <u>is working</u> on a project in China, which <u>means</u> she <u>flies</u> out to Beijing about once a month. She <u>already speaks</u> fluent Spanish, and she <u>is learning</u> Chinese. She <u>doesn't meet</u> the two other project managers in her department very often, because they are finishing a project in Saudi Arabia, but they all get on very well and <u>talk</u> two or three times a week by telephone. Jane is also following an MBA course; she <u>submits</u> coursework by email and <u>attends</u> three intensive weeks per year in London. Financially, Jane feels very lucky: right now, she is earning twice what most of her friends from university are bringing home, and the company is paying for her MBA. In many ways, Jane <u>believes</u> she has the perfect job.

**2** Start by reading the notes on present perfect simple in the *Refresh your memory* box with students. If they seem unsure of the tense, work through exercise 6 in *Grammar and practice* on page 124 in the Student's Book (answers on page 117 in this book).

Remind students of the use of the past simple (to describe actions in a completed period of time) and get them to explain how the present perfect is different (the time period includes the present).

Students can do this exercise with a partner. Check answers with the whole class. Elicit from students or explain to them why each answer is correct.

**ANSWERS:**

| | | |
|---|---|---|
| 1  has been | 2  left | 3  worked |
| 4  has never regretted | | 5  immediately put |
| 6  has received | 7  was | 8  called | 9  arrived |
| 10  has already worked | 11  invited | 12  has just asked |

**3** Read the notes on the present perfect simple and continuous in the *Refresh your memory* box with students. If they seem unsure of the two tenses, work through some or all of exercises 7–12 in *Grammar and practice* on page 124 in the Student's Book (answers on page 117 in this book).

Students do this exercise individually and then compare their answers with a partner. Check answers with the whole class.

**ANSWERS:**

| | |
|---|---|
| 1a has preferred | 1b has been looking |
| 2a has just paid | 2b has been hoping |
| 3a has been trying | 3b has repeatedly postponed |
| 4a has been playing | 4b has never occurred |
| 5a has sometimes wondered | 5b has been thinking |
| 6a hasn't been spending | 6b has already had |

Do exercises 13–14 *Grammar and practice* on page 125 in the Student's Book (answers on page 118 in this book) for further practice on all of the tenses practised in this module.

### Present perfect and past simple

**4** Read the instructions with the whole class and give students a few minutes to skim read the table.

With lower-level classes, elicit the questions that students will need to ask, e.g.:
*When does Mr/Ms _____ graduate?*
*What kind of work experience has he/she had?*
*What was his/her grade on the management potential test?*
You could also complete the information for the first two candidates with one or more Student Bs to get lower-level classes started.

Circulate while students are completing the table and assist where necessary. Make a note of any incorrect use of tenses for remedial teaching when the activity is over.

Give students a few minutes to choose the most suitable candidate and then take whole-class feedback. Get students to give reasons for their choice.

**SUGGESTED ANSWERS:**

1  Ms Bianco or Mr Green, assuming he spoke Spanish in CA and FL. Mr Salmon hasn't graduated yet.
2  Miss Rose or Mrs Grey (but she hasn't worked in marketing).
3  Mr Schwarz. Mr Braun scored C-.
4  Miss Plum, assuming she spoke French in Quebec.
5  Miss Rose (if she wasn't chosen for 2) or Ms Violeta.
6  Ms Bianco (if she wasn't chosen for 1) or Mr Da Silva.

## Listening: present perfect simple and continuous

**5** 🔊 2:04–2:13 Play the recording, pausing after each situation to allow students time to write. Ask them to compare their answers with a partner. Take whole-class feedback. Check that students are using the tenses appropriately and forming their sentences correctly.

### SUGGESTED ANSWERS:

1 He's just been offered a job. / He's been having an interview.
2 They've just passed their exams. / They've just been looking at the exam results.
3 She's interviewed 17 candidates. / She's been interviewing since 8.00.
4 He's just run ten kilometres. / He's been doing recruitment tests.
5 Jon has failed his exams.
6 They haven't decided which candidate to choose. / They've been discussing candidates.
7 Nick hasn't finished his CV. / He's been working on his CV for a long time.
8 Paula has just been to an interview. / She's attended 27 interviews.
9 Mr Singh has spilt coffee over the interviewer's papers.
10 Sally has written 100 job applications. / She's been writing job applications since this morning.

### RECORDING SCRIPT

🔊 2:04–2:13

**1**
A: Well, the job's yours if you want it.
B: Well, thank you very much, I'm delighted to accept.

**2**
C: Congratulations! Don't forget, the degree ceremony's next Friday!
D: Thank you, sir!
E: Thank you very much!

**3**
F: Nearly finished now.
G: Wow. Seventeen candidates in one day! And it's almost dinner time. What time did you start?
F: Eight o'clock this morning!

**4**
H: Ten kilometres! Phew! When they said 'recruitment tests', I thought they meant IQ and graphology, not an army assault course!

**5**
I: Have you seen the results, Jon?
J: Yeah.
I: Oh. Oh, I'm so sorry.
J: It's all right. It's not the end of the world.

**6**
K: I still think Ms Brown has more relevant experience than the others.
L: Look, we're not getting anywhere like this. Why don't we meet again tomorrow? And, remember, we can always ask all four candidates back for a second interview if we still can't decide.

**7**
M: Nick? Are you coming out for a drink?
N: Nah. Gotta finish my CV.
M: You still working on that CV?! I mean, how long can it take to say you've got no skills, no qualifications, and you've never done an honest day's work in your life?!
N: Very funny.

**8**
O: Hey, Paula, how did the interview go today?
P: Oh, so-so. Pretty much the same as the last twenty-six.

O: Ah. Well, I've got to hand it to you Paula, you certainly don't give up easily.

**9**
Q: Look out!
R: Oops, too late. Oh dear, it's all over your papers. Sorry about that, these cups are very easy to knock over, aren't they?
Q: Never mind.
R: Hope it wasn't anything important. Er, are you here for the interviews, then?
Q: Yes, as a matter of fact I am. I'm conducting the interviews, actually. It's Mr Singh, isn't it?
R: Oops!

**10**
S: Ninety-eight, ninety-nine, one hundred. There we are! Finished!
T: Finished what, Sally? You don't mean …?
S: Yep. Job applications. Started this morning.
T: One hundred job applications?! You're kidding!

## Asking questions

**6** Write *sports club* and *community arts centre* on the board and ask students to tell you what kinds of jobs might be available in each place (e.g. sports club: receptionist, tennis coach, swimming instructor, yoga teacher, etc; community arts centre: receptionist, marketing manager, exhibitions organizer, etc.).

Explain that students are going to interview each other for jobs at these places. Give them a few minutes to read the instructions and think about the questions they might ask. While they are speaking, circulate and check that they are forming the questions and using tenses correctly. Make a note of any mistakes for remedial teaching later.

### EXTENSION ACTIVITY

This activity focuses on the four tenses practised in this module. Demonstrate what to do by preparing three or four sentences about yourself, one or more of which is false. Write the sentences on the board or read them aloud, e.g.:
*I have been teaching for 10 years.*
*I am training to run a marathon.*
*I have never visited Australia.*
*When I left school I spent a gap year working at a hotel in Germany.*

With a partner, students decide which sentence(s) is false. Then get students to raise their hands about each sentence, asking them to justify their choice if they can. Then invite learners to ask you questions to find out more about each statement.

Students then write their own similar sentences and, working in small groups, follow the same procedure as above.

## 4.4 Speaking
## Job interviews

This module focuses on language and expressions useful for answering questions at a job interview.

### Internet research

A search for *interview advice tips questions* will reveal a number of websites offering advice on how to prepare for an interview and how to answer specific questions. They will also include information on interview problems, body language, group interview tests, panel interviews, and questions to ask an interviewer.

Get students to search a number of websites and write down one or two pieces of advice that they find especially useful. They can then share these with the whole class in a feedback session.

This research could be done before the roleplay in exercise 6 as it would be especially helpful for students roleplaying the candidate. Or it can be done at the end of the module as a follow-up activity.

## Discussion

**1** Ask students to work individually to answer these questions. Tell them to make notes on possible answers. Then get them to compare their answers with a partner. Take whole-class feedback and write any useful phrases or vocabulary on the board.

> **FURTHER PRACTICE**
>
> Get students to consider what an interviewer might be trying to find out by asking these questions, e.g.:
> *Are you ambitious? Are you making plans for your future career?*
> *How do you deal with conflict / difficult situations?*
> *Will you make a good leader / manager?*
> *Are you self-aware? Can you identify your own shortcomings?*
> *How do you handle stress? Will you be effective under pressure?*

## Listening

**2**  **2:14–2:18** Play the recording. Pause after each extract to allow students time to decide which question applies in each case. When they have finished, check answers. Ask students to tell you which words or phrases helped them to answer the questions.

> **ANSWERS:**
>
> 1 A
> 2 B, C, D, E
> 3 B, E
> 4 C
> 5 D

### RECORDING SCRIPT

🔊 2:14–2:18

**A**
Interviewer: Where do you see yourself in five years' time?
A: Well, that's a difficult question to answer; let's just say that I see myself as a top performing employee in a leading company, like this one. I plan to gain experience and learn new skills. Hopefully, in five years' time, I would be ready to move up to a position with more responsibility.

**B**
Interviewer: How do you cope with people who resent your success?
B: Do you mean how do I manage working with someone who doesn't like me? Well, fortunately that hasn't happened very often. But, yes, I'm able to cope with being unpopular. I remember doing a summer job in a food processing factory. The person I was working with had been there for twenty years, and didn't much like the idea of working with a business student, especially a woman. On the first day, I made the mistake of finishing more pieces than him, and he took it really badly. Of course, I soon realized that he was just feeling insecure, so over the next few days, I made sure I asked him for advice about different aspects of the job; you know, made it clear I wasn't there to teach him any lessons. Well, gradually he came round, and in the end we got on really well.

**C**
Interviewer: How do you motivate people to do their best?
C: Well, I think there are two important aspects to this question. The first is to create a positive atmosphere. If people feel happy about what they're doing, they're much more motivated to work towards a common goal. So making sure they understand the objectives and the process, and that the atmosphere is pleasant and relaxed – those are really important. The second thing is to give feedback, especially when somebody does a good job, not just when they get something wrong. When I worked in a restaurant a couple of years ago, I realized that knowing how well you're doing is essential to staying motivated.

**D**
Interviewer: What are your weaknesses?
D: Well, of course, I'm aware that there are areas that I can improve on, but I have to say, as far as this job is concerned, I don't feel that I have any significant weaknesses. And if I do identify a problem, I take action to resolve it. Take time management, for instance. A couple of years ago, I realized I wasn't the most organized person in the world, so I followed a time management course. I applied what I learned, and now I would say that organization is one of my strengths.

**E**
Interviewer: Can you give an example of a situation you found stressful, and how you coped with the stress?
E: Yes. Last term, for example, I was on a work placement where my supervisor had to go off sick for three weeks, so the company asked me to take over responsibility for the project. It meant a huge workload, which was pretty stressful. Anyway, I sat down and planned out exactly what I had to do each day for those three weeks. I also planned an hour each evening in the gym. That really helped to ease the stress. I managed to finish the project on time, and in much better shape than when I started! Does that answer your question?

**3** Before playing 🔊 2:14–2:18 again, see if students can complete the expressions. Then check answers with the whole class. Get students to repeat the expressions following the intonation and stress used by the speakers in the recording.

> **ANSWERS:**
>
> Do you <u>mean</u>, how do I ...?
> That's a <u>difficult</u> question to <u>answer</u>; let's <u>just say</u> that ...
> I think <u>there are two</u> important <u>aspects</u> to this <u>question</u> ...
> Take ..., for <u>instance</u>.
> Does that <u>answer</u> your <u>question</u>?

**4** Students work with a partner to put the words in the sentences in the correct order. They can then practise saying the sentences aloud, focusing on appropriate stress and intonation. Play the recording again so that students can hear the sentences in context.

**ANSWERS:**

1. I applied <u>what I learned</u>.
2. I'm able <u>to cope with being unpopular</u>.
3. I see myself <u>as a top performing employee in a leading company</u>.
4. I plan <u>to gain experience and learn new skills</u>.
5. I would be ready <u>to move up to a position with more responsibility</u>.
6. I realized that knowing <u>how well you're doing is essential to staying motivated</u>.
7. I'm aware <u>that there are areas that I can improve on</u>.
8. I don't feel <u>that I have any significant weaknesses</u>.
9. I would say <u>that organization is one of my strengths</u>.
10. I managed <u>to finish the project on time</u>.

**5** Get a student to read the quotation aloud. Explain *enterprise* (a business company). Do the first part of the exercise as a whole-class activity. Read each question aloud and get students to decide whether it is type 1 or type 2. Check their understanding of:
*to get something done* (to achieve or complete something).

Circulate while students are asking and answering the questions and assist where necessary. Make a list of any useful vocabulary or expressions and teach them to the whole class after the activity is over. They could be used in the roleplay which follows.

**ANSWERS:**

a) What are your strengths and weaknesses? 1
b) Why do you want to work for us? 2
c) What is your greatest achievement? 1
d) How do you make sure things get done? 1
e) Why do you want to leave your present job? 2
f) Tell me about a time when you successfully handled a difficult situation. 1
g) What sort of environment would you prefer not to work in? 2
h) What are the most difficult kinds of decisions for you to make? 1

---

**FURTHER PRACTICE**

Point out that in an interview situation different questions can be answered in the same way. For example, in the listening task, *How you do motivate people to do their best?* and *How do you make sure things get done?* are different questions, but could both be answered in the same way. Similarly, *Can you give an example of a situation you found stressful?* and *Tell me about a time when you successfully handled a difficult situation?* could be answered by using the same information and examples.

Get students to think of alternative ways of asking the other questions in exercise 5.

---

## Roleplay

**6** Read the instructions and the job ads with the whole class and explain any new vocabulary or allow students to look them up in a dictionary.

Candidates should refer to the Internet research they did on interview tips and advice. If they have not done this, elicit from the whole class a list of topics that they could ask questions about (e.g. details about the job itself; information about the company and department; opportunities for training and developments; benefits, etc.).

Remind the interviewers to look back at the previous exercises in this module for help and ideas when they are preparing their questions.

Circulate and check that all students are using expressions and tenses correctly in their questions.

When the activity is over, get students to give each other feedback, either with a partner or as a whole-class activity. The interviewers can say which answers were most satisfactory and which were less satisfactory; the candidates can say which questions they found easy to answer and which ones were difficult.

## 4.5 Writing
## A CV

This module focuses on the content, organization and style of CVs.

### Internet research

An Internet search for *résumé style* will reveal information about a number of possible approaches to presenting information in a CV. For example, a chronological CV starts with your most current position and progresses back in time; a functional CV lists your major areas of experience and/or accomplishments; a skills CV emphasizes what you can do. Different styles will be appropriate for different individuals and different situations.

Students will find many sample CVs on the Internet. They could download some and evaluate which style would best suit their individual circumstances and the profession or industry they are interested in.

### Discussion

**1** Start by reminding students that *CV* stands for 'curriculum vitae', a Latin term meaning 'course of life'. *Résumé* has a similar meaning; it is more commonly used in American English.

Students discuss the questions in small groups. As the answer to most of these questions is likely to be 'it depends', encourage students to give reasons for their answers. Take whole-class feedback.

#### SUGGESTED ANSWERS:
The 'correct' answer to all of these is 'it depends'. There are valid arguments for both sides of each case.
1 Stating your objective will help employers decide if your CV is relevant, and gives the impression of a focused candidate. On the other hand, it may mean you are not considered for other equally interesting and suitable positions.
2 Some experts recommend not giving references until they are requested, so that you have time to contact the people concerned and inform them about the context, your objectives, etc. Others advise supplying genuine references rather than stating 'references available on request'.
3 In general, one page is enough, especially for new graduates; but if you need more space, it's better to use two pages rather than try to squeeze everything onto one page.
4 Decide which is more relevant. If your experience is more relevant to the job than your qualifications, put it first. However, many employers like to have a summary of your qualifications at the top of the page.

### Skim reading

**2** Give students a few minutes to put these categories in order individually or with a partner.

Students check their answers against the sample CV. To check answers with the whole class, read out sections from the CV and get students to give the category it falls under, e.g. *British* (personal details), *clean driving licence* (general / additional skills), *I coordinated an office reorganization project* (work experience).

#### ANSWERS:
| | |
|---|---|
| personal details | 1 |
| qualifications | 2 |
| work experience | 3 |
| voluntary roles / positions of responsibility | 4 |
| general / additional skills | 5 |
| references | 6 |

### Reading for detail

**3** This exercise highlights the degree of formality usually found in CVs. Get individual students to read each of the sentences aloud, while the rest of the class finds the matching sentence in the CV.

Focus on the useful verbs and verb phrases, e.g. *liaise, coordinate, run, represent, play an integral part in, be responsible for* which students can use in exercises 4 and 5.

#### ANSWERS:
1 ... involved liaising with a client's parent company in Germany.
2 Advanced computer literacy
3 I coordinated an office reorganization project.
4 I ran a language training programme for members of the department.
5 I represented over 400 members in faculty meetings.
6 I played an integral part in a team of consultants working on IS projects.
7 I was responsible for managing the outdoor exhibition of camping equipment.
8 This position required familiarity with networking solutions.
9 I am responsible for motivating the team.
10 ... chaired conferences with visiting speakers.

#### FURTHER PRACTICE
Use the sample CVs which students downloaded from the Internet and / or real job ads taken from newspapers to compile a list of useful 'action words' – i.e. verbs that that students could use in their own CVs to describe their achievements. Examples of the kinds of words that might be included in this kind of list are *administer, analyze, assess, build, create, design, develop, devise, direct, ensure, implement, improve, increase, instigate, introduce, manage, monitor, organize, produce, re-organize, solve, support, test.*

## Ordering and reformulating

**4** Students could do this task with a partner. Circulate while they are working and assist where necessary. Then get students to exchange their CV with another pair, who check the organization and choice of language.

**SUGGESTED ANSWER:**

---

**Justine Dominga Collier**

Date of birth    4 November, 1986, Auckland, NZ
Nationality    New Zealand
Address    14 Green Street, Newcastle NE13 8BH
Telephone    01879 122 7789

**Education**

2004–2007 BA in Economics at Newcastle University (Expected final grade 2:1)
2002–2004 Northern High School: 3 'A' levels – Mathematics (A), Economics (B), French (B)

**Work history**

Oct–Mar 2005 Internship with Arbol Oil
I played an integral part in the finance department. This position required familiarity with accounts software, and involved liaising with colleagues in South America.
June–Sept 2004 Information officer with Newcastle Social Security
I was responsible for managing a confidential personnel database. I coordinated a three-day visit for a representative of the Spanish government.

**Positions of responsibility**

2006 Secretary of Newcastle Junior Chamber of Commerce
I was responsible for communications and edited a monthly newsletter. I also liaised with guest speakers and the local authorities.
2005–present Voluntary work for the charity OUTLOOK
I devise and organize events for disabled children.
Social Secretary for the University Basketball team.

**Other**

Bilingual Spanish
First violin in a string quartet
Typing speed: 90 wpm
References
Mr Bowers, tutor, Newcastle University
Mrs Broadbent, Principal, Northern High School

---

**5** Students could use the results of the Internet research task to help them write or update their own CV. Otherwise, they could use the model in exercise 2 as the basis for their CV. Circulate while students are working and make a note of any useful new vocabulary or phrases that could be shared with the whole class.

## 4.6 Case study
### Gap years and career breaks

This module focuses on the reasons for and experience of taking time off from your career to do something different.

### Internet research

A search for *gap year* will reveal a wide range of websites suggesting ways of spending a gap year, including travel, adventure holidays, and voluntary work.

Carrying out this research before they start this module will be useful for students who do not have any knowledge or experience of gap years or career breaks.

## Brainstorming

**1** Explain that *gap year* usually refers to the time taken off at the beginning of a career, while *career break* refers to the time taken off at a later stage of life.

Do this as a whole-class activity. If students have difficulty getting started, give them the brief outline of a story to comment on, e.g.: *A friend of mine had been working for 7 years in a big company. He enjoyed the work, but the job was stressful and he wanted a break from the pressure and the routine. So he left his job and decided to take some time off and do something different …*

**SUGGESTED ANSWERS:**

Gap year: travelling, working, doing voluntary work, writing a book, building a house, studying, meditating, etc.
Advantages: gain experience and maturity, see the world, do something you can't do professionally, do something for people in need, give yourself time to make important choices, escape pressure or difficulty, save money for studies, etc.
Disadvantages: get out of step / lose touch with friends / colleagues, financial cost, acquire 'bad' habits, be perceived as less serious / ambitious, lose job or miss opportunities, etc.

Ask students if gap years and career breaks are common in their country. Do they know anyone who has taken a gap year or career break? What were their experiences? Would they consider taking one themselves?

## Listening

**2** 2:19–2:24  Play the recording. Pause after each speaker to allow students time to answer the questions. Then get students to comment – which of these gap year options would they have chosen to do themselves and why?

**ANSWERS:**

| | When | Where | Experience | Why |
|---|---|---|---|---|
| 1 | between 2nd and 3rd year at university | Nepal | positive | learned more than in 3 years at university |
| 2 | between school and degree course | Dublin | mixed | good for English and culture, but boring at school |
| 3 | in work | around the world | mixed | clearer idea of goals, regrets not helping people |
| 4 | before business school | car factory | negative | bored, wasted a year |
| 5 | after 20 years in same job | India | positive | changed outlook on life |
| 6 | before studying medicine | East Africa | mixed | very hard, but made a difference |

## RECORDING SCRIPT

 2:19–2:24

1   My gap year? Oh yes, it was a fantastic experience. It was between my second and third years at university. I went to Nepal to teach English. I think I learned more in that year than in three years at university. It was incredible. Everybody should do it.

2   I went to live with a family in Dublin for a year before starting my degree course. Of course, it was really good for my English, and interesting from a cultural point of view. But it was pretty boring going back to school for another year, even if it was in English.

3   I've had a great year. I've been around the world, working for two or three weeks, then moving on to the next place. I've just gone back to my job, and now I have a much clearer idea of where I'm going and what I want to achieve. My only regret is not doing something to help people. If I could do it again, I'd definitely volunteer for charity work, probably in Africa.

4   Yeah, I had a gap year before starting business school. I needed to earn some money, so I worked in a car factory. It was hell. I've never been so bored in my life. I suppose I learned some valuable lessons, but now I wish I'd done something more exciting, gone somewhere exotic. I feel I wasted a year of my life.

5   I'd been in the same job for about twenty years, and I decided I needed to step back and think about what I wanted to do with the rest of my life. So I took a sabbatical. Fortunately my company was very understanding. I travelled in India for six months, then wrote a book about my experiences. It completely changed my outlook on life. I'd recommend it to anybody.

6   I've just started studying medicine. I wanted to get away from my parents and see the world, so I've just come back from nine months in East Africa. It was really hard. I almost came home after the first week. I'm glad I stayed, because I felt I made a difference to people's lives – a very small difference, but a difference all the same. But if I'd known what it would be like, I'm sure I wouldn't have gone.

## Scan reading

**3**   Read the title of the article with the whole class and get them to explain what they understand by the two expressions *change the world* (make a difference to other people's lives) and *want a change* (do something different, for yourself).

You could do this task by reading the first question aloud and giving students a few minutes to find the answer in the text. They should then raise their hands when they have found the answer. Wait until most of the class have raised their hands and then call on a student to give you the answer. Continue in this way until students have answered all the questions.

**ANSWERS:**

1   People over 17 years of age, before, during or after a degree course, or in work.
2   Broaden your horizons, enhance your CV, step back from your studies to decide what you want to do with your life, do something concrete and tangible to help people in need in underprivileged areas of the world.
3   Education, conservation, medical support and care work.
4   Participants work as volunteers. Food and accommodation are provided, but participants pay their own travel costs.
5   Send in the application form together with your CV.

## Reading and discussion

**4**   Get students to read the four descriptions of gap-year placements silently. Then ask them some questions to get them thinking about what is involved in each placement, e.g.:
*What kinds of things do you think a classroom assistant in South Africa or Costa Rica would do on a daily basis?* (help the teacher with lessons; spend time with individual children; help with break times and lunch breaks)
*What kind of physical work might a conservation volunteer do in Malaysia?* (digging, cutting back vegetation, clearing land, caring for animals)
*What do you think it would it be like to teach in a school in Tanzania?* (classes may be large; facilities and resources may be limited; teachers have to teach all subjects so would need a wide range of knowledge and skills).

While students are discussing with a partner circulate and assist where necessary. Make a note of any new vocabulary or expressions and write them on the board at the end of the discussion. Take whole-class feedback on students' choice of placement. Ask them to explain the reasons for their choices.

## Writing and roleplay

**5**   This activity could take place over two lessons – completing the application form in one lesson, and conducting the interviews in another lesson. Alternatively, the application forms could be completed for homework before the class.

With lower-level classes, work through the questions on the application form, eliciting possible answers and making a list of useful words and expressions on the board. Remind them of the information provided in the previous exercises in this module which will help them to complete the answers.

With higher-level classes, before students do the interviewing part of the activity, brainstorm a short list of 'success criteria' to use when assessing each candidate. Possible criteria might be: previous experience of community or care work (for the placements in South Africa and Costa Rica); involvement in sports and extra-curricular activities (Tanzania); health and physical wellbeing (Malaysia), etc. Students could also refer to the vocabulary for personal skills and qualities in module 4.2 to help them, e.g. is the candidate a good communicator (Tanzania), a good team worker (Costa Rica), etc.

Remind students about the work they did on interviewing skills and techniques in module 4.4. Interviewers and interviewees should refer back to the questions and expressions practised there.

Circulate while students are speaking and make a note of any mistakes in the target language for remedial teaching later. You could also make a note of any particularly good questions or responses to share with the rest of the class when the activity is over.

# Review 3 and 4 answers

## Review 3

(page 56 in the Student's Book)

### 3 Products and packaging

**1**

1 competitive
2 attractive, effective, distinctive
3 critical, efficient, limited
4 original, impractical, technical

**2**

1 chance
2 view
3 sale
4 communication, process
5 field
6 needs
7 issues
8 solution

**3**

1 generate new ideas in focus groups
2 screen out unfeasible or unprofitable ideas
3 launch the product onto the market
4 draw up specifications for the product
5 conduct market studies
6 draw sketches and build mockups
7 go into production on a large scale after tests
8 test the product by using it in typical situations

**4**

1 length
2 width
3 height
4 weight

**5**

1 USP
2 feature
3 specification
4 benefit
5 function

**6**

2 Here's the email that arrived this morning.
3 The team leader is an interesting man who comes from Spain.
4 The team leader who I met yesterday is an interesting man.
5 The team leader is an interesting man whose background is in IT.

**7**

1 Here's the email (that) I got this morning.
4 The team leader (who) I met yesterday is an interesting man.

**8**

2 travel insurance document
3 packaging design concept
4 household-cleaning product

**9**

1 go on
2 answer
3 objective
4 Finally
5 I'll
6 listening
7 into
8 feel
9 reasons

**10**

Possible order:
Beginning of presentation 3, 7, 5, 1, 4, 8
End of presentation 9, 6, 2

**11**

1 Can we come back to that later?
2 I'm not sure that's a direction we want to go in.
3 That's more the kind of thing I had in mind.

## Review 4

(page 57 in the Student's Book)

### 4 Careers

**1**

1 make a career choice
2 reach your long-term goal
3 prefer money rather than job satisfaction
4 learn new skills
5 gain experience
6 get a performance-related bonus
7 send off a job application
8 apply for a gap-year placement

**2**

1 targets
2 objectives
3 aim

**3**

1 know-how
2 knowledge
3 skill
4 experience
5 background
6 aptitude

**4**

1 be dismissed / be fired / be sacked
2 be dismissed
3 be laid off / be made redundant
4 be made redundant

**5**

1 short-listed
2 resign
3 attend
4 appointed
5 hired
6 apply

**6**

1 am interviewing
2 interviewed
3 've / have interviewed
4 interview
5 need
6 Has anyone seen
7 put
8 'm / am talking

**7**

1 have been writing / have finished
2 have written / have been trying

**8**

1 strength
2 weakness
3 responsibility
4 performance
5 commitment
6 achievement

**9**

1 responsibilities
2 performance
3 strengths
4 weaknesses
5 achievement
6 commitment

# 5 | Making deals

## Subject background

There are often two misconceptions about negotiating. The first is: 'Negotiating is all about making offers and finding compromises.' The typical image is buying a carpet in the bazaar. But, in fact, this is really the stage of 'bargaining', and negotiating also includes the earlier stages of establishing rapport, information gathering, stating needs, etc. Even in the bazaar the serving of mint tea is an essential part of the process – a chance to get a sense of the other person as an individual before the hard bargaining begins. The second is: 'Negotiating is all about supplier-customer situations.' But, in fact, the textbook negotiation of a purchasing manager buying materials from a supplier is a specialized situation in business. The same language may be used when negotiating with colleagues and bosses about day-to-day work procedures.

In negotiation roleplays in the classroom, another common mistake that is made, especially amongst those with little or no work experience, is trading concessions and finding compromises issue by issue. In real business, negotiators often leave everything open right up to the end, at which point everything falls into place as a whole.

Issues that might be subject to negotiation include: price, minimum order, discount, delivery, quality standards, payment terms, extras, penalty clauses, other contract details, procedures, documentation, after-sales service, timing, guarantees, etc.

There is always a good deal of preparation before a negotiation. This might consist of:
- Setting broad objectives for what you want to achieve. What are your main priorities?
- Identifying the other person's needs. Initial contact by phone and email will allow you to do this – ask lots of questions.
- Listing all possible variables. Divide them into quantifiable (price) and unquantifiable (design). For each variable, write down i) your best possible outcome, ii) a realistic outcome and iii) the worst position you will accept (beyond this point you walk away).
- Deciding on possible concessions. What are you prepared to give?

Some of the above can be simulated in the classroom by students with the same role preparing together first, or at least reading (and adding to) a role card for homework.

In the negotiation itself, there is a psychological element to the trading of concessions.
1 Maximize your concessions:
- stress the costs to you (*Well, I could do that, but it would involve …*)
- refer to a major problem your concession will solve (*Well, if I agreed to that it would remove the need for you to …*)
- imply that the concession is exceptional (*I really don't know what my boss would say.*).
2 Minimize their concessions:
- acknowledge a concession briefly without putting any value on it (*Right, let's do it that way.*)
- devalue their concession (*Right, that's a small step forward I guess.*)
- amortize their concession into smaller units (*Well, at least that saves me X per month.*) rather than quoting the total figure.

Other key techniques during the negotiation include:
3 Summarize frequently.
4 Take notes.
5 Use silence. It gives you time to think and – you never know – the other person might fill it with a concession.
6 Where agreement is easy, use this to promote good feeling (*That's a good suggestion / Yes, let's do it that way.*).

## Useful websites

Here are three Internet sites that have articles on a whole variety of business topics, including negotiating:
http://www.salesvault.com/artman/publish/index.shtml
http://www.expertmagazine.com/artman/publish/index.shtml
http://www.mindtools.com
(For this last one go to the 'Communication Skills' area of the site.)

## 5.1 About business
### E-tailing

This module focuses on the ways in which companies are trying to increase online sales through specific marketing techniques.

### Internet research

Students can find out more about how conversational agents are used from these websites (oddcast.com uses illustrated 'salespeople' and pulse3d.com uses a 'talking puppy'). Get students to try out two or three different examples and assess how successful they are. In class, get students to work in small groups to exchange their findings and note down the main points. Then take whole-class feedback.

Students could do this research before they start this module or before they do the discussion activity in exercise 6.

---

**LEAD-IN ACTIVITY**

To start students thinking about the topic, ask them the following questions:
*How many purchases have you made online in the past month or so?*
*What were they?*
*Were you satisfied with the experience?*
*If you haven't bought anything online, why not?*

Explain that the topic of this unit is e-tailing, and ask them to guess which two words it is formed from (*electronic* and *retailing*).

---

### Discussion

**1** Question 1: Give students a few minutes to discuss this question. Then take whole-class feedback and make a list of the pros and cons of website and store shopping on the board.

Question 2: Ask students to think about why less than 5% of people visiting a website turn into paying customers. This will help them to come up with ideas for how e-tailers could persuade people to buy from websites. Take whole-class feedback and make a list of ideas on the board.

### Scan reading

**2** Students read the article and look for examples of what e-tailers are doing to encourage visitors to websites to buy products. Add these ideas to the list you made on the board in exercise 1. Get students to comment on how effective they think these ideas would be. If they have any personal experience of live web chats with sales reps or animated characters, get them to comment on their reaction to them.

With lower-level classes, you could read the article one paragraph at a time. Pause after each paragraph to check understanding and elicit the ideas it contains.

### Reading for detail

**3** Students do this sequencing exercise alone, and then compare answers with a partner.

---

**ANSWERS:**

[4] Animated sales reps are cheaper than real people and can increase sales by one third.
[6] Though interactive discussion boosts sales, e-tailers have to be cautious.
[1] Only a very small percentage of visits to websites produce sales.
[5] Customer tracking is often badly perceived by online shoppers, who may prefer to shop privately.
[2] Live web chats with sales reps double online sales.
[3] Customer-tracking systems can provide help for customers when it is appropriate.

---

Ask students further questions about the text to help them engage with the topic. Some questions (with possible answers in brackets) might be:
*Why do you think live web chats with sales reps double online sales?* (They give customers more information about the product / make them feel more confident about the purchase.)
*What do animated characters do?* (They act as sales reps and use a databank of voice answers to reply to common customer questions.)
*Why do some companies use them?* (They can't afford as many live online reps as larger companies.)
How successful are they? (They can help to increase sales.)
*Why don't online shoppers like customer tracking?* (They feel that it is an invasion of their privacy.)

### Roleplay

**4** Give students a few minutes to read the instructions for the roleplay and re-read the article quickly, if necessary, to remind themselves of the main points that they will need for the roleplay.

With lower-level classes, get students to write out the questions in full before they start.

Circulate while students are speaking and assist where necessary.

---

**FURTHER PRACTICE**

To provide additional focus on the ideas and vocabulary presented in this module, get students to write a short report or article using the answers they received from their partner in the roleplay.

---

### Listening

**5** 2:25 Before they look at this exercise, ask students if they can guess what a *conversational agent* might be. Some students may make the connection between this term and *animated character*, which is used in the article. Students will know what it means if they have done the Internet research task before this module.

Read the questions with students and play the whole discussion through. Get students to compare their answers with a partner. Then check answers with the whole class. Get students to correct the false statements.

## ANSWERS:

| 1 T | 2 T | 3 F | 4 T | 5 F | 6 T | 7 F |

## RECORDING SCRIPT

 2:25

**Johnny:** Now, ladies and gentlemen, tonight we're going to talk to Hermelinda Ray, who is an e-tailing consultant, and who's going to tell us what's new in the world of internet shopping. Hermelinda, welcome to the show!

**Hermelinda:** Thank you, Johnny. It's my pleasure to be here.

**J:** Now, tell me, Hermelinda, what exactly does an e-tailing consultant do?

**H:** Well, basically, my job is to help e-tailers to grow their businesses by improving their websites, their products and services, and increasing their sales.

**J:** I see. I guess a lot of people, like me, do a lot of window-shopping on the Internet, but we don't often buy anything.

**H:** That's right Johnny. And that's one of the main challenges for e-tailers today, especially because they have to pay to advertise their sites to increase traffic. But only a small percentage of that traffic results in sales, and so when you visit a site without buying anything, your visit is actually costing the e-tailer money!

**J:** OK, now you're going to tell us about a new way to increase sales: conversational agents?

**H:** Uh-huh.

**J:** So, what exactly is a conversational agent?

**H:** A conversational agent, or virtual host, is what computer specialists call an avatar. It's an animated character that appears on the customer's screen, and can answer questions and chat with the customer, just like you would chat with a sales rep in a store.

**J:** But it's not a real person, right?

**H:** No. Having real people to chat with customers online is too expensive for small e-businesses. A conversational agent is a computer programme which uses artificial intelligence to interact with customers.

**J:** OK. But does it work? Do people really want to chat to a machine?

**H:** Oh, yes. Of course, some people are happier with the idea than others, but depending on the product and the type of customer, conversational agents can increase sales by as much as 50%.

**J:** Really! 50%?

**H:** Yes. The longer customers spend on the site, hearing and asking questions about a product, the more chance there is they'll buy it. It builds their confidence in the product. And research has shown that people trust what they hear from a conversational agent much more than what they simply read on a website.

**J:** Well, we thought you should judge for yourselves, so Hermelinda has very kindly brought along a sample for us.

**Recorded voice:** Hi, I'm Laurie! I'm here to help you find your way around the site. I'll answer all your questions about our products. Click on a question on the left. Would you like to tell a friend about us? Click on the referral zone so your friends can experience our site for themselves.

**J:** Well, ladies and gentlemen, would you buy a used car from that lady? All right, let's have a big round of applause for Hermelinda Ray, and for Laurie, the conversational agent!

## Discussion

**6** Question 1: After students have discussed this question in small groups, take a poll of the whole class by getting students to raise their hands to show which of the three options they prefer. Ask a few students what their reasons for their choices are. Students who are unsure, or want to answer 'It depends' should explain their reasons.

Question 2: Get students to give some concrete examples of e-tailing sites they think would be appropriate / inappropriate for conversational agents. Get in-work students to comment on whether they think they would work in their own business.

Question 3: Groups could choose one or more of these websites, depending on time. Get them to give as detailed a description of the character as possible – appearance, gender, clothing, etc. Get each group to describe their character to the whole class. Students could then vote on the character that they think would work best in each case. For example, the agent for General Motors could be a 40-something year-old mechanic, dressed in overalls who really seems to know what he's talking about. An alternative would be a slick looking, smartly-dressed male or female salesperson. They should seem trustworthy.

# 5.2 Vocabulary
## Negotiating and e-tailing

This module focuses on key expressions for negotiating and describing the process of an e-tail transaction.

### Internet research

*Principled negotiation* is the name given to the approach to negotiation described in the book, *Getting to Yes*, first published in 1981 by Roger Fisher and William Ury. The book advocates four basic principles of negotiation:

- separate the people from the problem
- focus on interests, not positions
- devise a variety of options that will benefit everyone concerned
- insist that the agreement is based on objective criteria.

Principled negotiation is a *win-win* approach, with the aim of reaching a lasting agreement.

Students will find several websites which explore these principles in more detail. They could do this research before they start module 5.2 or at the end of the module, to supplement the work done here. This research will also be useful for the negotiating activities and exercises which appear in later modules of the unit.

## Discussion

**1** Do this as a whole-class activity. Get students to brainstorm ideas and write them on the board. Encourage students to think of positive and negative aspects to shopping in an e-store and shopping in a high-street store.

### SUGGESTED ANSWERS:

In an e-store you can't (usually) negotiate the price.
In a high street store you can't (usually) read what other people think about the product, know how many items the store has in stock, easily compare prices in other stores, find out what other products people who bought this one also bought, set the product aside for a later purchase, or make a wish list for your friends to choose a present for you.

## Collocations

**2** Students could complete these exercises individually or with a partner. Allow them to use dictionaries, if they wish. Circulate while they are working and assist where necessary. Check answers with the whole class. Then ask students to pick out any collocations that are new to them or that they are unsure of, and review their meaning and use.

### ANSWERS:

| | | | |
|---|---|---|---|
| 1 an order | 2 a price | 3 a discount | 4 the benefits |
| 5 the details | 6 a proposal | 7 negotiation | |
| 8 a deposit | 9 fee | 10 costs | 11 a deadline |
| 12 a compromise | | | |

## Listening

**3**  2:26–2:33 Students work with a partner. Play the extracts from negotiations one at a time and give students a few minutes to note down their answers. Check answers with the whole class and get students to tell you the words or phrases they heard which helped them to get the answer.

With lower-level classes, do the first one or two extracts with the whole class. Elicit answers from the whole class and write them on the board. Accept all possible answers.

---

With lower-level classes, write the possible answers in random order on the board, numbered 1–8. Students then listen and choose the best answer from those on the board.

Circulate while students are writing their own extracts. Then circulate again while they are working with a partner and assist where necessary. Get some students to read their extracts aloud for the whole class to identify the collocations.

### SUGGESTED ANSWERS:

1 A supplier is taking an order.
2 A buyer is trying to bring the price down.
3 A buyer is asking for a bigger discount.
4 A seller is rejecting a proposal.
5 Someone is saying that availability is open to / subject to negotiation.
6 A seller is asking the buyer to pay / to put down a deposit.
7 A customer is refusing to extend a deadline / is complaining that a supplier has missed a deadline.
8 A negotiator is seeking / offering a compromise.

## RECORDING SCRIPT

2:26–2:33

1 So that's five hundred at 12 euros a box, then. And you need them by Wednesday, you say?
2 Considering this would be a regular order, I think two and a half thousand is still a bit expensive.
3 How about if we paid cash? Could you give us an extra 2%?
4 No, I'm sorry, that's my final offer. I can't go any lower than that.
5 And then we'd need you to be available five or six weeks a year. Or maybe a bit less. Anyway, we can talk about it. Nothing's decided yet.
6 Yes, we usually ask for 20% now, and the balance on delivery.
7 Look, this just isn't good enough! If you don't deliver until tomorrow morning, it'll be too late!
8 Well, there's not much between us now. What do you say we split the difference?

### FURTHER PRACTICE

Get students to close their books. Using the nouns in the boxes in exercise 2, write a list of scrambled words on the board and get students to unscramble them, e.g.:

| | |
|---|---|
| *mpemrcoiso* | (compromise) |
| *giiatnotnoe* | (negotiation) |
| *eieddnla* | (deadline) |
| *topeisd* | (deposit) |
| *nbeiftes* | (benefits |
| *ldsiaet* | (details) |
| *dostnuci* | (discount) |
| *orpplaso* | (proposal) |
| *ipcer* | (price) |
| *sotsc* | (costs) |
| *efe* | (fee) |
| *errod* | (order). |

When they have unscrambled the letters, students should give one or more of the verbs that collocate with them.

## Pronunciation

**4** 2:34–2:38 Play the recording and get students to underline the schwas in each case. Then get them to compare their answers with a partner. Write the phrases on the board and get individual students to underline the correct words on the board. Then practise saying the phrases aloud with the whole class.

Play  2:34–2:38 again. Pause after each phrase so that students can repeat it quietly to themselves, either with their eyes closed or by reading the words from the book.

Play the whole extract  2:26–2:33 again (extracts 1,2,3,5 and 6 in exercise 3) so that students can hear the complete sentence in context.

For homework, students could record themselves saying the extracts aloud (using the recording script which can be found at the back of the Student's Book). They could then play this back and assess their own delivery.

**ANSWERS:**
1 five hund<u>red at</u> 12 euros <u>a</u> box
2 two <u>and a</u> half thous<u>and</u>
3 <u>an</u> extra two <u>per</u> cent
4 five <u>or</u> six weeks <u>a</u> year
5 We usually ask <u>for</u> 20% now.

## RECORDING SCRIPT

2:34–2.38

1 five hundred at 12 euros a box
2 two and a half thousand
3 an extra two per cent
4 five or six a year
5 We usually ask for 20% now.

**5** If necessary, explain *browse* (to examine something in a casual way). Students work with a partner to put these sentences in the correct order. Check answers with the whole class by calling on students to read the sentences aloud. Remind them to use schwas, where appropriate.

**ANSWERS:**
[4] The customer prices similar products on other sites.
[10] The product is shipped to the customer's address by mail or express carrier.
[12] The seller exchanges the product or gives a refund.
[6] The customer goes to the check-out and pays by credit card.
[7] The website records the transaction and generates an invoice.
[5] The customer selects a product and places it in a cart.
[11] The customer sends the faulty product back under guarantee.
[8] The customer's credit card account is debited.
[2] The customer clicks on the link to the seller's site.
[1] The prospective customer looks up the product on a search engine.
[3] The customer browses the site and identifies the product which interests him.
[9] The website sends an instruction to the warehouse to ship the product.

**6** Students complete this exercise with a partner. Check answers with the whole class.

**ANSWERS:**
1 a) product   b) site   c) product   d) credit
2 a) transaction   b) invoices   c) refunds   d) product
   e) link

Alternatively, do this activity as a listening task. Students close their books. Write the words in bold on the board. Tell students you are going to read two separate emails aloud and that they should choose the best word to fill the gap when you pause.

With higher-level classes you could present all the words together. With lower-level classes, keep the two lists separate. Then get students to open their books and read the two emails.

## Listening for detail

**7** 2:39 Give students time to read the minutes silently, or read them aloud with the whole class.

Higher-level classes could try to predict what similar words or phrases they might hear in the recording.

Then play the recording. Pause from time to time, if necessary, to allow students to note down their answers.

**ANSWERS:**
1 get to <u>work</u>
2 pointed out the <u>benefits</u>
3 the <u>issues</u> you'd like to discuss
4 clarify your <u>remarks</u>
5 summarize the <u>situation</u>
6 make an <u>offer</u>
7 work out a <u>compromise</u>
8 consider <u>alternative solutions</u>
9 break for <u>lunch</u>
10 find <u>common ground</u>

## RECORDING SCRIPT

2:39

Ben: OK then, Jacky. Let's get to work. You've pointed out the benefits of your policy, but there are still one or two issues I'm not happy with.
Jacky: All right, then. What exactly are the issues you'd like to discuss?
B: First of all, I'd like you to clarify your remarks about returns.
J: OK. To summarize the situation, our policy insures you against any damage caused during shipping. It does not cover any problems resulting from incorrect assembly or operation by the customer.
B: I see. So, basically, if it's the customer's fault, you don't pay?
J: Right.
B: And are you prepared to extend your cover to include installation difficulties?
J: Well now, Ben. We could certainly make an offer, but there'll be extra costs.
B: Well, considering the size of the contract we're talking about here, I was hoping we could work out a compromise. If not, I might have to consider alternative solutions.
J: I'm sure that won't be necessary, Ben. Why don't we break for lunch, and I'll have my team do a simulation? I'm sure we'll find common ground.

## Discussion

**8** In-work students could talk about a situation at work, if this is appropriate; pre-work students could talk about an agreement with a family member or friend, in a holiday job, or during a work placement.

Circulate while students are working and check that they are using the target language correctly. Make a note of any difficulties for remedial teaching later.

**EXTENSION ACTIVITY**

To follow up this discussion, get students to write some minutes, using those in exercise 7 as a model, in which they report the agreement their partner described to them.

## 5.3 Grammar
### Conditionals and recommendations

This module focuses on the uses of the first, second and zero conditionals and on verb patterns with *recommend*, *suggest* and *advise*.

### Internet research

Students will find numerous quotations about negotiating if they search the Internet. Below are a few examples.

'In business, you don't get what you deserve, you get what you negotiate.'
(Chester L. Karrass)
'Never cut what you can untie.'
(Joseph Joubert)
'The most important trip you may take in life is meeting people half way.'
(Henry Boyle)
'Negotiating is finding out what the other person needs and working out the best way to give it to them.'
(Philip Laut)

You could use these as discussion points in class if students do not have time to conduct a search themselves. Get students to think about what they mean and how they could use them in real situations. You could do this as preparation for or follow-up to exercise 8, when students work with a partner to negotiate an agreement.

### Test yourself: Conditionals

**1**, **2** and **3** Start by reading the first part of the *Refresh your memory* box with the class. Students work alone to complete exercises 1–3 and then compare their answers with a partner. Check answers with the whole class by getting individual students to read each answer aloud. If students seem unsure of the conditionals or would like further practice in them, work through some or all of exercises 1–13 in the *Grammar and practice* section (page 126–127 in the Student's Book, answers on page 118 in this book).

**ANSWERS:**

Exercise 1
| 1 | would go | 2 | don't go | 3 | won't go | 4 | went |
| 5 | would you go | 6 | go | 7 | doesn't go | 8 | will you go |

Exercise 2
1 a) possible   2 c) sure   3 b) probable

Exercise 3
1 providing   2 unless   3 only if

### Test yourself: *recommend / suggest / advise*

**4** Follow the same procedure as in exercises 1–3. Get students to try to formulate the ways in which these three verbs are used. They can then turn to the *Grammar and practice* section (page 127 in the Student's Book, answers on page 118 in this book) to check their answers. There is also a further practice exercise on that page.

**ANSWERS:**

1   What options would you recommend ~~me~~?
2   I suggest you ~~to~~ take the dust-proof control unit: it's specially designed for industrial environments.
3   Would you advise ~~me~~ choosing the 750W or the 1,000W motor?
4   We generally suggest ~~you~~ allowing for a little extra power.
5   We recommend ~~you~~ not exceeding 9,000 rpm in the first two weeks.
6   I would advise ~~that~~ you to check the oil level at least once a week.
7   Our parent company recommends ~~it~~ that we do not buy from non-ISO-certified suppliers.
8   In that case, I would suggest your Quality Manager ~~to~~ visit us before placing an order.

### Reformulating

**5** Higher-level classes could do this exercise orally. Lower-level classes might need to write the sentences down first. Students can turn to the *Grammar and practice* section (page 127 in the Student's Book, answers on page 118 in this book) for further practice of *unless*, *if*, *providing* and *as long as*.

**ANSWERS:**

2   Our production manager is willing to make the changes, providing you supply a prototype.
3   We are reluctant to consider a larger discount, unless you pay in advance.
4   We would be prepared to sponsor the exhibition, but only if we had a large stand in the entrance hall.
5   Unless we can get the sub-components in time, it will be impossible to meet the deadline.
6   As long as several other top CEOs were present, our president would agree to attend.

### Discussion

**6** While students are speaking, circulate and check that they are using the target language correctly. Make a note of any errors for remedial teaching when the discussion is over.

Students who finish early could formulate one or two questions of their own to ask and answer.

### Listening

**7** 2:40 Play the recording through once and get students to do the exercise. Ask how many things Petra has agreed to do (two) and how many things Jan has agreed to do (three). If students have the correct numbers, get them to tell you the answers. If not, play the recording again so that they can check their answers.

To focus on the language and expressions used, get students to listen to the recording and read the recording script (Student's Book, page 141) at the same time. Get them to underline examples of the target language (conditionals and recommendations).

## RECORDING SCRIPT

 2:40

Petra: OK, we have to decide how to divide this list of responsibilities between us. What are your priorities?

Jan: Well, I'd really like to go the conference in Madagascar. Could I suggest that you go to Siberia? If you agreed, I'd be willing to take my holidays in January and let you take yours in August.

P: I'm sorry, but I'd really like to go to Madagascar too. I couldn't agree to your proposal, unless you were prepared to take your holidays in January and go to the exhibition in Kazakhstan.

J: Hm. Well, I might consider going to Kazakhstan. I've got an uncle who lives there…

P: Great!

J: … providing you looked after the foreign customer at the tennis tournament – I know nothing about tennis!

P: OK, we're making progress. So, can I just summarize the position so far? You can go to Madagascar, as long as you also go to Kazakhstan, and you let me take my holidays in August. OK?

J: OK. But only if you do the tennis weekend.

P: All right, no problem, I'll handle the tennis, if you take your holiday in January.

J: And you go to Siberia.

P: Oh, now wait a minute, I never agreed to that! I couldn't possibly go to Siberia unless you were able to …

## Negotiating

**8** Remind students of the work they did in module 5.2 on negotiating and about the idea of principled negotiation. Circulate while students are speaking and assist where necessary.

---

**FURTHER PRACTICE**

For further writing practice, get students to write a short summary of the agreement they reached in exercise 8 along the lines of the summary in module 5.2, exercise 7.

---

## 5.4 Speaking
## Negotiations – bargaining

This module focuses on the language and skills needed for successful negotiating.

### Internet research

A search under *cross cultural negotiation* will reveal a wide range of articles and information. The kinds of factors that need to be considered in cross-cultural negotiation include cultural differences in eye contact, personal space and touch, time, meeting and greeting, gift-giving, negotiating styles, and the nature of business relationships.

Get students to focus on one or two topics and gather as much information as they can on them. They then prepare a brief summary for oral or written presentation to the class. Then compile the material into a folder which is made available to the whole class or give each student a copy.

This research could be done as a follow-up to the work in this module.

### Discussion

**1** Students should first decide what their 'bottom line' is, i.e. what they want to achieve, what they want to get out of the sale, e.g. a minimum price they will accept or a concession that they are prepared to make, such as having the bicycle serviced before selling it or delivering the item to the buyer's house.

When the time is up, get students to say if they think they won or lost the negotiation. How much did they deviate from their initial plan?

Discuss the notions of *win-lose, lose-lose,* and *win-win* in negotiations and get students to explain what they understand by these terms (reminding them that they explored *win-win* in module 5.2). How would they describe their own negotiation? How did each person feel at the end of the process – satisfied or dissatisfied?

**ANSWERS:**

Negotiations can generally be categorized as win-lose, lose-lose, or win-win.

### Listening

**2** 2:41 Read the questions with students and play the conversation through. Explain any new vocabulary, e.g. *logistics* (the organization of supplies and services for an operation). Play the recording. Pause the recording if necessary to allow students to note down their answers. Get students to compare their answers with a partner and then take whole-class feedback.

**ANSWERS:**

1 Harry Petersen's company sells sheet music.
2 The package includes website design, building and management, processing sales, dealing with payments and logistics.
3 Harry intends to deliver products electronically as PDF files.
4 Holman will charge a monthly fee.
5 Harry will have no capital investment to make, no new staff to hire, no overheads, and a small monthly fee to pay compared to the money coming in.
6 The next step is to define exactly what Harry wants the site to do.

## RECORDING SCRIPT

 2:41

Part 1

Ingrid: So, Mr Petersen, you want to set up an e-business to sell music – MP3s and so on?

Harry: Oh, please call me Harry, everybody does. No, not MP3s – sheet music. You know, printed music for musicians to play, like song books, orchestral parts, and so on. At the moment we sell through our network of shops in Denmark, but I'm getting more and more enquiries from other countries, and I'd like to set up an e-business to reach customers worldwide.

I: I see. You want to compete in a global market?

H: Exactly. But the problem is, we don't have the skills, the staff, or the money to do it ourselves.

I: Well, Harry, that needn't be a problem. My company, Holman Multimedia, is used to working with small businesses, and we have a complete e-tailing package solution. You don't have to worry about anything at all. We will design, build and manage your website, and process your sales. We deal with the payments, and we can even handle the logistics for you if you want. Although I suppose most of the sheet music will be sent electronically as PDF files, right?

H: That's right – it's much easier for us, and the customer gets immediate delivery.

I: Exactly. So all you have to do is make sure you have the product in stock, and count your profits!

H: And pay you a monthly fee, is that right?

I: That's right, Harry. No capital investment for you, no new staff, and no overheads. And once you start selling music all over the world, that monthly fee is going to look insignificant compared to the money coming in.

H: OK, Ingrid, er, can I call you Ingrid?

I: Yes, of course.

H: All right, I think we're in business. So what's next?

I: That's terrific, Harry! OK, well, would you mind telling me exactly what you want the site to do? You see, it all depends just what you …

**3**  2:42  While listening to this version of Part 2 of the negotiation, ask students to note down the things Harry says which help them identify his failure to negotiate (*There's no way I could pay that; No, I couldn't agree to that; No, I can't commit myself to three years*).

Play the recording and check answers with the whole class. Ask students to comment on why Harry's choice of words were not helpful in the negotiation (words like *No, no way, can't* sound very 'final' and don't offer room for discussion). Point out that Harry's failure to negotiate also means that Ingrid is less open to negotiating her own terms, i.e. she does not offer any alternatives.

### ANSWER:

Harry says no. He rejects all Ingrid's proposals and doesn't try to negotiate.

## RECORDING SCRIPT

 2:42

Part 2, Version 1

H: All right, Ingrid, I think we agree on what we need. Now let's get down to the nitty-gritty – how soon can you deliver, and how much is it going to cost?

I: OK, look. I'm going to write down a figure per month here, just so it's clear, then you can tell me what you think. There, how do you feel about that?

H: Wow, as much as that! There's no way I could pay that.

I: Well, that figure is based on what you say you need, Harry. I might possibly be able to bring it down a little, but only if

we had a three-year contract.

H: A three-year contract! No, I couldn't agree to that.

I: Well, in that case, I can't bring the monthly fee down, I'm afraid.

H: Hm. And what about lead time? Could you have the site up and running by next month?

I: No. I'm afraid development time is around three months.

H: Isn't there any way you could have the site online in two months?

I: Well, I don't think there's much point in talking about lead time unless we can agree on the monthly fee. You're sure you won't consider a three-year contract?

H: No. I can't commit myself to three years.

I: OK, Harry, you have my phone number. If you change your mind, you know where to find me.

**4**  2:43  Ask students to listen and answer the questions. Get them to compare their answers with a partner.

Higher-level classes could comment on the tone of this version, in comparison with Version 1. For example: the discussion is longer because both Harry and Ingrid question, bargain, and make offers; their language is more tentative as they discuss the options, e.g. *Hm, Well, I'd be reluctant to, I don't really want to …*, etc; both of them seem satisfied with the outcome.

### ANSWERS:

1  Harry negotiates and offers a compromise.
2  Ingrid will bring down the monthly fee if Harry signs a three-year contract.
   She will guarantee a maximum down time of 24 hours per month if Harry chooses the platinum service level.
   She will have the site up and running by next month if Harry pays a year's fees in advance.
3  Harry agrees to pay six months in advance and to sign a three-year contract.
   Ingrid agrees to have the site online in two months, bring the monthly fee down 5% and include the platinum service.
4  Ingrid avoids the question of penalties by saying nobody has penalty clauses and producing a bottle of champagne.

## RECORDING SCRIPT

 2:43

Part 2, Version 2

H: All right, Ingrid, I think we agree on what we need. Now let's get down to the nitty-gritty – how soon can you deliver, and how much is it going to cost?

I: OK, look. I'm going to write down a figure per month here, just so it's clear, then you can tell me what you think. There, how do you feel about that?

H: Wow, as much as that! Is there any way we could bring it down a little?

I: Well, that figure is based on what you say you need, Harry. I might possibly be able to bring it down a little, but only if we had a three-year contract.

H: Well, I'd be reluctant to agree to a three-year contract unless you could guarantee a maximum down time of 24 hours per month. Could you do that?

I: Let me reassure you on that point, Harry. Our sites and servers are very, very stable, and average down time is less than 24 hours per year – and so we're happy to guarantee less than 24 hours per month, as long as you choose our platinum service level – but of course, it's more expensive.

H: Well, I don't really want to increase the budget. Hm. What about lead time? Can you have the site up and running by next month?

I: Not unless we hire another developer. I suppose we could do it, providing you paid a year's fees in advance.

H: Hm.

I: Normally, development time is around three months.

H: Look, let's split the difference. I can pay six months in advance on condition that you have the site online in two months. And if you can bring the monthly fee down 5% and include the platinum service, I'll agree to the three-year contract.

I: You're a tough negotiator, Harry. But, OK, I think we can agree to that.

H: It's a deal. Oh, but wait a minute, what about penalties – you know, if you can't deliver for any reason, or if the site is offline for more than 48 hours, for example?

I: Oh, you don't need to worry about that, Harry. It never happens. In fact, nobody in the industry has penalty clauses these days. Now, I just happen to have a bottle of champagne in my bag here – if you can just sign – here, here and here – I'll open the champagne and we can celebrate your new e-business!

**5** Play  2:43. Pause at appropriate places to allow students time to complete the sentences. Check answers with the whole class. Draw attention to the use of conditionals and get them to identify likely and unlikely future events and how modals are used.

**ANSWERS:**

1 I <u>might possibly</u> be able to bring it down a little, but <u>only if we had</u> a three-year contract.
2 I'd <u>be reluctant</u> to agree to a three-year contract, <u>unless you could</u> guarantee a maximum down time of 24 hours per month.
3 ... so <u>we're happy to</u> guarantee less than 24 hours per month, <u>as long as you choose</u> our platinum service level.
4 I suppose <u>we could</u> do it, providing <u>you paid</u> a year's fees in advance.
5 ... let's <u>split</u> the difference.
6 I can pay six months in advance <u>on condition that you have</u> the site online in two months.
7 ... if you <u>can just sign</u> – here, here and here – <u>I'll open</u> the champagne.

**6** Elicit from students or explain the meaning of any unknown terms in the table, e.g.:
*tentative* (something which is not definite or final)
*counteroffer* (an offer which opposes or challenges the first offer)
*compromising* (giving up a particular demand so that an agreement can be reached which satisfies both parties to some extent).
Do this as a whole-class activity. Check answers by getting students to read the sentences aloud.

Students discuss their answers to the question about the conditional tenses with a partner. If necessary, refer students to the notes and exercises in the *Grammar and practice* section (page 127 in the Student's Book, answers on page 118 in this book) to remind them of the use of these tenses.

**ANSWERS:**

| Tentative offers | Counter offers | Firm offers | Compromising |
|---|---|---|---|
| I might consider reducing the price if you increased your order. 1 | It would be difficult for me to increase my order unless you guaranteed the price for two years. 2 4 | I am ready to sign a contract today if you can guarantee the price for two years. 3 6 7 | Would you agree to a compromise? Is that an acceptable compromise? 5 |

The second conditional (*if* + past ... *would*) is used in tentative offers and counteroffers to make a hypothetical, exploratory offer with no commitment.
The first conditional (*if* + present ... *will*) is used in firm offers to express a definite commitment.

## Pronunciation

**7** 2:44–2:46 Encourage students to say the sentences aloud as they decide which words are stressed. Circulate while students practise the sentences with a partner.

Get students to close their books and repeat each sentence after you, putting the stress in the appropriate place. As these are long sentences, read out chunks, e.g. *I might possibly be able / to bring it down a little / but only if / we had a three-year contract.*

**ANSWERS:**

1 I might <u>possibly</u> be able to bring it down a little, but <u>only</u> if we had a three-year contract.
2 I <u>might</u> consider reducing the price, <u>if</u> you increased your order.
3 I'd be <u>reluctant</u> to agree to a three-year contract, <u>unless</u> you could guarantee a maximum down time of 24 hours per month.

## RECORDING SCRIPT

2:44–2:46

1 I might possibly be able to bring it down a little, but only if we had a three-year contract.
2 I might consider reducing the price, if you increased your order.
3 I'd be reluctant to agree to a three-year contract, unless you could guarantee a maximum down time of 24 hours per month.

---

**FURTHER PRACTICE**

Write the sentence stems on the board and some word prompts and get students to make their own sentences using them, e.g.
Sentence stems:
*I might possibly ... but only if we ...*
*I might consider ... if you ...*
*I'd be reluctant to ... unless you could ...*
Word prompts:
*homework, car, lunch, laptop, concert, tennis racket,* etc.

Example: *I'd be reluctant to lend you my laptop unless you could help me with my English homework.*

---

## Negotiating

**8** With lower-level classes, read the instructions with the whole class and elicit from them the kinds of things they might say at each stage of the negotiation. Remind them of the value of trying to reach a *win-win* conclusion.

While students are speaking, circulate and assist where necessary. Check that they are using the conditional tenses correctly and stressing the key words appropriately.

**9** Allow students time to prepare and practise their conversation. When they have finished get students to raise their hands to indicate how many ideal, acceptable and unacceptable options they managed to get. Then get one or more confident pairs to present their conversation to the rest of the class.

Alternatively, with higher-level classes, get one or two pairs to do their negotiating in real time, i.e. without preparing it beforehand. The rest of the class listens and comments on the performance, giving two things that worked successfully and two things that could be improved.

---

### EXTENSION ACTIVITY

Sometimes in negotiations it is necessary to 'read between the lines', i.e. to look for or discover a meaning that is not openly stated. By paying attention to what might be implied, students can pick up on signals from others and use them to further the negotiation. Below are some example statements, with possible answers in brackets.

*It would be difficult for us to meet that demand.*
(*… but we might be able to compromise on other demands.*)
*It is not our normal practice to give discounts.*
(*… but on this occasion / under certain circumstances we might be able to give a discount.*)
*Our price for that quantity is X*
(*… but we might be able to give you a lower price for a bigger quantity.*)
*We never negotiate on price.*
(*… but we could negotiate on other things.*)
*These are our standard contract terms.*
(*… but we might be able to change some of them.*)
*We are not prepared to discuss that at this stage.*
(*… but we could discuss it later.*)

Write the sentences on the board (the underlined text). Students work with a partner or in small groups and write down what they think is really being said (the text in brackets). Take whole-class feedback. Accept all possible answers.

---

## 5.5 Writing
## A proposal

This module explores the structure and content of a business proposal and requires students to write their own proposal.

### Internet research

Searching under *how to write direct mail* will produce several websites which list tips and techniques for writing effective direct mail. Some of the tips include the following: get to the point; be clear and concise; sell benefits not features; use a conversational style; keep the language simple; include a guarantee; include testimonials.

Students may find that some websites appear to give contradictory advice, e.g. 'keep to one page' in one place, but 'write a long letter' in another.

Get students to compile a list of useful tips. This could be a short list of five to eight key or fundamental points. If students have more time, they could compile a more complete list. If they find contradictory advice, get them to review this and reach their own conclusion.

This research could be done before students do this module or at the end, as part of the extension activity.

### Discussion

**1** Get students to explain the similarities and differences between *mailshots* and *spam* (both are advertising material; both are unsolicited; mailshots are sent by post, spam is sent electronically). Ask if students know another common term for this kind of advertising (*junk mail*).

Students discuss the question in small groups for a few minutes. Take whole-class feedback. Get students to give reasons for their answers.

---

### EXTENSION ACTIVITY

To personalize the activity, ask students these questions:
*Do you receive mailshots or spam? How do you feel about them?*
*Have you ever bought anything as a result of a mailshot or spam email?*

---

### Scan reading

**2** Read each question aloud and get students to scan the letter for the answer. When they have found the answer, they should raise their hands. When most of the class has raised their hands, ask one student to give you the answer, and then ask two or three other students if they agree or would like to add anything. Repeat this procedure with the rest of the questions.

#### ANSWERS:
1  The proposal is for a merchant account for an e-business.
2  Prestige and respect for Mr Bellows' e-business; transparent control of sales, cash-flow and administration fees; independent power of decision on refunds; low charges.
3  $12 per month, minimum transaction fees of $10.
4  Because PZpay has more than 1,800 satisfied members in 26 countries.

## Analysis

**3** Read the section headings and descriptions with the whole class. Ask students to tell you which are likely to be the first and last sections (*Introduction*, *Conclusion*). Without looking at the article, get them to try to put the remaining sections in the correct order.

Then give students a few minutes to read the article and check their answers.

**ANSWERS:**

3 Solution
4 Benefits
1 Introduction
8 Conclusion
6 Qualifications & references
5 Process & schedule
2 Needs / background
7 Costs

## Writing

**4** Get students to read the sentences quickly and identify the tenses used to express the options and contingencies (conditionals). If necessary, they could review module 5.3 or the relevant *Grammar and practice* section (page 126–127 in the Student's Book, answers on page 118 in this book).

Point out the use of *should* in sentence 3. This could also be *If you should …* and is used to suggest that something is unlikely or not particularly probable.

Students can refer to the proposal on page 66 to help them with words and expressions that they could use to complete the sentences.

Get two or three different groups to read each completed sentence aloud.

**SUGGESTED ANSWERS:**

1 If you would like to see similar projects we have managed, we would be pleased to put you in touch with some of our customers.
2 In the unlikely event that you were less than 100% satisfied with the result, we would offer a full refund.
3 Should you require on-site support, our engineers are available seven days a week.
4 If you would like to see some examples of our work, I would be delighted to organize a demonstration on your premises.
5 In the unlikely event of a breakdown, we would provide a replacement while your server was repaired.
6 Should you require greater capacity, our engineers can perform an upgrade on-site.
7 If you wish to place an order, we require a deposit of 25%.

**5** Read the notes with the whole class. To help students get started, brainstorm some ideas about what they might do to improve the website.

Ask students to work with a partner to write the proposal. Circulate while they are writing and assist where necessary. Get them to write a first draft, making use of the headings listed in exercise 3. They then exchange their texts with another pair for feedback.

When they are reading each other's texts, students should check that the proposal is well structured, and should also look for the appropriate use of language.

Then ask students to revise their texts. Display the finished texts on a table or on the wall so that students can read them all. If you wish, get them to choose the best proposal, i.e. the one they think would be accepted by Poster Passion.

**MODEL ANSWER:**

Dear Ms Nash-Williams,

Thank you for taking the time to talk to me by telephone today. As agreed, please find below a proposal for a 'MaxiMedia' website, which I believe will increase your traffic and sales dramatically.

Your current website is out of date and unable to compete with your competitors' sites. You are looking for an exciting, interactive site which will attract teenagers and improve sales of your posters.

We recommend our 'MaxiMedia Experience' range of interactive sites, which incorporate music and video presentations. If you subsequently required online games, you would be able to upgrade to the 'MaxiMedia Gamer' range with no additional set-up fee.

A 'MaxiMedia' site will increase traffic to your e-business, since teenage customers will enjoy exciting music and video on your website. In addition, they will be able to download thumbnails of your posters and free ringtones. In the unlikely event of a technical difficulty, MaxiMedia guarantee to solve the problem within two hours. Our charges are amongst the lowest on the market, meaning that your business will be more profitable from day one.

We provide a complete, ready-to-use website installed on your server. Please allow 30 days for development and installation. Should you encounter any difficulties, our helpline is available 24 hours a day, seven days a week to assist you.

With more than 400 satisfied customers and several design awards, MaxiMedia is one of the top site designers in over the country. I will be happy to put you in contact with other MaxiMedia customers in your area.

The design fee for a 'MaxiMedia Experience' site is just €3,000, with monthly technical support fees of only €15. You will find full details of our terms and conditions in the attached quotation.

We look forward to meeting you to discuss design options: I will call you next week to fix a date. Should you have further questions, please feel free to call me on 0800 113 647.

Sincerely yours,

### EXTENSION ACTIVITY

If possible, bring to class a selection of English-language mailshots. Get students to analyse the structure, language, style, etc. and to say how effective they think the mailshots are. This activity could be done in conjunction with the Internet research – students use the list of techniques they compiled on how to write effective direct mail as a checklist to evaluate the authentic examples.

## 5.6 Case study
## St John's Beach Club

Students negotiate a deal between a company and a buyer to get the best price for a company incentive trip.

### Internet research

Students will find a wide range of employee incentive programmes, with examples including birthday gifts, day trips, parties, tickets for sporting events, theatre and concerts, days out, weekend trips, etc.

This research could be done before class, so that the information feeds into the Discussion activity.

### Discussion

**1** Do this as a whole-class activity, getting students to brainstorm ideas. Write a list of advantages and disadvantages on the board.

---

**EXTENSION ACTIVITY**

To personalize the activity, ask students to tell you about any incentives they themselves or anyone they know have received.

---

### Reading

**2** Give students a few minutes to read the memo and look at the brochure. Then, get them to close their books. Ask the four questions. Students open their books and check their answers.

To develop the theme of incentives, get students to brainstorm some examples of what kinds of team-building events and competitions might be offered in a resort of this kind.

**ANSWERS:**

1   The top ten performing sales reps and their partners.
2   No. ('As usual ...')
3   The memo was sent in the third quarter to encourage sales reps to make an extra effort in Q4.
4   Suggested answer: corporate clients, young, active professional people with available income and a taste for luxury.

### Listening for detail

**3** 2:47 Read the statements aloud before you play the recording. Pause at appropriate places to allow students time to note down the reasons for their answers.

**ANSWERS:**

1   F. 'Shall we use my office?' 'No, here is fine.'
2   F. Loretta doesn't have the time.
3   T. Loretta has asked him (i.e. told him) to allocate the budget.
4   T. $26,500 + 5% is almost $28,000.
5   F. He is going to get one of their best negotiators to negotiate with a couple of travel agents.
6   T. Ten reps + partners + Malcolm and his wife, + maybe two more reps + partners.
7   F. A week, plus perhaps a couple more nights.

---

**RECORDING SCRIPT**

 2:47

Loretta: Oh, Malcolm, there you are. I just wanted a quick word.
Malcolm: Sure. Shall we use my office?

---

L:  No, here is fine. I think I'll have a coffee too.
M:  Black, no sugar?
L:  Yes. Thanks, Malcolm. I saw your memo about the incentive trip – it sounds great. I wish I was going!
M:  Well, why don't you? It would be an excellent opportunity to get to know the sales team better.
L:  Yes, it would, wouldn't it? But I just don't have the time, I'm afraid. Anyway, the reason I wanted to catch you was to confirm the budget.
M:  Ah, yes.
L:  Mm. I spoke to Charles. I've asked him to allocate a global budget of $28,000. That's for everything except travel, which is a separate budget. That's up about 5% on last year. How does that sound?
M:  That sounds great. Thanks, Loretta. I'm going to get one of our best negotiators to talk to a couple of travel agents, see what sort of deal we can get. The hotels usually work with several agents, and some of them are prepared to negotiate better terms than others.
L:  Uh-huh. Try to persuade them to throw in some extra benefits too. After all, if we use the full budget, we're giving them a lot of business. Sometimes you can get a free upgrade to an executive suite, that kind of thing. How many people are you taking?
M:  Well, the top ten sales people, plus myself, and partners – that makes 22. But if we can negotiate a really good package, I'd like to take one or two more sales reps along. They've all worked fantastically hard this year.
L:  Yes, I agree. It would encourage the reps who almost made it into the top ten. I always think it's hard on number 11! It'll be about a week, like last year, I suppose?
M:  Well, again, if we can squeeze a couple more nights out of the budget, that would be great. But we'll see.
L:  OK, Malcolm. Let me know what you decide.
M:  Sure. Thanks, Loretta.

**4** Students could make a guess at how the sentences end, on the basis of the first listening. They may be able to suggest one or two words for each one. Write them on the board as prompts. Play 2:47 again. Check answers with the whole class.

**SUGGESTED ANSWERS:**

1   Loretta would get to know the sales team better if she went on the trip.
2   If they only talked to one travel agent, they might not get such a good deal.
3   Loretta thinks the agents may give a free upgrade if they use the full budget.
4   If they can negotiate a really good package, Malcolm would like to take one or two more sales reps along.
5   They'll stay longer than a week if they can squeeze more nights out of the budget.

### Negotiating

**5** Give students a few minutes to read the instructions. Circulate and assist where necessary. Get students to review the work they have done in this module and in the rest of the unit which will help them with this task, e.g. conditionals and recommendations (5.3), making offers, counteroffers, firm offers, and compromising (5.4).

While students are speaking, circulate and monitor their use of language, pronunciation and stress, and how the negotiation is developing. Make notes to use for feedback at the end.

When students have finished the task, get them to evaluate their performance in terms of language use and negotiating skills, e.g. by answering the following questions:
*Which part(s) of the negotiation are you happy with?*
*Which part(s) could you have done better?*

This unit deals with the topic of what is commonly referred to as Corporate Social Responsibility (CSR). This is an expression used to describe two related features of business practice.

1 A company's obligation to be sensitive to the needs of all of its stakeholders (so not just shareholders, but also employees, customers, suppliers, community organizations, subsidiaries, local neighborhoods, etc.).

2 The principle of 'sustainable development', which says that businesses should make decisions based not only on financial / economic factors, but also on the social and environmental consequences of their activities.

So CSR covers:
- business and the environment (reporting and regulation of waste, sustainable production, recycling)
- people in the workplace (equal opportunities, encouraging employee involvement, promoting diversity, health and safety, labour standards, family-friendly policies)
- community affairs (developing programmes for effective engagement with local communities)
- reputation management (using good practice as part of the marketing message of the company, as well as PR when things go wrong).

There is a lot of activity in the field of CSR.
- At the European level there is the European Alliance for CSR, launched by the EU in 2006 (link given below).
- At the national level there is a UK government body for CSR (link below).
- There is a private sector initiative in the UK called 'Business in the Community' (link below).
- At the individual company level, there are many big names proudly stating their activities in this field on their websites.
- There are many university courses devoted to the subject.

It is clear that CSR has become an established and important area in the business world. Indeed, good practice in CSR is now a key part of many companies' marketing strategy. Businesses stress their green and community credentials in their advertisements, and most annual reports these days would be incomplete without the CEO making reference to their company's beneficial effects on society and the environment.

But not everyone is happy with the idea that business has a role to play in CSR. Some people would argue that this is the proper responsibility of government, not business. Where are the limits? Consider these areas:
- human rights
- fair trade
- sustainable consumption.

These areas are on the borderline between social policy (the responsibility of government) and business policy.

In general, companies are usually happy to comply with social and environmental legislation. But they want to see a 'level playing field' with other companies also having to comply. Acting alone, a business has few guidelines on how to proceed (it is not their job to set social policy) and by raising standards they run the risk of increasing costs (and thereby losing profitability, causing layoffs, etc.).

A few companies are happy to take the lead and be pioneers in this field. The Body Shop is perhaps the best-known example, but BP is at the forefront of developing green energy and Marks & Spencer is famous for its diversity, employee involvement and CSR policies generally.

The EU organization referred to above has a website with a useful glossary:
http://www.csreurope.org/
The UK government body is:
http://www.csr.gov.uk/
And the UK private sector initiative is:
http://www.bitc.org.uk/index.html

## 6.1 About business

## Corporate social responsibility

This module focuses on the issues around corporate social responsibility and examines the approach taken by one multinational in particular.

### Internet research

Students could conduct these Internet searches before they start this module. For example, searching for *CSR* will provide them with information which will feed into Discussion (exercise 1) and Reading and discussion (exercises 3–4); searching for *Starbucks bean stock* and *Starbucks standards business conduct* will provide them with extra information for Part 1 of Listening for gist (exercise 5).

Before the class, assign groups of students to conduct one of the searches. Each group can then report their findings to the class at the appropriate point in the exercises.

---

**LEAD-IN ACTIVITY**

Ask students some questions about their everyday lives, e.g.:
*What did you have for breakfast and where did it come from?* (e.g. coffee – Brazil, orange juice – Florida)
*What are you wearing and where it was made?* (e.g. shirt – China)
*How did you get to work?* (e.g. by Japanese car), etc.

Get students to comment on the fact that many of these things come from other countries. Ask these questions:
*Why are these things produced in other countries?*
*What impact does this have on their own local / national economy?*
*What impact does it have on the countries in which they were produced?*
*How does it affect the environment?*

---

### Discussion

**1** Do this as a whole-class activity, writing students' ideas on the board. If necessary, explain *conflicts of interest* (when two or more things are in opposition to each other).

**SUGGESTED ANSWERS:**

Employees, customers, shareholders, the community
Shareholders generally want profitability, which is usually in conflict with employees' and sometimes customers and the community's interests.
Employees and the community want jobs, which may conflict with the customer's wish for low prices.
The community would like companies to be socially responsible and ecologically neutral, which may conflict with growth, job creation and mass production to achieve low prices and profitability.

---

**EXTENSION ACTIVITY**

To personalize the activity, ask students to tell you:
a) about the different groups their own company has a responsibility towards.
b) any personal experience they have of conflicts of interest (either in their working life or in their life outside work).

---

### Scan reading

**2** Get students to read the text quickly to find the answers. Give them just one minute to do this as there will be more detailed analysis of the text in later exercises.

Then give students a few more minutes to read the text again more carefully. Remind them to check any new words in the *Wordlist* on pages 155–156 in the Student's Book or in their dictionaries. Circulate and assist where necessary.

**ANSWERS:**

customers and end-users (doctors, nurses and patients)
employees
the community
stockholders

### Reading and discussion

**3** If students need help getting started, brainstorm with the whole class possible decision-makers, e.g. national government, local government, EU, courts, stockholders. Students work in small groups. Take whole-class feedback.

Focus on the meaning of *fair* (treating each person equally and according to the rules or the law), and on *reasonable* and *just*, which have similar meanings. These adjectives describe a wide range of the activities revolving around corporate social responsibility.

**ANSWERS:**

This is a matter of personal opinion and political sympathies. The following points may arise in discussion:
1  Today, prices for health care products are regulated by government in many countries.
2  Companies whose profits are perceived as being excessive attract criticism, principally from the media.
3  Many western governments have implemented minimum wage legislation, and labour tribunals decide disputes over compensation.
4  Perhaps a distinction should be made between justice, as defined by the judiciary, and ethics, as defined by philosophers and the community.
5  Using tax specialists to find the most favourable way to apply tax laws defined by government is generally considered 'fair'; exploiting tax loopholes might be judged 'unfair' by the media and the community.
6  This seems to be decided by stockholders themselves, and can cause the problems discussed by Marc Gunther below.

**4** Students work in small groups. You could assign questions 1–3 to half of the class and questions 4–6 to the other half.

Questions 1–3: Students should list examples of the three aspects of corporate social responsibility. Take whole-class feedback and write students' ideas on the board.

Questions 4–6: If necessary, explain *PR* (Public Relations – the company department which works to present a good image of the organization to the public). Students should be prepared to give reasons for their answers.

Take whole-class feedback. If you divided the questions between the class, students who did not prepare answers to the questions, should listen carefully and add any further ideas of their own.

**SUGGESTED ANSWERS:**

The core dilemma in points 1–3 is where to draw the line.
1  Disaster relief, the Red Cross, Aids research, soup kitchens, holidays for underprivileged children, churches, museums, orchestras, sports clubs
2  Hospitals, orphanages, shelters for the homeless, parks and gardens, zoos, tennis courts, art galleries
3  Eliminate pollution from manufacturing, use only recyclable materials, use clean vehicles and machinery, encourage employees to use public transport
4–6 are completely subjective and all views are valid.

## Listening for gist

**5**  2:48–2:50 Play the whole interview from beginning to end so that students get an overview of the content.

Part 1: Point out that students will need more than one word to complete each blank. Play Part 1 as many times as necessary to allow students to write their answers. Then get them to compare answers with a partner. Check with the whole class. Get students to read individual sentences aloud. If other students disagree, they should raise their hands and give their own answers. Play the recording once more to allow students to check their answers.

Part 2: With lower-level classes, play Marc Gunther's first speech, then pause to allow students to complete questions 1 and 2. Tell them that they will not hear two of these three words in the interview – they must work out if these topics have been mentioned from what Marc Gunther says.

If necessary, explain that *bottom line* refers to profit. This expression also occurs later in the unit. Then play the rest of Part 2 so that students can answer questions 3–5.

With higher-level classes, play Part 2 without pausing.

Part 3: Read the statements aloud or get students to read them aloud. Then play the recording. Check answers with the whole class. Get students to correct the false statements.

### ANSWERS:

**Part 1:**
1. look after the environment
2. avoid exploiting developing countries
3. environmental groups
4. company owners
5. everyone who works there
6. global warming
7. planting trees to offset their emissions
8. gasoline powered cars
9. hybrid vehicles

**Part 2:**
1. profitability (bottom-line considerations), recruitment
2. They want their jobs to have meaning. They want to make the world a better place.
3. employee first, customer second, shareholder third
4. Happy employees will attract customers, the business will work and shareholders will benefit
5. If a customer argues with an employee, the assumption is that the employee is right and the customer is wrong.

**Part 3:**
1. T
2. F – they wanted to, but they were under pressure not to
3. F

### RECORDING SCRIPT

 2:48 – 2:50

**Part 1**

I: Despite all the scandals of recent years, Mark Gunther thinks that corporate behavior is improving. He's a senior writer at *Fortune* magazine and author of a book contending that companies are becoming more socially responsible. Gunther is tracking companies that treat employees well, look after the environment and avoid exploiting developing countries.

MG: If you just think back 15 or 20 years ago, the workforces were much less diverse than they are now; now you see businesses working very closely with environmental groups in a whole lot of areas. Employees have become company owners in a way they never had been before. You have a company like Starbucks that gave away what it calls 'bean stocks' to everyone who works there, including part-timers, and that aligns the interests of the company with its employees.

I: I wonder if part of the question here is which company you focus on, because you just said businesses are getting along better with environmentalists, there are certainly examples of that; there is also an administration in office that has battled with environmentalists over business questions, and there are businesses that are doing things that dismay environmentalists across the country right now.

MG: Right and of course it is hard to generalize, but even on the environment, I mean the Bush administration has not even acknowledged really global warming as a serious man-made problem. If you look at the US utility industry, you have utilities that are out there planting trees to offset their emissions, you have companies like UPS and FedEx which have huge transportation costs looking for ways to drive hybrid vehicles and get off the gasoline powered cars; I'd argue that the big companies in America are much more green than the Bush administration at the moment.

**Part 2**

I: What is motivating companies to do that?

MG: Purely bottom-line considerations, this is not about altruism. It's about, predominantly I think, attracting and engaging the best employees, no one really wants to go to work every day to enhance shareholder value, we really want to go to work and be in a place where we feel aligned with the company's goals, where we feel there's some meaning to what we do, and where we feel we can make the world a little bit of a better place every day.

I: Somewhere you've written that, er, Southwest Airlines will favour its employees in some cases over its customers?

MG: Southwest is very explicit about the hierarchy. They put the employee first, the customer second, and then the shareholder third, and the theory is if you have happy, engaged, motivated employees, they're gonna attract customers and therefore your business is going to work, and shareholders are going to benefit, and by the way, if you go to a Southwest gate, get into an argument with someone there, the presumption when word gets back to Southwest headquarters in Dallas is that you were wrong, the customer was wrong and the employee was right because they hire people very carefully and train them and they trust their people 100%.

**Part 3**

I: Well, let's talk about a long-term trend that's been tracked by some business writers who will say that in the nineteen-fifties and sixties American corporations believed that they should take care of their employees, believed that they should take care of their customers as well as their shareholders, but that from the seventies, eighties onward, they've been pressured to just take care of the stock price, just take care of the share-holder, and in fact they get sued when they don't do that, or they get taken over when they don't do that.

MG: My argument is we are now correcting back from that. That we are not as short-term driven, that we are starting to think more long-term about building sustainable businesses and this short-term model not only doesn't work for businesses in the long run, it doesn't work for our society in the long run.

### EXTENSION ACTIVITY

Get students to investigate the activities of their own company or local companies in the areas of good works and charities, civic improvement, and protection of the environment and natural resources from company websites or printed materials. Alternatively, collect some relevant brochures and reports from local companies, and distribute them in class. Students should extract relevant information from them, then make a short presentation to the class describing the activities of the company in these areas.

## 6.2 Vocabulary

## Meetings, ethical behaviour and social performance

This module presents and practises vocabulary in three areas and develops the themes of corporate social responsibility.

### Internet research

A search for *Rhonda Abrams* will reveal that she offers advice and mentoring for entrepreneurs and small businesses. She is an advocate for the small business and her website offers help in many areas of setting up a business.

Students could do this research before they listen to the presentation in exercise 5 or afterwards as a follow-up activity to this module.

## Meetings

**1** Ask students to do this exercise with a partner. To check answers, get students to read the complete sentences aloud. Monitor stress and pronunciation.

**ANSWERS:**

| | | | | | |
|---|---|---|---|---|---|
| 1 c) | 2 a) | 3 e) | 4 b) | 5 f) | 6 d) |
| 7 j) | 8 l) | 9 k) | 10 g) | 11 i) | 12 h) |

**2** Again, ask students to work on this with a partner. Check answers with the whole class. Then get students to tell you what might be happening at a meeting which would give rise to the rest of the phrases, e.g.:

Phrase 3: at the end of a discussion which does not reach an agreement / decision.
Phrase 5: in the middle of a meeting; perhaps when participants are starting to look tired.
Phrases 6 and 10: if a participant starts to talk at length about something unimportant.
Phrase 9: at the end of a discussion when everyone agrees.
Phrase 11: when there is some additional information to feed into the meeting.

**ANSWERS:**

at the beginning of a meeting: 1, 2, 7, 8
at the end of a meeting: 4, 12

## Adjectives

**3** Students do this exercise individually or with a partner. Allow them to use dictionaries, if you wish. To check answers, read the text aloud and pause at each word in **bold**. Call on students to give you the correct definition for the word before continuing.

To focus on meaning, get students to divide the adjectives into two groups:
1 positive qualities (*reliable, trustworthy, accurate, prompt, altruistic*)
2 negative qualities (*deceptive, confusing, misleading, dishonest, false*).

**ANSWERS:**

1 prompt
2 dishonest
3 misleading
4 deceptive
5 trustworthy
6 reliable
7 confusing
8 false
9 altruistic
10 accurate

## Collocations

**4** Students could complete these exercises individually or with a partner. Circulate while they are working and assist where necessary. Check answers with the whole class by getting students to read the whole extract aloud.

When students have finished, get them to pick out any words or phrases which are new to them or that they are unsure of, and review their meaning and use.

**ANSWERS:**

1 supporting a charity
2 think long-term
3 identify with an issue
4 contribute funds
5 obey the law
6 uphold standards
7 respecting human dignity
8 recognizing merit
9 limit the impact
10 acknowledge the problem
11 negotiate a settlement
12 compensate the victims

### FURTHER PRACTICE

Some of these collocations are used in the Johnson & Johnson credo on page 70, in either the same or similar ways. Get students to scan the credo for these collocations so that they can see them in another context.

## Listening for detail

**5**  2:51 Get students to read the expressions aloud and check for correct pronunciation. If necessary, explain:
*integrity* (the quality of being honest, having strong principles)
*lawsuits* (the process of bringing a dispute or claim before a court of law so that it can be settled)
*fines* (money paid as a punishment for breaking the law).
Play the recording. Get students to tell you how many phrases they did *not* hear. If they disagree on this, play the recording again. Check answers with the whole class. Get students to make sentences with the expressions that were not used.

**ANSWERS:**

Phrases not heard are:
obeying the law
responsibility to your customer
misleading, confusing, or even false advertising or sales techniques

### RECORDING SCRIPT

2:51

Rhonda Abrams: Thank you. Thank you very much. Every entrepreneur hopes to do well. We'd all like to make a lot of money and have a big, profitable customer base. But over the years, I've realized that most entrepreneurs want to do more. They'd not only like to do well; they'd like to do good. They'd like their business to contribute to their community, respect the environment, play a positive role in the lives of their employees and customers.
I'm not naïve or simplistic. I strongly believe that building an honest, responsible business, with a healthy bottom line, in and of itself makes a valuable contribution to our economy and society. Such businesses buy supplies and materials, often employ others, and obviously meet a need of their customers. Over the years, however, I learned that companies with a sense of integrity and purpose actually have a competitive edge over companies that are solely focused on the bottom line. I want to tell you about four ways they achieve this. First of all, being

socially responsible helps you attract and retain employees. Having a strong corporate culture committed to good corporate citizenship enables employees to feel that they are part of something important. Company programmes allowing employees to use job time to be involved in community causes are viewed as a valuable benefit. Prospective employees look at a company's values and social commitment when comparing job offers.

Secondly, being socially responsible helps you attract and retain customers. People like to do business with companies they respect. Some customers will be attracted by specific company policies, such as looking to buy products that aren't tested on animals or are recycled. But all customers are attracted to companies that consistently deal with them honestly and fairly.

Thirdly, being socially responsible helps you reduce employee misbehaviour. Businesses that act with integrity and honesty toward their employees, customers, and suppliers are more likely to have their employees also act with integrity and honesty towards the company and their fellow workers. An atmosphere of honesty helps keep everyone honest.

And, finally, being socially responsible helps keep you out of trouble. Being a good corporate citizen – whether in your advertising, employee treatment, or environmental policies – makes it less likely that your company will get in trouble with regulatory agencies, taxing authorities, or face lawsuits or fines. When your company does good – treats employees, customers, and suppliers fairly, as well as participating in community and social activities – you'll find you also do well. Good companies can become great companies.

## Discussion

**6** Students work in groups. You could get students to discuss all of the company departments or assign one or two to each group. Students who work in any of these departments could share what happens in their own companies.

If students need help in getting started, refer them back to the credo on page 70 and to the listening task in exercise 5 to spark off ideas.

Circulate while students are discussing and assist where necessary. Take whole-class feedback.

**SUGGESTED ANSWERS:**

**R&D:** using recyclable, non-toxic, sustainable materials, designing eco-friendly products
**Production and quality:** respecting health and safety legislation and best practice, avoiding waste and pollution
**Marketing & sales:** respecting advertising standards, not taking advantage of customers, giving fair deals, being honest
**HR:** avoiding discrimination of any kind, protecting the local community from redundancy, encouraging education and training
**Purchasing:** not applying unfair pressure on suppliers, paying a fair market price, encouraging local suppliers
**Finance:** paying taxes, ploughing back profits into the business, supporting community projects, honesty

### FURTHER PRACTICE

Prepare a quiz which tests the vocabulary practised in this module. You could divide students into two teams and award points for correct answers or simply do this as a quick-fire practice session to review the vocabulary at the end of this lesson or the beginning of the next one. Some example questions are given below. Answers are in brackets.

*This word means the same as:*
*on time* (prompt)
*correct* (accurate)
*not easy to understand* (complicated)
*not true* (false).

*Form the opposite of these words:*
*honest* (dishonest)
*reliable* (unreliable)
*short-term* (long-term).

*Complete these collocations:*
*obey* … (the law)
*recognize* … (merit)
*compensate* … (the victims)
*negotiate* … (a settlement).

*Make a sentence using these words or phrases:*
*side-tracked*
*misleading*
*unanimous decision*
*handout*
*competitive edge.*

## 6.3 Grammar
### The passive and reported speech

This module focuses on the meaning and use of the passive and reported speech within contexts related to corporate social responsibility.

### Internet research

Students might search a number of newspapers and news magazines online, e.g. *Financial Times, International Herald Tribune, Wall St Journal, South China Morning Post, Japan Times, Time,* or *Newsweek* to find interesting comments and quotes from people and companies in the news. To focus on the topic of this unit, get students to search for stories related to corporate social responsibility. Students could also look out for the vocabulary and grammatical structures they have practised here in the articles they read.

This research could be done at the end of this module as a follow-up activity.

### Test yourself: The passive

**1** Start by reading the first part of the *Refresh your memory* box with the class. Students work alone to complete exercise 1 and then compare their answers with a partner. Check answers with the whole class by getting individual students to read the sentences aloud. If students seem unsure of the passive or would like further practice, work through some or all of exercises 1–6 in the *Grammar and practice* section (page 128 in the Student's Book, answers on page 118 in this book).

**ANSWERS:**
1 Illegal levels of nitrates are sometimes released into the river.
2 Too many mistakes are being made at the moment.
3 Unfortunately a poor decision was made in hiring unqualified staff.
4 Children were being employed to make T-shirts in Asia.
5 We have been accused of industrial espionage.
6 The company had been warned about the risks.
7 Conflict with the unions can be avoided by making small concessions.
8 You might be asked some delicate questions.
9 It was agreed that production staff should work a four-day week.
10 It has been decided that 300 employees are going to be made redundant.

### Test yourself: Reported speech

**2** and **3** Follow the same procedure as for exercise 1. Get students to define the reporting verbs, if they can, from the contexts of the original sentences. Alternatively, explain the meanings, e.g.:
*announce* (make something known publicly)
*admit* (recognize or agree that something is true)
*reassure* (remove someone's fears or doubts about something)
*enquire* (ask)
*reply* (answer)
*warn* (inform someone in advance about something)
*emphasize* (stress something in order to make the meaning clearer)
*argue* (express an opposite opinion).
Point out that these verbs convey more nuances of meaning than simply using *say, ask* or *tell*.

**ANSWERS:**

Exercise 2
1 CEO Ben Straw announced that nitrate levels in the local water supply were slightly higher than normal.
2 Mr Straw admitted it was possible that the factory was responsible.
3 Plant manager Jane Lee explained there was / had been a small chemical leak last Friday.
4 Mrs Lee reassured the meeting that they had taken measures to ensure that this situation could not / cannot reoccur.
5 Mr Straw said they were negotiating a settlement with the town council.
6 He promised the meeting that they would announce full details in a press statement in a few days' time.
7 Mrs Green, a local resident, asked if there had ever been a problem like this before.
8 Mrs Lee replied that she could not remember any other leaks in 30 years at the factory.
9 Pat Holz, a union representative, enquired when they planned to re-open the factory.
10 Mr Straw warned that some staff might be laid off for a few days.

Exercise 3
2 The CEO argued that developing countries were extremely grateful for the investment and the jobs that they brought.
3 The CEO explained that they made fair profits and paid shareholders good dividends, but they had never exploited their employees.
4 The CEO accepted that they could and would do more to develop sources of alternative energy.
5 The CEO commented that he did not feel that higher petrol prices would reduce traffic and pollution.

**4** Read each of the four extracts aloud or get students to read them silently. Then, one by one, read the statements 1–10 aloud. After each one, ask students to say who made the statement and to say what the phrase is that helped them work out the answer.

**ANSWERS:**
1 CEO Klaas Roos – labour costs in Europe could not be justified
2 Employees at Plazachem's Tashkent plant – they claimed that several fatal accidents had occurred
3 Ms Gronko – discussions were being held with local representatives
   Mr Sanchez – no decision had yet been reached
4 Mr Sanchez – negotiations may be protracted
5 Ms Gronko – she was unable to give a figure
6 Mr Sanchez – the complexity of the legal situation
7 Mr Sanchez – no decision had yet been reached
8 Ms Gronko – all villagers forced to leave their homes by the new road would be compensated
9 CEO Klaas Roos – announced an end to manufacturing in Europe
10 Plazachem management – journalists are reported to have been refused entry
11 CEO Klaas Roos – Asian textile imports could no longer be matched for price
12 Plazachem's receptionist – Plazachem management declined to comment

## Listening and reporting

**5**  **2:52–2:57** Play all six extracts so that students get an overview of the conversation. Ask the following questions to check comprehension:

*Why are 100 people being made redundant?* (new automated machinery means that operators are no longer needed)

*What three things the company doing to help the redundant workers?* (setting up an outplacement service; making redundancy payments; helping people who want to start up their own businesses).

Play the recording again. Pause after each extract to allow students time to note down their answers.

With lower-level classes, brainstorm with the whole class which reporting verb(s) they could use. Point out that there may be more than one possible answer. Check answers with the whole class.

**SUGGESTED ANSWERS:**

2 Mr Bullard explained that new technologies had revolutionized the industry. He emphasized that the company would no longer need so many operators.

3 I agreed that it was difficult to remain competitive, but I enquired what Mr Bullard was intending to do to help people.

4 Mr Bullard told me that the company was setting up an outplacement service, and said that he was sure most people would find work very quickly.

5 I asked how those people who didn't find jobs would survive. I commented that they didn't have a lot of savings, and asked whether the company was offering financial help.

6 Mr Bullard reassured me that each person had received a generous redundancy payment, and he added that the company was making interest-free loans and advice available for people wanting to start their own businesses.

**RECORDING SCRIPT**

🔊 2:52–2:57

1

Leila Belabed: Mr Bullard, the mayor is very upset. You've just dismissed 100 people from the factory! Have you forgotten that when your company arrived, you promised to create jobs for our town?

2

Geoffrey Bullard: Well, of course I understand that you are upset, Ms Belabed. Unfortunately, new technologies have revolutionized our industry. You must understand that with new automated machinery, we will no longer need so many operators.

3

LB: I know that it is difficult to remain competitive, but what about these people and their families? It's a disaster for them. What are you intending to do to help them, Mr Bullard?

4

GB: Please call me Geoffrey. Of course we share your concerns. We are setting up an outplacement service to help people find new jobs, and I'm confident that most of them will find work very quickly.

5

LB: But what about those who don't, Mr Bullard? How will they survive? These people don't have a lot of savings, you know! Are you offering them financial help?

6

GB: Yes, of course, Ms Belabed, you don't need to worry about that. Each person has already received a generous redundancy payment. And we're also making interest-free loans and advice available for those who want to start their own businesses.

**6** Students work with a partner to rewrite these announcements in informal language. Read the sentences aloud with the whole class. Before they start, elicit or explain some of the features of informal language they might use here, e.g. active voice, imperatives, contractions, etc. Check answers by getting students to read their revised announcements aloud.

**SUGGESTED ANSWERS:**

2 Could you please use the stairs while the lift is being repaired?

3 We are sorry, but we can't give you your money back unless you have the receipt.

4 We can only give you your deposit back when you've brought all the equipment back to reception.

5 They're holding all the meetings in the training centre until they've finished redecorating the conference room.

6 I'm afraid we can't reimburse your expenses unless your manager has approved them.

## Roleplay

**7** To help students get started, brainstorm some products or services with the whole class, e.g. an item of clothing, a computer, a night at a luxury hotel. If possible, bring some pictures to class to stimulate ideas. Ask in what ways they might be dissatisfied with the products and services they have listed (e.g. the item of clothing has shrunk in the wash).

While students are working, circulate and monitor. Make a list of any common mistakes in the target language for remedial teaching later.

## 6.4 Speaking
## Meetings – teamwork

This module explores appropriate language and behaviour at meetings and provides contexts for students to discuss issues of ethical behaviour.

### Internet research

A search using "*golden rules of meetings*" will find a number of websites which explore how to run effective meetings. Typically these will include the following advice:
- Be clear about the purpose of the meeting.
- Invite the right people.
- Start and finish on time.
- Be prepared.
- Don't get sidetracked.
- Don't hold unnecessary meetings.
- Finish meetings with a clear statement of the next steps and who will take them.

Students could do this research before they do the work on meetings in this module. They could then aim to implement some of these rules in exercises 8 and 9, e.g. the third and fifth rules.

Alternatively, they could do this research as a follow-up to the work done in this module.

### Discussion

**1** Students discuss this question in groups. Take feedback from the whole class, getting students to give reasons for their answers.

Useful words and expressions that may arise from this discussion are:
*bribe / bribery* (money, services, etc. offered to someone in return for (often) dishonest help)
*backhander* (an informal word for a bribe)
*corruption* (dishonest behaviour).

In-work students may be able to share information about their company's corporate gift policy, which sets out what kinds of gifts are acceptable. Pre-work students could comment on what kinds of gifts might be acceptable or unacceptable. If necessary, provide some prompts, e.g.: a corporate pen; dinner at a top-class restaurant; a gold watch; cash; tickets to a sporting event, concert or play; a weekend at a beach resort.

#### ANSWERS:
It will often depend on the relationship with the customer, but in most cases everything except cash and employing a relative would be acceptable.

### Listening

**2** 2:58 Before students listen to the recording, get them to predict the ways in which someone might behave inappropriately at a meeting. Write a list of the students' ideas on the board.

Play Version 1 and get students to check what they hear against the list on the board, noting down any other things they hear.

#### ANSWERS:
Stanislas constantly interrupts, tries to impose his point of view, uses inappropriate register, goes off the topic and gets involved in an argument with another attendee.

## RECORDING SCRIPT
 2:58
Version 1
Anna: Do we all agree on that then? All right. That brings us to the next point on the agenda – company policy on gifts from suppliers. Now, in the past we used to turn a blind eye, but now I tend to think that we need …
Stan: Well, it's stupid!
A: I'm sorry, Stanislas. Did you want to say something?
S: Yes. It's stupid. Really, really stupid. Well, it is, isn't it, Anna?
A: Well, I'm not quite sure why Stanislas feels so strongly about this issue, but the fact is, we had a major problem with our packaging supplier recently. It seems they had been sending regular 'goodwill packages' to our buyer's home.
S: What?!
Jon: Gifts, Stan. Cases of vodka, I believe.
S: Vodka?! Oh, I see.
A: Yes. Well, apparently, the suppliers thought the contract was guaranteed for life, and unfortunately Mr Vieri, from our purchasing department, 'forgot' to mention our policy of calling for new tenders every three years.
S: So, we should sack Vieri, that's what I think!
J: Stan, I see your point, but you can't just sack someone for making one mistake after twenty years with the company!
S: No, you're wrong, Jon! It's not right, and he has to go.
J: But Stan, don't you think that everyone should have a second chance? I mean …
A: Jon, Stan, I think we're getting side-tracked here. The question today is not how we deal with Mr Vieri, but what our company policy should be in future.
S: Yes, but his behaviour was unethical, do you understand? Unethical! So he must be fired!
Magali: Could I just come in here?
A: Yes, Magali, do you have any views on this issue?
M: I'm sorry, Anna; when you say this issue, do you mean our policy, or Mr Vieri's vodka?
A: Listen, perhaps we should break for coffee. I think we're all getting a bit tired. Could we come back to this later?

**3** Play 2:58 Version 1 again while students write down any inappropriate words and expressions they hear. Students should also listen for tone of voice, stress, intonation, etc.

#### SUGGESTED ANSWERS:
1 Well, it's stupid!
2 Well, it is, isn't it, Anna?
3 What?!
4 That's what I think!
5 No, you're wrong.
6 Do you understand?

**4** 2:59 Play Version 2. Students listen and note down the differences in vocabulary and tone of voice and in the way the meeting proceeds. They then compare their answers with a partner. Take whole-class feedback.

#### ANSWERS:
Stanislas uses more appropriate language and the meeting is more constructive.

## RECORDING SCRIPT

🔘 2:59

Version 2

**Anna:** Do we all agree on that, then? All right. That brings us to the next point on the agenda – company policy on gifts from suppliers. Now, in the past we used to turn a blind eye, but now I tend to think that we need …

**Stan:** Sorry to interrupt, but …

**A:** Yes, Stan. Go on.

**S:** Well, I must say, I think accepting gifts from suppliers is unwise. Would you agree, Anna?

**A:** Well, Stanislas, on the whole, yes, I would. Now, recently we had a major problem with our packaging supplier. It seems they had been sending regular 'goodwill packages' to our buyer's home.

**S:** Sorry, Anna. I don't see what you mean.

**Jon:** Gifts, Stan. Cases of vodka, I believe.

**S:** Vodka? Oh, I see.

**A:** Yes. Well, apparently, the suppliers thought the contract was guaranteed for life, and unfortunately Mr Vieri, from our purchasing department, 'forgot' to mention our policy of calling for new tenders every three years.

**S:** Well, I feel strongly that we should dismiss Mr Vieri!

**J:** Stan, I see your point, but you can't just dismiss someone for making one mistake after twenty years with the company!

**S:** I'm afraid I can't agree, Jon! It's not right, and he should leave the company.

**J:** But Stan, don't you think that everyone should have a second chance? I mean …

**A:** Jon, Stan, I think we're getting side-tracked here. The question today is not how we deal with Mr Vieri, but what our company policy should be in future.

**S:** Yes, but wouldn't you agree that his behaviour was unethical? So he should be dismissed.

**Magali:** Could I just come in here?

**A:** Yes, Magali, do you have any views on this issue?

**M:** I'm sorry, Anna. When you say this issue, do you mean our policy on gifts, or the wider issue of corporate ethics? You see, it seems to me that we need some kind of global charter or code of conduct which would cover all possible …

**5** Play 🔘 2:58 Version 2 again so that students can complete the expressions. Check answers by getting students to read the complete sentences aloud, using appropriate intonation.

### ANSWERS:

1 Sorry to interrupt, but …
2 Would you agree, (Anna)?
3 Sorry, (Anna), I don't see what you mean.
4 Well, I feel strongly that (we should dismiss Mr Vieri).
5 I'm afraid I can't agree, (Jon).
6 Yes, but, wouldn't you agree that (his behaviour was unethical)?

**6** and **7** Do these exercises as whole-class activities.

With lower-level classes, play 🔘 2:58 Version 2 again so that students can hear the expressions again in context.

### ANSWERS:

Exercise 6
1 That brings us to the next point on the agenda.
2 I tend to think that we need …
3 I see your point, but you can't just dismiss someone …
4 Don't you think that everyone should have a second chance?
5 I think we're getting side-tracked here.
6 Could I just come in here?
7 Do you have any views on this issue?
8 When you say this issue, do you mean our policy on gifts?

Exercise 7

| Giving an opinion | Asking for opinions | Managing the discussion |
|---|---|---|
| In my opinion … It seems to me that … I feel strongly that … I tend to think that … | What's your feeling? Would you agree? Do you have any views on …? | Do we all agree on that, then? Perhaps we should break for coffee. Could we come back to this later? That brings us to the next point on the agenda. I think we're getting side-tracked. |

| Disagreeing tactfully | Interrupting | Asking for clarification | Persuading |
|---|---|---|---|
| I agree up to a point, but … I'm afraid I can't agree. I see your point, but … | Sorry, but could I just say …? Sorry to interrupt, but … Could I just come in here? | So are you saying that …? Sorry, I don't see what you mean. When you say … , do you mean …? | Isn't it the case that …? Wouldn't you agree that …? Don't you think that …? |

**8** Read the four issues aloud with the class.

With lower-level classes, brainstorm some opinions on each issue with the whole class and write them on the board. Students can use these in their conversations.

Circulate while students are speaking and assist where necessary. Check that students are using the target language appropriately. When they have finished, get some pairs of students to present their conversation to the class.

**9** Each group should choose one person to chair the meeting. Give students a few minutes to read the instructions and think about what they might say. Remind them to review the language and expressions in this module and in earlier modules which might help them with this task.

While students are speaking circulate and assist where necessary. When they have finished, get the chairperson in each group to report to the whole class what was decided in each case.

To follow up, students could write a brief summary of their decision in each case.

### EXTENSION ACTIVITY

Students discuss how they would deal with the following behaviour at meetings:

- someone who never speaks
- someone who dominates the meeting by talking too much
- someone who always arrives late
- someone who can't stick to the point
- someone who constantly interrupts
- someone who often does not come to meetings and does not inform you in advance.

Students work in groups or pairs and note down what they would say or do in these situations. Check answers with the whole class.

## 6.5 Writing
## Reports and minutes

This module provides practice in using the appropriate grammar and vocabulary for writing reports and minutes of a meeting.

### Internet research

A search for *email ethics* will reveal a wide range of information on the use and abuse of email within companies, including real-life stories about employees losing their jobs because of inappropriate use of email; suggestions for a code of ethics for email use; tips for avoiding problems with email at work, etc.

This research could be done as a follow-up activity after students have completed exercises 4 and 5.

### Discussion

**1** Get students to explain the meaning of *community projects* (schemes or activities which improve the quality of life for people living in a certain area) or explain it yourself, and make a list of some examples of community projects, e.g. building a children's playground, establishing a community garden, planting trees, providing books for schools, etc.

Get students to work in groups to brainstorm ideas. Take whole-class feedback.

**SUGGESTED ANSWER:**

Companies often rely on the local workforce, so it's in their best interests to invest in the community so that they have a happy, committed and loyal workforce. It will also raise their profile with local councilors and government which could be useful for them.

**EXTENSION ACTIVITY**

To personalize the activity, get students to add to the list any community projects they know of in their own locality.

### Brainstorming

**2** Do this as a whole-class activity. Write the words in the box on the board and elicit alternatives from students, who should also spell the word as you write it on the board.

**SUGGESTED ANSWERS:**

but: however, although
and: in addition, also
so: therefore, this means
say / tell: inform, explain, etc.
think: imagine, believe, etc.

### Skim reading

**3** Question 1: Students read the report silently, underlining the answers to the first question.

With lower-level classes, you could tell students in advance how many arguments there are for and against. Check answers with the whole class.

Question 2: Get students to close their books and listen for the answers to question 2 while you read the minutes aloud. Check answers with whole class. Students then open their books and read the minutes silently to double-check their answers.

**ANSWERS:**

1   Arguments for:
    Benefits to the company's image justified more active and extensive support, in particular after the recent difficult negotiations.
    Substantial benefits in terms of motivation and job satisfaction.
    A positive effect on expansion of our manufacturing facilities and recruitment of our workforce locally.
    Need for good relations with local communities benefits in developing team spirit.
    Arguments against:
    Group policy is to give encouragement, but only limited financial support.
    Concerns about the size of the investment and the project's impact on productivity.
    Risks involved for production, for example, absenteeism and quality issues.
    The project could become an excuse to take time off work.
2   a) Head Office decided to support Mirratec's decision.
    b) Mirratec decided to approve the project.

**EXTENSION ACTIVITY**

Put students into groups of three and get them to roleplay the meeting that was reported in the minutes on page 78 in the Student's Book. Before they start, each student should re-read the minutes to check what was said by the person they will be roleplaying. They can also review the language practised in 6.4. Circulate while students are speaking and monitor the use of language, pronunciation, and how effectively the meeting is run.

### Scan reading

**4** Read through the list of titles in the left-hand column with the whole class. See if students can guess what the missing words are. Then give them a few minutes to read the report and the minutes and complete the answers.

**ANSWERS:**

| Function | Linking words |
|---|---|
| Addition | besides, moreover, in addition, furthermore |
| Conclusion | lastly, in conclusion, finally |
| Consequence | so, therefore, consequently |
| Contrast | but, however, even so |
| Equivalence | that is to say, namely, in other words |
| Example | for instance, such as, for example |
| Generalization | in most cases, as a rule, on the whole |
| Highlighting | mainly, chiefly, in particular, especially |
| Stating the obvious | of course, naturally, obviously, clearly |
| Summary | to sum up, overall, in brief |

### Writing

**5** Give some brief information about Josiah Wedgwood. (He was an influential 18th century businessman who founded the world-famous Wedgwood china company. He pioneered innovative products, efficient production methods, and effective marketing strategies for his products.)

Students do this exercise with a partner. Check answers with the whole class by getting students to read the sentences aloud with the appropriate linking word in place.

Josiah Wedgwood was a pioneer in social responsibility, building a village for his workforce. <u>In addition</u>, his products combined technology with classical culture.
More than a century later, George Cadbury developed social housing for his chocolate factory workers. <u>Consequently</u>, Cadbury's became one of Britain's most respected companies. Both men were pioneers of corporate social responsibility. <u>However</u>, they were also accused of paternalism.
Today, sustainable development policies aim to manage the effects of business on employees, the community, and <u>especially</u> on the environment. Multinationals like Shell are focusing on the idea of being good neighbours, <u>in particular</u>, by consulting local stakeholders before beginning new projects which may affect them.

## Reading for detail

**6** Do this as a whole-class exercise. Students read the report silently, underlining the impersonal structures. When they have found five, they should raise their hands. When most students have raised their hands, check answers with the whole class.

**ANSWERS:**

it was felt that ...
it is recommended that ...
it is hoped that ...
it is believed that ...
It is expected that ...

**7** Ask students do this exercise alone and then compare their answers with a partner. Check answers by getting students to read their sentences aloud.

**ANSWERS:**

1 Christopher agreed that productivity was a concern.
2 Christopher stressed that only a small number of staff would be directly involved.
3 Christopher claimed that most department managers didn't expect any problems.
4 Christopher reported that there was a similar project in Greece where they had actually improved productivity.
5 Christopher suggested that team spirit would be much better when the community centre had been built.

## Listening and writing

**8**  2:60 Play Jan's first speech and pause the recording. Ask students what they think *diversity* in the workplace means (employing people from different parts of society and ensuring a representative mix of ages, gender, mobility, ethnic background, etc.).

Play the rest of the recording and get students first to listen, without making notes, so that they can get an overview of the whole discussion. Then play the recording again, pausing at appropriate moments while students take notes. They then compare answers with a partner. Circulate and assist where necessary. Check answers with the whole class to ensure that everyone has the correct information.

Students then write their summary. When they have finished, they should exchange their summaries with another pair and check each other's work. They should underline or circle any mistakes or things which are unclear and pass the summary back for correction and improvement.

When students have finished, display the summaries on a desk or wall and allow students to read them all.

## RECORDING SCRIPT

2:60

Jan: All right, then. Let's move on to point two on the agenda: diversity. As you know, our workforce is still 80% male. What's more, we have very few employees from ethnic minorities. The general feeling within the group is that we need to take measures in order to reflect the increasing diversity in society ...

Ines: Sorry to interrupt, Jan, but when you say 'measures', do you mean positive discrimination? Hiring women in preference to men, for instance? Because that's all very well in sales and admin, but I really, really can't see women doing the heavy jobs in production. And anyway, I'm not sure that positive discrimination is the right way to approach the problem.

Christopher: No, I don't think it is either. It seems to me that we would just go from one extreme to another – you know, all our employees would be middle-aged female immigrants with disabilities!

J: Point taken, Christopher. But, seriously, that's what we want to avoid – extremes. In fact, what we need are measures to ensure that we don't discriminate against anyone on whatever criteria, whether it's their age, their race, their gender, their religion, or anything else.

C: But Jan, don't you think that's just an HR problem? I mean, they're the people who interview the candidates, not us. Nine times out of ten, we only see a short-list of people they've already approved. It's even worse when we recruit from the agencies. And that's another problem, by the way: half of the people they send us are absolutely hopeless. I don't know how they select them, but honestly ...

J: Yes, Christopher. I know the agencies are a problem, but I think we're getting sidetracked here. Could we agree that we'll talk about the agencies next Monday?

C : OK.

J: Good. So, getting back to diversity. Ines, what can we do to attract more applications from women?

I: Well, for a start, we should offer more part-time positions. Flexible hours, longer holidays when the schools are closed, a four-day week. You know, jobs that women with families can manage. That's really obvious. I've been saying this for years! I mean, why don't we start by allowing our present staff to go part-time if they want to? I can think of at least four women who'd be delighted to work part-time! That would mean we could offer more part-time jobs to new candidates.

J: Yes, Ines, thank you. That's an excellent idea. Shall we get HR to work on it? Christopher?

C: That's fine by me.

J: All right, that's decided then. All right, shall we break for coffee now, or take point three first?

## 6.6 Case study

## Phoenix

This case study brings together the themes and language practised in the unit requiring students to roleplay interest groups at a public meeting about the site of a new vehicle recycling centre.

### Internet research

Students will find detailed information about what is involved in *automobile recycling contamination* (only 82% of a car is recycled which means 18% of them go into landfill. This search could supplement the information in exercises 2, 3 and 4. It would be useful to do this research before you start this module. However, it is not essential, and could be done as a follow-up to this module.

## Discussion

**1** Students work in groups to answer this question. First elicit from the whole class or explain the meaning of *recycling centre* (a place where used or waste materials are processed and converted into reusable material) and ask what kinds of things might be recycled (fridges, building materials, garden waste, cars). To focus on the topic of the case study, ask students to answer the question about a car recycling centre. Take feedback from the whole class.

## Reading

**2** Read the text aloud or get a student to do it. To help them answer the questions students can refer back to the vocabulary and expressions they practised earlier in the unit.

### SUGGESTED ANSWERS:

1  The company tries to present itself as a responsible member of the community, protecting the environment by providing a valuable service, and applying an ethical code of fair practice in its dealings with all its partners.

2  Depending on how high-tech their equipment is, it may be very clinical and relatively clean, or very dirty, dusty, heavy, noisy, unpleasant and dangerous.

### ROLEPLAY PREPARATION

Read the roleplay preparation notes with the whole class and divide the class into three groups. Students should work in their groups for the remaining exercises in this module.

## Listening

**3**  2:61  This exercise provides the background information for the meeting in exercise 6.

Question 1: Read this question aloud and play the first part of the meeting up to '… attract new business and jobs to the area'. Check answers with the whole class.

Question 2: Play the rest of the meeting. First get students to tell you where sites A, B and C are and write notes about the locations on the board. If necessary, play the second part of the recording again so that students can answer question 2.

Question 3: Explain *charm* (the power to please or attract people) and *diplomacy* (art or skill of dealing with people by gentle or tactful means) and get the whole class to brainstorm what 'Operation Charm and Diplomacy' might involve in this context.

### ANSWERS:

1  Port Katherine is a good choice for Phoenix because:
a)  it's close to Perth.
b)  it's far enough away not to attract too much attention from the environmentalists.
c)  the population is only about 3,500, so there shouldn't be too much local resistance.
d)  the local authorities are desperate to attract new business and jobs to the area.

2  For the Planning Department, site A is likely to be politically sensitive, but is conveniently close to the highway on the edge of town.
Site B will probably produce the most income for the community and seems to have no major disadvantages.
Site C would involve major demolition and road-building work, so is less suitable.
For the Residents' Association, site A is a problem because it's close to a school.
Site B seems to be a good choice as it will not disturb residents.
Site C may involve a lot of demolition and building, which could disrupt residents' lives in the town centre.
For Phoenix, site A is the best: it's close to the highway, the price for the land is reasonable and it's a nice flat site to build on. The disadvantage is that it's right next to the local school.
Site B is on a business park, but it's a bit expensive, and taxes will be higher.
Site C is an old factory site near the harbour in the town centre. Access would be a problem, unless they built a new road, and they'd have to demolish the old building.

3  'Operation Charm and Diplomacy' is an attempt to establish good relations with the local community by stressing the company's environmentally friendly ethics and mission statement in order to outweigh the disadvantages and break down resistance in people's minds.

### RECORDING SCRIPT

2:61

Justin: … so we all agree that we need to keep an eye on that one. All right, that just leaves point six on the agenda: the new site for the South West. Helen, can you bring us up to date?

Helen: Yes, Justin. There's good news: we've identified three possible sites in a place called Port Katherine.

Glenn: Never heard of it!

H: Well, it's a small town about 30 miles south of Perth. It's exactly what we were looking for: close to Perth, but far enough away not to attract too much attention from the environmentalists.

G: Well, that's good news! We don't want another disaster like Cairns. Those Greens have absolutely no idea what this country would look like if we didn't recycle cars!

J: Yes, all right, Glenn. Shall we let Helen finish?

G: Oh, yes. Sorry, mate.

J: Helen?

H: Thank you. Port Katherine's population is only about three and half thousand, so Glenn will be happy to know there shouldn't be too much local resistance. And the local authorities are desperate to attract new business and jobs to the area.

J: Sounds good. You said there were three possible sites?

H: Yes, that's right. I've put all the details in this handout. There you are, Glenn.

G: Oh, yeah. Thanks.

H: Now, site A is a good one. It's a greenfield site just on the edge of town. There are several plus points. Firstly, it's close to the highway, so access for our trucks is easy. Secondly, the price of land is reasonable. And thirdly, it's a nice flat site to build on.

J: Any negatives?

H: Well, just one. It's right next to the local school.

G: Uh-oh!

H: But I don't think it's going to be a problem. I spoke to someone at the planning department, and they were very enthusiastic. Sites B and C are also possible, but they have other problems. Site B is on a business park, so no problems with residents, but it's a bit expensive and taxes will be higher. Site C is actually in the town centre.

G: Oh yeah, perfect! Twenty ton trucks in the high street!

H: Actually, Glenn, it's not that bad. It's on a big old factory site near the harbour. We'd have to demolish the old building, and access would be a bit of a problem, but they could build a new road. It's possible.

J: OK, thanks, Helen. Excellent work. I'll send somebody out there to start talking to the locals.

G: 'Operation Charm and Diplomacy', eh?

J: Yes.

H: Hm. Better not send Glenn, then!

## Reading and discussion

This section provides key information that each of the three interests groups will need to present its case in exercise 6.

**4** and **5** Circulate while students are doing these exercises and assist where necessary. You could set a time limit for the opening presentations, e.g. 5 minutes per group. Encourage students to refer to the previous modules in the unit to help them in their preparation, e.g. 6.2 and 6.4. Students could write notes on cards to help them with their presentations.

**ANSWERS:**

Group A: Port Katherine Planning Department

1 The email is from Duncan Gillespie, one of the Mayor's staff.

2 Your role is to organize and chair the meeting, and to try to find an agreement which suits everyone.

3 It's important to keep the residents happy because the elections are coming up soon. If they are unhappy, the Mayor may not be re-elected.

4 The project is important because the town desperately needs new jobs and investment.

5 Site B is the best choice for financial reasons.

Group B: Port Katherine Residents' Association

1 Members feel strongly about preserving the environment and the safety of their children.

2 Demonstrations, protests, lobbying, sabotage?

3 Because the elections are approaching and the mayor wants to be popular.

4 Ideally, you would prefer the centre not to be in Port Katherine at all. The industrial environment of Site C seems to be the best choice.

5 Make sure site A is not chosen.

Group C: Phoenix

1 Make friends and sell the benefits of the recycling centre.

2 Improving facilities at the school, redeveloping the port area in the town centre, attracting new businesses to the business park?

3 To develop the largest recycling centre on the continent.

4 Site A is the best if the residents' resistance can be overcome. Site B is possible, but more expensive. Site C depends on the town agreeing to build a new road.

5 The cost argument against site B may not receive much sympathy from the residents and the authorities; the contamination argument is delicate and may increase resistance to the project. The cost for the town of a new road is probably a good argument to use against site C. The disruption to the city centre is more delicate, as this argument can also be used against site A.

## Roleplay

**6** Play the part of chairperson of the meeting yourself – welcome the participants and introduce the three presenters; summarize the discussion at the end.

Hold the meeting, following the agenda. While students are speaking, make notes of any common errors for remedial teaching later. You could also make a note of any particularly good uses of the target language to share with the rest of the class when the activity is over.

When they have finished, students could also assess their own performance, commenting on one thing they think they did well and one thing that could be improved.

## Writing

**7** Students should refer to earlier work in the unit on the passive and reported speech (6.3) and writing reports (6.5). Students could exchange their first drafts with another group for feedback before finalizing it.

# Review 5 and 6 answers

## Review 5

(page 82 in the Student's Book)

### 5 Making deals

**1**

1  a) website        b) eyeballs
   c) search ads
2  a) web chats     b) purchase
3  a) databank      b) browsers
4  a) expectation   b) merchandising
   c) approach

**2**

tracking / consent / violation / privacy

**3**

1  look up a product on a search engine
2  pay by credit card
3  place the product you want in a cart
4  click on a link to get to the seller's site
5  browse the site to find any interesting products
6  debit the customer's credit card
7  send back a faulty product under guarantee
8  ship the product from the warehouse

**4**

1  offer
2  find
3  put on
4  put back
5  take
6  meet

**5**

1  miss the deadline
2  place an order
3  reach a compromise
4  are entitled to a discount

**6**

will increase / would increase / do you give

**7**

If we increased our order, would you give us a discount?

**8**

If we increase our order, will you give us a discount?

**9**

1  if + increased
2  unless + guaranteed
3  providing + agree

**10**

1  recommend
2  advise me to do
3  suggest
4  advise you
5  suggested to him

**11**

1  agreed, below
2  Should, available
3  unlikely, replacement
4  charges, lowest
5  wish, require

## Review 6

(page 83 in the Student's Book)

### 6 Company and community

**1**

1   shareholder value
2   compensation
3   facilities
4   charities
5   environment
6   exploiting
7   sustainable
8   equal opportunity
9   complaints
10  align

**2**

1  acknowledge any problem that exists.
2  act with integrity towards employees.
3  compensate victims for any damage caused.
4  limit the impact of any problem.
5  negotiate settlements which satisfy everyone.
6  obey the law or face a lawsuit or fine.
7  recognize merit when staff perform well.
8  uphold standards of common decency.

**3**

1   apology for absence
2   approving the minutes
3   stick to the agenda
4   introduce the first item
5   getting side-tracked
6   come back to this
7   have any views
8   see your point
9   Wouldn't you agree
10  take a vote
11  break for coffee
12  unanimous decision
13  any other business
14  close the meeting

**4**

1  tries
2  are made
3  was lost
4  took
5  was found
6  dismissed

**5**

as a rule = on the whole
clearly = obviously
consequently = therefore
especially = in particular
finally = in conclusion
in addition = moreover
in brief = to sum up
in other words = that is to say

**6**

1  in addition / moreover
2  especially / in particular
3  as a rule / on the whole

# 7 | Mergers and acquisitions

**Subject background**

**A** merger is when two companies join together as equals to form one, and the process is mutually consensual, whereas an *acquisition* (or *takeover*) is when a larger company buys a smaller one, and the smaller company may not be happy because its identity will be lost. In practice the differences are not so great, firstly because nearly always one partner will be more powerful, and secondly because the legal and practical arrangements are very similar.

The term *M&A* is common in place of *mergers and acquisitions*, and it is used a lot in the context of investment banking, where advising on and organizing M&A activity is a very lucrative part of their business.

What is involved in deciding on a merger or acquisition? The initial idea will come from the board of directors – it is a very long-term strategic decision and operational managers are unlikely to put forward the idea of joining together with a company who they see as a competitor in their day-to-day work.

So, the board has to make a decision that for reasons of growth, or increased competitive advantage, or extending their product line into other related areas, they will look for a target company to merge with or buy. The next step is to analyse the potential target. This means not only understanding its products and its customers, but also its cost structure,
a) because the aim is to make substantial savings when the two companies join together and
b) any future investments that might be necessary if it were bought.

Eventually you arrive at two figures – the first is what the company is worth to the current owners, and the second is what it is worth to the company making the acquisition. The difference between the two arises because of the benefits (added value) that the acquisition will bring. If those benefits are clear and substantial, the takeover will go smoothly – the acquiring company will start to accumulate shares in its target until it has a controlling stake. Existing shareholders of the target company are likely to be happy – the price of their own shares will be rising because of the increased demand as shares are being bought, and because of the future prospects for synergy between the two companies.

People inside the target company will be less happy – they will be worried about their jobs. The larger company who is buying them is unlikely to need two marketing directors, two finance directors, and all the extra middle managers. Indeed, one of the main arguments in favour of the acquisition will have been precisely this – to make cost savings by merging budgets and running the same business with fewer employees. In relation to the board of the target company – they may be prepared to fight for their independence if the takeover is hostile, or they may be pleased (perhaps they had decided to sell off this part of the business in order to focus on their core activities).

After the acquisition has happened, success is by no means certain. The first problem is cultural – the two organizations may have a different way of doing things, and there may be personality clashes between the two groups of managers. The second is poor implementation – reorganization, new job descriptions, unfamiliarity with the customers and markets of the other company will all lead to a period of confusion, and any expected cost savings may not materialize.

**Useful websites**

For more details on M&A, look at the 'investopedia' website – this is generally one of the best sources of financial information for language teachers on the net:
**http://investopedia.com/university/mergers/**

## 7.1 About business

### Risks and opportunities in M&A

This module explores issues around mergers and acquisitions; students examine the pros and cons of taking over a business and practise making effective presentations using visuals.

### Internet research

A search under *surviving a merger* will bring up numerous articles offering advice on what employees can do when their company is taken over, including the following:

- develop a plan of action in case you are made redundant
- re-assess your position in the company and take advantage of any opportunities for promotion
- be willing to accept change
- work out ways of managing the effects, e.g. confusion, increased workload, low morale, by trying to remain positive
- being supportive of colleagues' who lose their jobs or suffer in some way as a result of the takeover, etc.

This research could be done after the extension activity at the end of exercise 5 or after students have finished the module, as a follow-up activity.

### Discussion

**1** Getting married could be seen as a kind of merger or acquisition! Get students to make a list of the kinds of things that happen to two people's separate lives when they get married and in what ways these are similar to two companies merging.

#### SUGGESTED ANSWERS:

How a merger is like and unlike a marriage:
Usually, both people in a marriage bring assets (car, stereo, house, an income) into the marriage so their combined wealth is greater than their individual wealth. In the same way a merged company will have more assets than the individual companies had had.
A newly-married couple have to learn to live with each other and work out the best way to do things as a couple. One person might be good at housework while the other might be better at doing the household accounts. In the same way employees in a merged company have to learn to live with each other and accept that there may be different ways of doing things in the newly-merged company.
Married people have to pull together and work hard to make the marriage a success – the same can be said of a newly-merged company.

How mergers and acquisitions are perceived by the following:
Employees – they get worried about redundancies, having to move office, etc. Workforces are generally resistant to change.
Shareholders – they like mergers if it means that they will profit from M&As.
Customers – they sometimes worry about losing contact with the company as they know it, especially if they are loyal, established customers. They might worry about a change in the quality of the company's products or services.
The general public – they can view M&As with suspicion or they may not even know that a particular company has merged with or acquired another company.

### Skim reading

**2** Read the four questions aloud. Give students a few minutes to read the article and find the answers. Check answers with the whole class. Remind students not to worry at this stage about any unknown words – they will have time in exercise 3 to deal with these.

With lower-level classes, split the text into four parts and get students to look for answers to the questions section by section, i.e. read paragraphs 1 and 2 and look for the answer to question 1; read paragraph 3 and look for the answer to question 2; read paragraph 4 and look for the answer to question 3; read paragraph 5 and look for the answer to question 5.

#### ANSWERS:

1 American executives. Because merger and acquisition deals are worth astronomical sums, and many mergers result in a net loss of value.
2 Techniques based on best practice in the conception, planning, due diligence, negotiation and integration stages, and common acquirer errors.
3 Improving earnings, asset growth, developing synergies, making economies of scale, increasing market share; cross-selling, diversification, or taking on debt to make the acquirer a less attractive target.
4 Reasons which involve excessive pride or arrogance on the part of management, e.g. wanting to build too big an empire, too quickly.

### Reading for detail

**3** Circulate while students are discussing the true / false statements. Get them to underline the parts of the text that helped them find the answers. Remind students to check any unknown words in the *Wordlist* on page 157 in their books or use their dictionaries.

If necessary, explain that *B-schools* are business schools.

#### ANSWERS:

1 True – 70% of half the 1,500–2,000 mergers in the world: 1,500 / 2 x 0.7 = 525
2 True – American executives are queuing up to go back to school for M&A classes
3 False – Classes are 'open enrolment' - the only condition of attendance is your, or rather your company's, ability to pay the fees.
4 False – Guest speakers illustrate some of the most common acquirer errors.
5 False – You might think that B-school professors would discourage their students from taking on mergers. But you'd be wrong.
6 True – Developing synergies and making economies of scale are conveniently long-term goals.
7 True – Empire-building is a wrong reason, but diversification and increasing debt can be good reasons.
8 True _ CEOs need to be brought back down to earth and follow their heads rather than their hearts.

#### EXTENSION ACTIVITY

Ask students to look at the tortoise / hare picture on page 85 in their books. Ask them to discuss in small groups or with a partner what it represents in relation to the subject of mergers (the idea that the two companies with very different natures have to become 'one animal' – e.g. the hare = a fast-moving company that is focused on quick growth which merges with the tortoise = a company with a slow growth rate that focuses on maintaining its customers).
You could ask students to think of other animal metaphors (elephant and mouse = big and small; tiger and cow = aggressive and complacent; owl and kitten = old, wise, serious and young, immature, fun / playful, etc.).

## Listening for gist

**4** 3:01 Get students to predict what the 'five Gs' might be. Write their answers on the board. Play the whole interview through and get students to put up their hands when they hear a 'G'. Pause the recording and check answers. Write the words on the board. Get students to give you the correct spellings in each case, if they can.

**ANSWERS:**

Goals, Gains, Genes, Geography and Growth

## RECORDING SCRIPT

3:01

**Interviewer:** If mergers are so difficult to do well, why bother with external growth at all? Why not just grow internally?

**Bernard Degoulange:** Well, the most common reason, and probably the best reason for a merger, is that your customers are asking you for something you can't deliver. Let's say you sell champagne. If people are satisfied with your champagne, they're going to start asking you for whisky, simply because everybody would like to be able to get the solution to all of life's problems from the same place. Now, if you can't give your customers the whisky they're asking for, you have a problem. Because however satisfied they are with your champagne, they're going to go somewhere else for whisky, and that's when you risk losing those customers.

**I:** What advice would you give on finding the right company to acquire?

**BD:** Personally, I have five points that I want to examine when looking at a possible acquisition: the five Gs. If I don't get good answers to at least four of them, I don't do the deal. The first of the five Gs is Goals. Are our goals compatible? Are both companies trying to achieve something similar? If not, keep looking. Secondly, Gains. I want to know if there will be real gains in terms of economies of scale. And will these gains compensate for perhaps not being able to react as quickly to new trends in the market because of the size of the organization? Being bigger is not always better. The third point is Genes. That's genes with a G, not with a J! By genes, I mean company culture. There's no point in trying to merge a traditional, hierarchical family business with a fast-moving start-up with a laid-back management style. It just won't work, the cultural genes are too different. It's not enough to find a partner whose strengths compensate for your weaknesses, and vice versa; there has to be a real synergy in culture and personality.

**I:** Yes, if that synergy isn't present, there's a risk that neither company's customers recognize the firm that they used to trust.

**BD:** Exactly.

**I:** OK, so, Goals, Gains and Genes. What are the other two Gs?

**BD:** Geography and Growth. Are the companies based in the same city or geographical area? If not, communication between headquarters is much more difficult, and the Gains are harder to achieve.

**I:** And Growth?

**BD:** Will the merger provide technology or skills that you don't have now, which would take too long to develop yourself, and which will unquestionably allow your company to grow? If the merger will open new markets, which would otherwise be inaccessible, then it makes sense.

**I:** When you've identified the right partner, how can you make sure the merger goes smoothly?

**BD:** The most important thing is to look after your people: employees, management and of course customers, but especially employees. First of all, you have to keep them focused and productive. A merger is a wonderful opportunity for everybody to take their eye off the ball – and so it's a wonderful opportunity for the competition to jump in and take market share from both companies in the merger. Secondly you have to help employees get over their feelings of loss and perhaps anger as quickly as possible, and accept the new situation. Whenever there is a merger, two companies die and a new company is born. It's essential to help people get through that traumatic period, to explain how things will change and what their new roles will be, and to get them to accept the new organization and their new identity. It's essentially about communication, sometimes counselling, and compensating those who leave the company, whether by choice or not.

## Listening for detail

**5** 3:01 Students work with a partner to note down the answers to the questions. Play the recording as many times as students need to hear it. With lower-level classes, pause the recording after the answer to each question to give students more time to write. Check answers with the whole class.

Make a note of the answers to question 3 on the board to make sure everyone has the same information. This will be a useful reference for exercise 6.

**SUGGESTED ANSWERS:**

1 Probably the best reason for a merger is that your customers are asking you for something you can't deliver.

2 If people like your champagne, they're going to start asking you for whisky. If you can't give your customers whisky, they're going to buy it from someone else, and then you risk losing your champagne customers too.

3 Goals: the goals of both companies must be compatible.
Gains: there must be real gains in terms of economies of scale, big enough to compensate for becoming less reactive.
Genes: company cultures must be compatible.
Geography: head offices of the two companies should be geographically close.
Growth: the merger must unquestionably allow the company to grow.

4 The opportunity for the competition to jump in and take market share from both companies, because people are distracted by the merger.

5 Because two companies die and a new company is born.

6 By communicating and counselling, explaining how things will change and what their new roles will be, and getting them to accept the new organization and their new identity.

---

### EXTENSION ACTIVITY

Ask if students have any personal experience of mergers and acquisitions.

For pre-work students, get students to think about the impact of a takeover on the employees. Ask e.g.:
*What would be traumatic about it?*
*How might employees feel?*
*Why might some people be made redundant?*
*Why might some employees want to leave voluntarily?*

---

## Discussion

**6** Students work in small groups to make a list of pros and cons, using the five Gs as a starting point, but adding any other ideas of their own. Get students to make a decision about whether they will take over Kadris' Kebabs. Circulate while they are working and assist where necessary.

When they have finished, get each group to say whether they would proceed to a takeover or not and give reasons for their decision, incorporating the five Gs into their answers.

## 7.2 Vocabulary
### Business performance

This module practises a range of words and phrases for describing business performance, talking about cause and effect, and describing information in graphs.

### Internet research

An Internet search of *bulls bears* will reveal that bulls buy shares hoping to sell them at a higher price later, while bears sell shares hoping to buy them back later at a lower price. Bulls may be seen as optimistic because they hope the market will improve. Bears may be seen as pessimists because they are hoping for a fall in the market price. Other 'animals' that students may find mentioned in connection with the stock markets are chickens, pigs (or hogs), and sheep.

Students could do this research as a follow-up to this module to find out further information about stock markets.

### Discussion

**1** Ask students to work with a partner. Remind them to use clues in the extracts to help them match the headlines to the sentences and to work out whether good or bad news is being reported. Check answers with the whole class, getting students to tell you how they arrived at their answers.

To focus on the meaning and use of the phrases in the headlines, get students to tell you:
which two phrases are opposites (*in the black / in the red*)
which three phrases mean that a company has failed (*go under / go bankrupt / go to the wall*)
which two phrases mean that the company didn't make a profit (*cover costs / break even*).

**ANSWERS:**

1 Titanic Enterprises go under h) – bad news
2 Air New Zealand in the black g) – good news
3 Oldies Records cover costs c) – good news
4 Honecker Ltd go to the wall b) – bad news
5 Brizal Coffee break even d) – good news
6 Marks & Engsel go bankrupt e) – bad news
7 Liverpool FC in the red a) – bad new
8 Predictor Inc make a profit f) – good news

### Giving financial information

**2** Ask students to do the first part of this exercise alone and then compare their answers with a partner. Check answers with the whole class by getting students to read the sentence aloud. Ask them to say whether it describes an increase, a decrease, or stability. Monitor pronunciation.

Follow the same procedure with the second part of the exercise. Check answers by reading sentence 1 aloud yourself, and getting students to read the correct matching sentence from a)–h).

To focus on meaning, get students to divide the verbs into three lists headed *Increase, Decrease, Stable* and *Other* (i.e. words which don't fit into the other three categories), e.g.:
Increase: *jump, rise, double, peak, climb, reach a high*
Decrease: *fall, slide, dip, slump, drop, deteriorate*
Stable: *stabilize, level off*
Other: *fluctuate, vary*

**ANSWERS:**

1 c) ↗   2 g) ↘   3 f) ↗   4 a) →
5 b) ↘   6 d) ↗+↘   7 h) ↘   8 e) ↗

**3** Do this as a whole-class activity. Get students to read out the correct sentence to match each of the four graphs.

To check students' understanding of the differences in meaning between *by / to, of / to, of / from* in this context, get them to draw graphs showing the correct meaning of the other sentence in each case.

**ANSWERS:**

1 b)  Sales increased to $3M.
2 a)  There was a decrease of 10%.
3 a)  Prices fell by €15.
4 b)  There was a rise from 30%.

**4** Students work with a partner. They take turns to read the first part of the sentence, while their partner reads the matching second half.

Ask students which group in exercise 3 (*Increase / Decrease / Stable / Other*) the following verbs would go into: *improve, go up, grow, shoot up* (*Increase*).

**ANSWERS:**

2 a)   3 b)   4 c)   5 h)   6 e)   7 f)   8 g)

**5** With lower-level classes, first get students to sort out the verbs + adverbs from the adjectives + nouns. Check answers with the whole class.

**ANSWERS:**

verb + adverb (smallest to largest)
-   grow slightly      improve significantly      go up sharply
    shoot up dramatically      +
adjective + noun (smallest to largest)
-   a slight increase      moderate growth
    a considerable improvement      a sudden surge      +

**6** Students work with a partner. Check answers by getting students to read the completed sentences aloud.

Although several of these phrases can be used interchangeably, the second part of the exercise demonstrates the differences among some of them.

**ANSWERS:**

1   due to / as a consequence of / as a result of / because of
2   resulted in
3   as a result / as a consequence
4   thanks to / due to / as a consequence of / as a result of / because of
5   resulted in
6   As a result / Ss a consequence
*due to, as a consequence of, as a result of, because of, thanks to* explain causes.
*resulted in, as a result, as a consequence* introduce effects

---

**FURTHER PRACTICE**

To check that they can use the phrases correctly, give students a number of sentence starters to complete, using the phrases in exercise 6, e.g.:

*I didn't finish the report on time; as a result _____.*
*Thanks to _____, I got the promotion I wanted.*
*As a consequence of the takeover, my department _____.*
*Due to _____, I had to relocate to London.*
*Because of _____, I decided to look for another job.*

Check answers with the whole class, accepting any reasonable answers.

## Listening for detail

**7** 3:02  Before students listen, get them to look at the axes on the blank graph so that they know what will be discussed (time, money) and to look back at the vocabulary they have practised in exercises 1–3.

With lower-level classes, draw a simple graph on the board, e.g. showing a fluctuation in number of students at a school / doing a particular course, etc. The vertical axis could represent the number of students in units of 10. The horizontal axis should represent a range of years, e.g. 2001 to 2006. As a whole class get students to describe the graph. Encourage them to use as much language as possible from the module, e.g. *There was a sudden surge in students numbers in 2005 with 100 students compared to 80 the year before.*

Play the recording as many times as students need to hear it to complete the graph. To check answers, get individual students to tell you about sections of the graph, using the phrases used in the recording or their own words, e.g. *In 1988 the share price was $15. In 1989 it dropped suddenly to $12. Then it reached $50 in 1991*, etc.

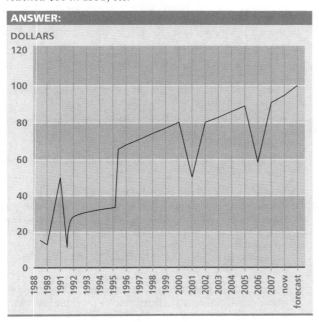

## Presenting

**8**  Circulate while students are speaking and check that they are using the target language correctly. Make a note of any mistakes for remedial teaching later. Get students to check their answers by comparing their completed graphs with their partner's original graph.

---

### FURTHER PRACTICE

Get students to write a short summary of the information in one or both of the graphs in exercise 8.

---

### RECORDING SCRIPT

 3:02

Anchor: Oxter Holdings today confirmed that they have increased their bid for Fraxis Corp. to $98 per share. Nelson Brown has the details of the New York industrial designer's Wall Street success.

NB: Fraxis Corp. was floated in 1988 at just $15 per share. After a sudden drop of $3 in 1989, the stock rose gradually over the next two years to reach $50 in early 1991, when Fraxis acquired one of their smaller competitors, Nimmco. The market was not enthusiastic about the takeover, and Fraxis fell sharply by over 40%. It then recovered slightly and levelled off around the $30 dollar mark for the next three years. In 1995, Fraxis CEO Alex Firman announced an alliance with the European market leader Haffmann; the reaction was immediate. The stock price soared to $65 as institutional investors rushed to share in the profits. The alliance has been a great success; with the exception of temporary dips to $50 in 2001 and $59 in 2006, Fraxis has climbed steadily to peak at $95, shortly after Oxter's first offer of $90 a share was rejected last week. Analysts believe that Fraxis are unlikely to accept anything less than $110, so expect to see the price jump to $100 plus when trading opens on Monday.

## 7.3 Grammar

### Future forms and expressing likelihood

This module focuses on ways of talking about the future and discussing forecasts and predictions.

#### Internet research

A search for *Alvin Toffler* will reveal that he is an American writer and futurist. He is well known for his ideas on, among other things, technology, communications, the digital revolution and corporate and political affairs, and their impact on society. He is the author of the best-selling *Future Shock* and *The Third Wave*, and many other books.

Students could research aspects of Alvin Toffler's work and ideas and make either oral or written presentations on them. This research could be done before or after exercises 4–6.

### Test yourself: Future forms

**1** and **2** Start by reading the notes on future forms in the *Refresh your memory* box with the class. Students work alone to complete exercise 1 and then compare their answers with a partner. Check answers with the whole class by getting individual students to read the sentences aloud. If students seem unsure of the future forms or would like further practice, work through some or all of exercises 1–9 in the *Grammar and practice* section (pages 130–131 in the Student's Book, answers on page 119 in this book).

**ANSWERS:**

Exercise 1
1 are going to 2 are going to 3 will
4 I'm going to 5 I'll sell
Exercise 2
1 b) are flying 2 b) will take 3 a) is attending
4 a) will prosecute

### Test yourself: Expressing likelihood

**3** Follow the same procedure as for exercises 1 and 2. Check answers by getting students to read the complete sentence aloud, followed by the percentage of probability they estimated. For further practice, students could complete exercises 10–12 in the *Grammar and practice* section (page 131 in the Student's Book, answers on page 119 in this book).

**ANSWERS:**

| | |
|---|---|
| 50% | 1 We have a 50/50 chance of success. |
| 20% | 2 We're unlikely to get a better offer. |
| 0% | 3 There's no way my boss will agree. |
| 100% | 4 Artip will definitely be sold. |
| 50% | 5 Costs are rising: it's possible our competitors will put their prices up. |
| 20% | 6 It's going to be a tough negotiation, but they might just accept our offer. |
| 100% | 7 It's in everybody's interest: the merger will definitely go ahead. |
| 10% | 8 There's not much chance our suppliers will deliver by next week. |
| 90% | 9 You did a good job: you're almost certain to get a raise. |
| 50% | 10 Their cultures are different, but I suppose they could find common ground. |
| 90% | 11 Wait a few months: the asking price is bound to come down. |
| 70% | 12 There's a good chance we'll meet the deadline. |
| 90% | 13 It's highly likely that taxes will increase. |
| 50% | 14 It's still uncertain, but they may announce a merger. |
| 70% | 15 Chris has all the right qualifications: she's likely to get the job. |
| 90% | 16 In the months to come, we fully expect sales to increase. |

### Discussion

**4** Read the events in columns A, B and C with the whole class.

With lower-level classes, write the phrases in bold from exercise 3 on the board so that students have easy reference to them, and brainstorm phrases students could use in defending their views, e.g. *We think ...; In our opinion ...; We reached this conclusion because ....* Students could also use some of the phrases they practised in module 7.2, e.g. *as a result, due to, as a consequence*, etc.

To get students started, demonstrate what to do with one of the events. Discuss students' views on the topic with the whole class. Make notes on the board and use them to prepare a very short presentation.

Circulate while students are speaking and assist where necessary. Get students to make their presentations. Students in the other groups should ask at least one question per group about what they hear. Make a note of any mistakes in the target language that you hear for remedial teaching later.

### Listening

**5** 3:03 Play the recording through once and get students to complete the exercise. Check answers with the whole class. Then play the recording again. This time, get students to note down the words and phrases that helped them arrive at their answers. Check answers with the whole class.

**ANSWERS:**

go freelance (U)     start evening classes (P)     stay at Artip (U)
find a new job (P)     Artip take-over (P)     read the job ads (P)
give up smoking and drinking (P)
retrain as a marketing assistant (P)
Ashley has forgotten to mention her engagement / wedding.

## RECORDING SCRIPT

 3:03

**Ashley:** Emma, Happy New Year!

**Emma:** Happy New Year!

**A:** What are you doing all alone over here? I haven't had a chance to talk to you all evening. Have some more champagne!

**E:** No, I shouldn't. I'm going to give up smoking and drinking this year. It's my New Year's resolution.

**A:** Really?! Well, you can start tomorrow. Come on, Em, it's New Year!

**E:** Oh, all right, just a drop. Thanks. Anyway, what about you, Ashley? What's the New Year going to be like for you? Have you made any resolutions?

**A:** No, not really. But I'm definitely going to find a new job. There's no way I'm staying at that company for another year.

**E:** Right. Have you got anything in mind?

**A:** No, but I'm going to read the job ads until I find something good. I'm bound to find something better than what I do now.

**E:** Oh, I'm sure you'll find something easily. Or you could go freelance, with the talent you've got …

**A:** Freelance?! Well, I suppose I could, but I think it's unlikely. It's far too complicated. No, I'm just going to choose about ten or twelve jobs to apply for, go along to the interviews, and we'll see what happens. I'm going to take my time, not rush into anything.

**E:** Right. I think that's very sensible.

**A:** So, what about you? Are you going to stay at Artip?

**E:** I doubt it.

**A:** Really?! Are you going to leave, or are they going to throw you out?

**E:** Well, both of those are quite likely, actually. The company's being taken over in February, so we don't know what will happen. I mean, they're bound to make redundancies, we just don't know how many. Anyway, I'm starting evening classes next week. I'm going to retrain as a marketing assistant.

**A:** Excellent! Well, here's to a successful New Year for both of us!

**E:** Yes, cheers! But, um, Ashley, isn't there another New Year's resolution you've forgotten to tell me about? Is that a real diamond? Who's the lucky man, then?

## Discussion

**6** As an alternative to pairwork, students could do this as a whole-class activity, milling about as if at a party, talking to several different people. Read through the question and the list together. Ask students what kind of questions they might ask each other.

With lower-level classes you could write the questions or question prompts on the board, e.g.:
*What are you planning to do with the rest of the day?*
*What are you doing at the weekend?*
*What (subjects, course, etc.) do you think you might do next term / year?*
*When do you think you'll retire?*

Tell students that they should remember or take simple notes on some of the answers for feedback at the end.

Give students time to mingle and talk, participating in the activity yourself. When they have finished, get some students to report back, e.g. *I spoke to Klaus about his plans for next year. There's a good chance he will do an MBA in the States.*

### FURTHER PRACTICE

Students discuss or write about plans, intentions and hopes for their town or city. Topics could include, shopping, leisure facilities, roads, public transport, taxes, government.

This module explores ways of presenting information through the use of visuals and practises expressions for explaining the information in them.

### Internet research

*Horizontal integration* refers to the activity of a company when it expands its business into different products that are similar to its current products, e.g. a hot dog seller expands into hamburgers. *Vertical integration* means that a company expands its business into areas that are at different points of the same production path, e.g. a car company expands into tyre manufacturing.

Students could choose one of the three industries mentioned – music, drinks, or TV – and gather information and examples about vertical integration.

This research could be done before the presentation activity in exercise 7 or as a follow-up to it.

### Discussion

**1** Read through the list of presentation tools and make sure that students know what they are. Encourage them to think about the pros and cons of each tool. Give students a few minutes to write their own answers and compare them with a partner. Take whole-class feedback.

Students could also consider which tool(s) might be appropriate for different types of presentations and audiences, e.g. an audience of more than 100 people in a large room; a small group of people around a table; a formal sales conference, etc.

Some students may decide that none of these tools is essential to a good presentation, and that other things are more important, e.g. tone of voice, body language, preparation, knowing your audience, etc. At this point you could remind students of the discussion they had in Unit 3 on the qualities of a good presentation.

### ANSWERS:

Answers will vary. It usually depends on the formality of the presentation, where it takes place, whether it involves any audience participation, the size of your audience (an overhead projector – OHP – will be better than a flip chart for larger audiences), what the presentation's about and what your audience expects.

### Listening for gist

**2** 3:04–3:08 Before students look at this exercise, get them to brainstorm the ways in which visuals can be used badly or ineffectively in presentations. Get them to think about their own experience – presentations they have seen (or have done themselves!) which have not worked well.

Read the sentences aloud or get students to read them. Compare these points with the ones students made themselves. Then play the recording through once while students listen and match. Get them to compare their answers with a partner.

Play the recording again so that students can check their answers. Check answers with the whole class by getting students to read the sentences aloud. Ask them to add some information about what each presenter did which failed to meet these guidelines, e.g. *Presenter 1 showed three slides one after the other very quickly. The audience may not have had enough time to look at them properly and there was probably too much information to take in.*

**ANSWERS:**

C Don't put too much data on slides: no more than six lines of text, and no more than six words per line.

A Too many visuals confuse the audience: don't overload them with slides.

D Don't be too technical; adapt to the target audience, and don't read out text on slides.

E Help the audience to understand by introducing, highlighting and explaining the most important information.

B Check all materials and equipment, and have backups for everything.

## RECORDING SCRIPT

 3:04–3:08

**Presenter A**

Now, my next slide shows how the number of takeovers is likely to increase over the next decade. This one gives a breakdown by sector. This next slide highlights the probable effects on company performance. And this one, this one and now this third slide show how share prices will fall.

**Presenter B**

Moving on to my next point, which is, er … yes, management buy-outs. No, sorry, just before that I'm going to show you another slide about corporate raiders. Ah, sorry, I can't seem to find it. Well, there's a hand-out which gives you the main points. I'll, er, make some copies when we finish. So, have a look at this slide which shows the confusion which resulted from … Ah, no, sorry, those are my holiday photos …

**Presenter C**

Now, then. Let's look at the next slide which shows some very interesting data. As you can see here – oh, or perhaps you can't see – yes, I'm sorry, the figures are rather small. Anyway, the sales forecasts are particularly good, in contrast to the data for the last three years, which is in the, ah, smaller table, over here on the right. Ah. You can't read that either?

**Presenter D**

If you look at the next slide, you'll see that we intend to collect data for the survey using a Grossman scheduled EMTI questionnaire modified from the standard CDF rapid assessment surveys procedure, and compensated for statistical significance using an unbiased reflex standard deviation algorithm.

**Presenter E**

OK, customer reactions to price and service levels after mergers: 30% of customers noticed an improvement; 49% said things had got worse. Erm, customer satisfaction by sector: almost 9% down in retail; stable in the service and financial sector; and 5% up for manufacturing companies.

**3** 3:09 Play the recording while students listen and choose the slide that is being described. Play the recording again. Get students to listen for the ways in which the presentation has improved, e.g. the speaker shows one slide and explains it clearly; he doesn't just read the contents aloud, he gives further information and interpretation of it.

**ANSWER:**

Slide C

## RECORDING SCRIPT

 3:09

How will our customers react to a merger? My next slide shows two charts which illustrate the problem. Recently, customers of large Spanish companies that had been involved in mergers were asked if they felt that prices and service had improved, remained the same or deteriorated as a result of the merger. As you will notice in the pie-chart, only a third of customers noticed an improvement, compared to almost half who said

that things had got worse.

Let's look at the second chart, which shows customer satisfaction by sector. As you can see, after a merger, customer satisfaction falls by an average of almost 9% in the retail sector, whereas it remains about the same in the service and financial sector, and rises by 5% on average for manufacturing companies.

The figures seem to suggest that, on the whole, customers are always likely to react negatively to mergers. This is due to a perceived drop in levels of service after a merger. The results indicate that retailers, where service is crucial to customer satisfaction, are particularly affected, as opposed to manufacturers, who benefit from mergers. Of course, this is the result of improved product quality and design, which are the most important factors for their customers.

## Listening for detail

**4** Before they listen, make sure students understand that the expressions are numbered in the same sequence as on the recording. Play 3:09 again. Pause if necessary to allow students time to complete the phrases. Check answers with the whole class. Get students to repeat the phrases, using the appropriate pronunciation, stress and intonation.

**ANSWERS:**

| Introducing a slide or visual | Highlighting |
|---|---|
| I'd like you to look at this slide. | As the graph shows, … |
| (1) My next slide shows two charts … | (2) As you will notice in the pie-chart … |
| (4) Let's look at the second chart … | (5) As you can see, after a merger … |

| Contrasting | Explaining and interpreting |
|---|---|
| In contrast to … | (7) The figures seem to suggest that … |
| (3) compared to almost half who said … | (8) This is due to a perceived drop … |
| (6) whereas it remains about the same. | (9) The results indicate that retailers … |
| (10) as opposed to manufacturers … | (11) This is the result of improved … |

## Presenting visuals

**5** Spend a few minutes discussing the pie chart, especially with lower-level classes. For example, you could ask students to give you some examples of what might be included under each heading:

*housing* (mortgage repayments, rent, utilities bills)
*transportation* (bus, train, petrol, car insurance, road tax)
*food* (meat, vegetables, fruit, fish, household requirements such as washing powder, etc.)
*disposable* (gym club membership, mobile phone costs, cinema or theatre tickets, weekends away, etc.)

While students are drawing their own pie charts, circulate and assist where necessary. Give them time to practise their presentation, using the words and phrases in exercise 4, before putting them into groups.

Circulate again while students are giving their presentations in small groups, monitoring use of the target language and making notes of any mistakes for remedial teaching later. Check also that students are following the four-point framework given in the exercise.

When students have finished, get some of them to repeat their presentations for the whole class.

## Pronunciation: Linking

**6**  3:10–3:13 Students work with a partner to mark the links between words. Encourage students to read the sentences aloud quietly while they are doing this.

Write the sentences on the board and get individual students to mark the links where they think they should go. Play the recording so that students can check their answers. If they want to make any changes to the answers on the board, they should do so now.

Play the recording again. Pause after each sentence so that students can repeat it quietly to themselves, either with their eyes closed or by reading the words from the board. They should also pay attention to stress, intonation, and pronunciation.

For homework, students could record themselves saying the sentences aloud (using the recording script which can be found at the back of the Student's Book). They could then play this back and assess their own delivery.

**ANSWERS:**

2 Only a third of customers noticed an improvement.

3 Customer satisfaction falls by an average of almost 9%.

4 This is essentially due to a drop in levels of
   service after a merger.

### RECORDING SCRIPT

3:10–3:13

1 Customers were asked if service had deteriorated as a result of the merger.
2 Only a third of customers noticed an improvement.
3 Customer satisfaction falls by an average of almost 9%.
4 This is essentially due to a drop in levels of service after a merger.

## Presentation

**7** Read the instructions with the whole class. Check that students understand *diversify* (vary your range of products/service in order to be more competitive) and *accelerate* (make something happen faster).

Brainstorm with the whole class the kind of businesses a manufacturer of tennis racquets might be interested in, bearing in mind the five Gs discussed in module 1.

Give students a few minutes to read their instructions. Circulate and assist where necessary. Remind students to use the *Wordlist* on page 158 at the back of the their books and their dictionaries, if necessary. Students could add some ideas of their own to the presentation, if they wish.

When the groups have decided which is the best candidate for acquisition, they should present their decision to the whole class, explaining the reasons for their choice.

As a follow-up activity, get students to write a short summary based on their oral presentation.

## 7.5 Writing

### Presentation slides

This module explores how to use PowerPoint slides and provides practice through reading and listening in preparing slides for presentations.

### Internet research

*Death by PowerPoint* refers to the poor use of PowerPoint for presentations and the effect this produces on audiences. Used ineffectively, presentation slides can make a presentation boring, for example if they are overused or are difficult to read or uninteresting.

Students will find websites offering advice on how to avoid 'death by PowerPoint', such as limiting the number of words on each slide, using simple, large fonts, using transitions wisely, customizing templates, and using pictures and graphs.

Students could do this research before they do this module, as a lead-in or after they have completed this module, to supplement the information given here.

### Discussion

**1** Do this as a whole-class activity, working through each item and getting students to comment on its suitability or unsuitability for a presentation slide. Get students to tell you where you might expect to find the two unsuitable items, e.g. footnotes might be found in an academic book or article; paragraphs are more suitable for a longer written text.

**SUGGESTED ANSWERS:**

no footnotes – they won't be legible
no paragraphs – just single lines of text

### Reading and analysis

**2** Ask students to work in small groups. After they have chosen the best way of presenting the information, get them to comment on the weaknesses of the two ways they rejected.

**ANSWERS:**

Slide B is the best: it highlights the key ideas the presenter wants to communicate. Each point can be understood without any commentary, but leaves room for the presenter to add interesting details.
Slide A has too much text and will be illegible. In fact, this is the oral commentary that the presenter might make on slide B.
Slide C is too succinct: there is not enough information for the key points to be understood without the presenter's explanations.

### Writing

**3** Students work alone, then compare their answers with a partner. Check answers with the whole class.

With lower-level classes, you could do this as a whole-class activity, writing the key words on the board.

If you wish, draw students' attention to the parts of the sentences that they have left out, as a way of focusing on general principles, e.g. omit introductory phrases, additional information, and examples; these can said during the presentation, but don't need to be written in the slides.

**SUGGESTED ANSWERS:**

1  One of the most challenging aspects of writing a presentation is the need to organize the information in a logical way.
→ Organize information in a logical way.
2  Choose attractive background and text colours that are comfortable for the audience to read.
→ Choose colours that are comfortable to read.
3  Presentation software can be fun to use. Be creative, but do not include too many effects which may distract your audience from your content.
→ Don't let creative effects distract from content.
4  Make sure the text is large enough that the audience can read it easily from the back of the room. Also, use a standard font that is not too complicated or distracting.
→ Use large, easy-to-read text and standard fonts.
5  Use positive statements like 'The figures show...' rather than vague language like 'The data could possibly suggest ...'
→ Prefer positive statements to vague language.

**4** Ask students to work with a partner to do this exercise. Encourage them to underline the key words first, as in exercise 3, and then compose the points for the slide, using their own words or rewriting, where necessary. Circulate while they are working and assist.

Get students to write neatly or type their five points on a sheet of paper, and display them on a table or wall so that everyone can see them.

**SUGGESTED ANSWERS:**

Three scenarios for our company's future.
Do nothing, continue to survive.
Invest in technology, develop new products.
Acquire Iticom, enter new markets immediately.
I recommend acquisition: risky, but enormous potential.

### Taking notes and writing slides

**5** 3:14 Read the instructions with the whole class and get students to predict what the strengths, weakness, opportunities and threats might be for a software company in today's market. Play the recording through once so that students get an overview of the presentation. Ask students how many slides they would want to prepare – they may say four (strengths, weaknesses, opportunities, threats), but as suggested here, they should also prepare an introductory, or 'overview' slide.

Then, play the recording again. Pause at the end of each section to allow students to make notes on the main points. Get students to compare their answers with a partner. Play the recording again so that students can check their answers. Then take whole-class feedback, ensuring that everyone has the right information to prepare the slides.

Students work with a partner again to prepare their slides. Circulate and assist where necessary. When students have finished, play the recording again and get students to listen and imagine the speaker is working through the slides as he delivers the presentation. This will allow them to check if their slides work effectively alongside the spoken presentation.

## SUGGESTED ANSWERS:

1 Overview:
   • Strengths
   • Weaknesses
   • Opportunities
   • Threats
   • Proposal
   • Questions and reactions
2 Strengths:
   • a reputation for innovation and quality
   • expert staff
   • careful financial management (chart)
3 Weaknesses:
   • not enough office space
   • costs (chart of development costs)
   • recruitment
   • size: too small and vulnerable
4 Opportunities:
   • recruit in eastern Europe
   • do development offshore
   • consolidation and diversification
5 Threats:
   • possible takeover target
6 Proposal:
   • take over Oranmore Video Games
     - growth and debt, less vulnerable
     - diversification, economies of scale
     - solve recruitment and space problems

## RECORDING SCRIPT

 3:14

Good morning everyone, and thank you for coming. Two months ago, you asked me to conduct a strategic analysis of the company's strengths, weaknesses, opportunities and threats. I'm here today to present my findings, and to make recommendations on the basis of those findings.

I intend first to give a short summary of the company's position, and then to invite you to ask questions and give your reactions to my proposals. If anything is not clear, please feel free to interrupt me.

First of all, I'd like to remind you of the company's main strengths. As you know, Galway Software has a reputation for innovation and quality in developing highly specialized customer applications. We are able to provide excellent service thanks to our small team of expert engineers and developers. What's more, our finances have been carefully and cautiously managed: as you can see from the figures on this slide, today the company is in good financial health with practically no debt.

However, although there are many reasons for satisfaction with the company's position, there are also a number of weaknesses which must be considered. The first, small weakness is office space. We just don't have enough. The second, more significant, weakness is costs. As this graph shows, our development costs have risen steadily, whereas market prices are falling. It is becoming increasingly difficult to maintain our profit margins. The principal explanation for these high costs is the high salaries we have to pay to attract experienced developers. A third, associated problem is recruitment: in spite of high salaries, we are finding it increasingly difficult to attract young engineers who prefer to join large international companies.

This brings me to perhaps the most significant weakness, and a problem which I want to come back to in a few moments when I talk about threats, and that is our size. As a small company in a very specific niche market, we are vulnerable. If things went wrong with just a few of our big customers, we could have serious difficulties.

But before looking at the threats, let's move on to opportunities. In particular, new technologies and a changing world economy are opening up exciting ways of re-thinking our business activities. For example, the new member states of the European Union in Eastern Europe have excellent schools and universities: their young engineers are talented, well-trained and keen to acquire experience in companies like ours. Another possibility is to do part of our development work offshore, in countries like India where labour costs are significantly lower than in Europe. Last, but certainly not least, we must look at opportunities in our own industry: competition is fierce, and a process of consolidation is under way. Many firms are forming alliances or launching takeover bids in order to exploit synergies, to make economies of scale and to diversify into new market segments. I believe these are opportunities we should not ignore, and I will be making a specific recommendation in the last part of my presentation.

So, I've talked about our strengths, our weaknesses and our opportunities. I want now to explain why one of the opportunities I have just described is also a serious threat. In the context of the consolidation I referred to earlier, Galway Software, as a small, successful, well-managed company with no debt, is a perfect target for a takeover. It is only a matter of time before a big international firm comes knocking at the door with its cheque book open. Unless we move first.

In the last part of this presentation, I am going to recommend that Galway Software should itself launch a takeover bid. There are many good reasons for this. Firstly, external growth with a reasonable amount of debt will make us less vulnerable. Secondly, a takeover will allow us to diversify into new markets, to expand our customer base and spread our risks, and to make economies of scale. And thirdly, the ideal candidate, Oranmore Video Games, is based just 20 miles away, currently has more developers than it needs, and has a lot of unused office space. I'm going to give you a handout which gives more details of why I believe we should acquire Oranmore …

## Writing slides

**6** This exercise allows students to personalize the work they have done on preparing PowerPoint slides to a subject which interests them. This could be related to their work, a hobby, or another topic of interest. They could, for example, choose to plan a presentation using the information they gathered in one of the Internet searches in this unit – on Alvin Toffler; vertical integration in the drinks industry; or bulls, bears and other animals on the stock market.

## 7.6 Case study
## Calisto

Students consider the options open to a business in trouble and make recommendations in a presentation about how to resolve them.

### Internet research

An Internet search for key words *"Avis: We Try Harder"* will reveal how this car rental company took on the market dominance of its rival, Hertz, in the 1960s and through clever market repositioning and brand-building dramatically increased its profits.

Students could do this research before they begin the case study as a lead-in activity and to provide ideas for the discussion and presentation in exercise 6. Or they could do it afterwards, to provide information on a real-world case study. They could write a short report on the story behind how Avis improved its market position.

## Discussion

**1** Do this as a whole-class activity. Explain *EBIT* (Earnings Before Interest and Tax: a commonly used way of measuring the profitability of a company).

Get students to compare the businesses in terms of their profits, costs, sales, etc. This analysis will feed into the exercises that follow.

### SUGGESTED ANSWERS:

Reysonido has lower operating costs than IMM and Calisto.
Reysonido has the lowest cost of sales while IMM's are very high.
IMM has the highest sales. (etc.)

## Reading

**2** Read the article aloud. Ask students to guess the meanings of *meteoric, newcomers, charismatic, slick,* and *trumpets* from the context, before they check the meanings in the *Wordlist* on page 158 in their books. Then check answers to the questions with the whole class. Ask students to suggest what kind of advertising Dylan might have used that could be described as 'slick' and what kind of discounting might be called 'aggressive'.

### ANSWERS:

1 By using direct sales, slick marketing and aggressive discounting.
2 The challengers have all lost market share and several smaller players have gone out of business.
3 IMM is the only company which has managed to reverse the trend of falling market share.

## Listening for gist

**3**  3:15 Get students to look at the notes before they listen to the presentation. Do the activity with the whole class. Play the recording. Pause at appropriate points to allow students to tell you, in a few words, what the options are.

See answer for exercises 3 and 4 on the next page.

## RECORDING SCRIPT

 3:15

President: As you know, this year Calisto has lost one point five million dollars. Obviously this situation cannot continue. Unless we take action now, we will go out of business next year. We have several options to consider. Our first option is to adopt the same strategy as IMM. IMM have reduced their operating expenses by 20% over the last two years. However, they have achieved this by ruthlessly cutting jobs: one fifth of IMM's staff have been made redundant. Here at Calisto we have a long tradition of looking after our staff, and I do not wish to choose this option unless there is no other alternative.

Our second option is to follow the example of our friends at Reysonido, and buy European technology which would reduce our cost of sales by 10–15%. However, we estimate that this investment would increase our operating expenses by half a million dollars a year. A third option is to cut our prices in order to increase sales. We estimate a price cut of 10% might increase next year's sales to $16.5 million – assuming, of course, that our competitors do not reduce their prices. However, our cost of sales would increase to just under nine million dollars.

My friends, there are three more options which I have not yet discussed with you, but which I would like you to consider carefully. Option number four is a merger. IMM have offered us three million dollars, which, in view of our desperate situation, is a very reasonable offer. If we agreed to a merger with IMM, the new company would be the new market leader, and be in a far better position to compete with Dylan. However, there would no doubt be some redundancies in order to make economies of scale.

As I said at the beginning of my presentation, I will take questions at the end. Now, option five. This is a high-risk strategy, but we must consider all possible solutions. In order to compete with Dylan, we need to be bigger; one way to obtain that critical size is by acquisition. Our fifth option is to acquire Reysonido.

Reysonido are likely to accept a takeover bid of around four million dollars. As well as synergy and economies of scale, this acquisition would also give us another bonus: access to the technology which means Reysonido's cost of sales is 10% lower than our own. Of course, we would need to borrow the money, and the repayments would represent around half a million dollars per year over ten years: not so unrealistic with combined sales of 25 million, I believe.

The final option is one which I sincerely hope you will not choose. That is, to close the company, and sell off our assets to pay our debts. I have kept it until last in order to stress that it is a serious option.

All right, I'm sure you are anxious to ask questions. After that, I would like us to consider all the options in detail; everybody's contributions will be valuable. Thank you.

## Listening for detail

**4** Play  3:15 again while students complete the notes. Check answers by getting students to form complete sentences, using a combination of their own words and the words they heard in the presentation, e.g. *Our first option is to cut jobs. IMM has adopted the same strategy. This would reduce our operating costs by 20%.* This will be useful practice for the discussion activity in exercise 5.

**ANSWERS:**

Exercises 3 and 4

| Options | Notes |
|---------|-------|
| 1 cut jobs | – same strategy as <u>IMM</u><br>– would reduce operating expenses by <u>20%</u> |
| 2 buy technology | – same strategy as <u>Reysonido</u><br>– would reduce production costs by <u>10–15%</u><br>– would increase operating expenses by <u>$0.5M</u> per year |
| 3 cut prices 10% | – next year's sales: <u>$16.5M</u><br>– cost of sales would increase to just under <u>$9M</u> |
| 4 merge with IMM | – price: <u>$3M</u><br>– advantages: <u>the new company would be the new market leader</u><br>– disadvantages: <u>some redundancies</u> |
| 5 acquire Reysonido | – price: <u>around four million dollars</u><br>– bonus: <u>access to technology, cost of sales 10% lower</u><br>– repayments: <u>$0.5M per year over ten years</u><br>– combined sales: <u>$25M</u> |
| 6 close the company | – sell off <u>our assets to pay debts</u> |

## Discussion and presentation

**5** Read the instructions with the whole class. Remind students of the work they have done in previous modules that will help them here, e.g. the vocabulary work in 7.2, future forms and expressing likelihood in 7.3, presentations in modules 7.4 and 7.5.

Set a time limit for the presentations, e.g. 5 minutes, so that each group has the same amount of time.

Circulate while students are working and assist where necessary.

When students are assessing which is the best presentation, they could use following criteria, which you could write up on the board as a checklist:
*Did the speakers present their information in a clear, structured way?*
*Did the slides follow the guidelines given in section 5?*
*Did the speakers support their arguments in a convincing way?*

Students could also add their own criteria, if they wish.

---

**FURTHER PRACTICE**

For homework, students can use the presentation in exercise 3 for further practice in preparing presentation slides (see module 7.5, exercises 4 and 5).

---

**W**hy export? The two most important reasons are likely to be under-used capacity (exporting will allow you to increase production, reduce unit costs and increase profits) and diversity (relying on just your own domestic market is risky because the market may decline, there may be seasonal factors, etc. Selling in other countries allows you to spread the risk and develop opportunities abroad).

Before getting started, there is a lot of initial research to be done on the foreign market. The main concerns will include:

- background information (economic situation, political stability, currency risk)
- market size and likely product demand
- competitors' products already in the market
- tariffs or import restrictions (duties, quotas, taxes)
- distribution channels and methods (agents, distributors, wholesalers, retailers)
- technical, safety, environmental and other standards required by law
- packing and packaging issues (climate and time in transit, handling methods, need for different packaging to suit local market)
- sales literature and support material (translations needed)
- servicing arrangements (if needed)
- customer satisfaction policy (money back/replacement schemes).

A major question is then going to be the nature of the distribution channel. Options to consider will include:

1 Direct selling from manufacturer to customer without an intermediary.
2 Domestic export firms operating in foreign markets (with their own agents, local offices, etc). These firms will take your goods on a wholesale basis and do all the sales and paperwork. However, you have no control over the market and your products may receive little attention compared to others.
3 Agents working exclusively for you in the foreign market. An agent receives a commission for sales made on your behalf. The advantages of using agents are that you gain the services of an experienced local person with contacts and market experience. The disadvantages are that the agent will take a high commission and may lose interest quickly if sales do not arrive quickly.
4 Distributors. A distributor is different to an agent. A distributor is a customer – they have rights (usually exclusive) to purchase your products and resell them in their market. They are like a foreign wholesaler. An agent is just an intermediary and never actually buys any products on their own account.

With agents and distributors there will be many issues to discuss and negotiate on an ongoing basis. These include:
- which products are to be sold
- prices in the foreign market
- performance targets
- payment of local marketing costs
- transportation (taking into account speed, cost, security and efficiency)
- getting paid (cash in advance, letters of credit, bill of exchange, open account, etc.).

There are other more specialized export options:
5 Licensing. This means selling or leasing some industrial or commercial expertise (for which you own the patent).
6 Franchising. This is a form of licensing for products which do not have patents.
7 Joint venture. This is a company owned jointly by two or more companies – for example a foreign company with a local partner.

On the net, a good starting point to research international trade are these two government sites (one UK and one US):
http://www.businesslink.gov.uk
http://www.unzco.com/basicguide
The World Trade Organization site is also useful (explore the link to Resources):
http://www.wto.org
For the activities of individual companies, look at:
http://www.corporateinformation.com

## 8.1 About business

### Export sales and payment

This module explores the theme of international trade and payments. Students also practise negotiating skills and using diplomatic language.

### Internet research

A search using *Big Mac Index* will reveal it is an informal way of comparing the purchasing power of two currencies. It was introduced by *The Economist* magazine in 1986 in a light-hearted way, and has been published more or less every year since then. One way of predicting exchange rate movements is that the rate between two currencies should naturally adjust so that a sample basket of goods and services should cost the same in both currencies. In the Big Mac Index, a Big Mac hamburger from the McDonald's fast food restaurant chain is used as the single sample item.

Students could be asked to compare their own currency with one or more others using the Big Mac example. This research could be done at the end of this module.

#### LEAD-IN ACTIVITY

To get students thinking about overseas sales and payments, ask if they have any experience of shopping in a foreign country or if they have bought anything online from a company in another country. What happened? How did they pay? Did they have any problems with payment, shipment or delivery?

Alternatively, ask students about the use of credit cards in their country. Are they widely used? How many credit cards do people usually have? What do they use credit cards for? Are there any problems in their country with consumer debt?

### Discussion

**1** Circulate while students are discussing the question and assist where necessary. Make a note of any useful vocabulary to share with the whole class at the feedback stage. Ask one student in each pair to give you one aspect of the difficulty of selling in overseas markets. Make a list on the board.

#### SUGGESTED ANSWERS:

quotas, import taxes, exchange controls, local regulatory bodies like FDA, local customs for payment terms, difficulty of providing after-sales service, language barrier, corruption

### Scan reading

**2** Check that students know what a pinball machine is (a game in which small metal balls are shot across a board and points are scored when the ball hits a pin with lights). Ask some questions to establish the context, e.g.:
*Are pinball machines popular in your country?*
*Where do you usually find them?*
*Do you play on them?*

Get students to read the first paragraph of the article. Ask some simple questions to set the context, e.g.:
*Why did Eisenhart Games expand into markets outside the US?* (because of competition from video games and computers in the US)
*What is Eisenhart's share of the Middle East market?* (35%)
If necessary, explain *take on board* (take notice of, learn).

With lower-level classes, students could read the article one paragraph at a time and identify the mistake.

#### ANSWERS:

1 wasting a lot of time chasing payments
2 trying to sell on price
3 not managing an agent
4 not taking an enquiry seriously

### Reading for detail

**3** Students work with a partner to find the answers. They should underline the relevant phrases in the article. Students could also pick out any examples that Daryl Vincenti gives to illustrate his points.

#### ANSWERS:

1 Use a credit agency to check out your customer's creditworthiness and to insure against non-payment.
2 Be flexible, learn to think outside the box.
3 Don't assume that what works well on your domestic market will automatically go down well in another.
4 Be prepared to modify product specifications to meet local conditions.
5 Focus on different aspects of the marketing mix.
6 Focus on one market, rather than trying to sell all over the world.
7 Make a firm commitment to export / put in a lot of time, get out there and meet your customers.
8 Remember that appearances can be deceptive.

### Listening for detail

**4**  3:16 Read the questions with the whole class. Students work with a partner to note down the answers to the questions. Play the recording as many times as necessary. Note that the terms *open account* and *letters of credit* are explained in exercise 5. Check answers with the whole class.

With lower-level classes, pause the recording after the answer to each question to give students more time to write.

#### ANSWERS:

1 Information and insurance.
2 There is information on over 50 million businesses worldwide, which allows N&H to provide information about financial performance, payment and possible problems.
3 They give a quick guide to how safely you can do business with a company or in a country.
4 70% of European firms, less than 5% of American firms.
5 Trading on open account with no need for letters of credit.
6 Between 0.25 and 1% of sales.

#### RECORDING SCRIPT

3:16

Interviewer: Mr Sullivan, Daryl Vincenti of Eisenhart Games recommends using a credit agency like yours. But can you tell us first what exactly credit agencies do?

JS: Well, basically, we offer a range of services in two main areas: information and insurance. Some of our clients are interested in information to help them manage credit risk, and others come to us for insurance. But many companies, like Eisenhart, need both information and insurance.

I: What sort of information can you provide?

JS: We have details of over 50 million businesses in countries all over the world. So, for example, we can help Daryl by telling him how businesses and countries in the Middle East are doing financially; we can tell him if his prospective customers pay, and how quickly they pay; and, in particular, we can warn him if one of his customers gets into financial difficulty.

I: And you give each company a rating which indicates how reliable they are?

JS: Yes, companies – and also countries – are given a rating. This gives us a quick guide to how safely you can do business with a particular company or in a particular country. Actually, there's much more than just the rating. Clients like Daryl receive detailed credit reports which help them decide if and how to work with different companies.

I: I see. Now, what about credit insurance? Is that something new?

JS: Well, it's relatively new over here in the States, but not in Europe. European companies have been using it for a long time. 70% of European companies use credit insurance, whereas in the States the figure is below 5%.

I: Why is that?

JS: Essentially because European firms have to export, because their internal markets are too small. Until now, the majority of American firms have done most of their business in America, so they didn't need credit insurance unless the customer was very risky. Nowadays, companies like Eisenhart need to export, so they're discovering the advantages of credit insurance. For example, it means that in Saudi Arabia, Daryl can trade on open account, with no need for letters of credit, which take a lot of time and are relatively expensive.

I: I see. Talking of expense, what does credit insurance cost?

JS: Well, of course, it depends on the contract. The more risk the insurer takes on, the higher the premium will be. But, on average, I would say, for international credit insurance, between 0.25 and 1% of sales.

## Reading for detail

**5** Give students a few minutes to put the methods of payment in order, then check answers with the whole class. Get students to give reasons for their answers, if they can.

**ANSWERS:**

[4] Open Account [1] Advance Payment [3] Bills for Collection
[2] Letters of Credit (L/Cs), also known as *documentary credits* (DCs)

## Discussion

**6** Students work with a partner. Check answers with the whole class. Students may have different answers, but should be able to give reasons for their choice.

**SUGGESTED ANSWERS:**

| | | | |
|---|---|---|---|
| 1 | Open account | 4 | Bill for collection |
| 2 | Bill for collection | 5 | Open account |
| 3 | Advance payment | 6 | Letter of credit |

**7** Students work with a partner. Remind them of the discussion in exercise 1 and the points raised in the article on page 97. Circulate and assist where necessary. Take whole-class feedback and make a list of problems and solutions on the board.

**SUGGESTED ANSWERS:**

Problems:
Different customer expectations, financing and producing to meet increased demand, transport, payment, currency exchange, pricing and margins, tax and VAT issues, managing agents / distributors, insurance.
Possible solutions:
Pricing – item might be too expensive for some markets and priced too low for others. Would need to check going rate of similar articles in individual markets and adjust pricing accordingly.
Transport – increased risk of damage to / loss of goods in transit – get insurance.
Problems with payment – could go for advance payment, etc.

## 8.2 Vocabulary

### International deals and payments

This module practises verb–noun collocations, phrasal verbs and other vocabulary to do with payments.

### Internet research

One definition of a *thesaurus* is that it is a list of words showing similarities, differences, dependencies, and other relationships to each other. It will include synonyms (words with the same meaning), antonyms (words with opposite meanings) and collocations (combinations of words that are used together). With care, a thesaurus can be used to broaden one's vocabulary and provide variety in one's writing.

Students could do this research before they do this module or as a follow-up activity when they have finished.

## Collocations

**1** Students complete the first part of this exercise individually or with a partner. Allow them to use dictionaries, if they wish. Circulate while they are working and assist where necessary. Check answers with the whole class.

**ANSWERS:**

| | | | | | |
|---|---|---|---|---|---|
| 1 | an invoice | 2 | goods | 3 | an application |
| 4 | conditions | 5 | a deal | 6 | a payment |

Then, ask students to pick out any collocations that are new to them or that they are unsure of, and review their meaning and use.

Do the second part of the exercise with the whole class, making two lists on the board under the headings: *Buyer* and *Seller*.

**SUGGESTED ANSWERS:**

1  the seller issues / the buyer queries / settles an invoice
2  the seller provides / loads / ships the goods
3  the buyer submits / the seller vets / approves an application
4  the buyer states / the seller meets / complies with the conditions
5  the buyer and seller negotiate / make / sign / a deal
6  the seller chases / the buyer makes / meets a payment

## Phrasal verbs

**2** and **3** Students work alone to do these exercises, then compare their answers with a partner. Check answers with the whole class by getting students to read the correct sentence aloud, followed by the definition.

**ANSWERS:**

Exercise 2
1  <u>Check up on</u> your new customer's creditworthiness.
2  <u>Take out</u> insurance if you have doubts about getting paid.
3  Do not let customers <u>get behind with</u> their payments.
4  <u>Chase up</u> invoices as soon as they become overdue.
5  Act quickly if your customer is <u>getting into</u> difficulties.
Exercise 3
a)  2 (take out)
b)  5 (getting into)
c)  1 (check up on)
d)  4 (chase up)
e)  3 (get behind with)

## Listening

**4** 🌐 3:17–3:21  With higher-level classes, play the five conversations straight through and get students to make notes on their answers.

With lower-level classes, pause after each conversation to allow students to decide on their answers.

Check answers with the whole class. Accept any reasonable answers, as long as students include the correct target vocabulary.

**SUGGESTED ANSWERS:**

1  A Slovakian company has submitted an application for credit.
   Bruno asks his colleague to check up on them.
2  They have to take out insurance to comply with the conditions in the contract.
3  Francesca's boss ask her to chase a payment from Kawasaki; she doesn't want them to get behind with their payments.
4  Mr Takahashi queries the invoice. He asks for more time to settle the invoice; the company seems to be getting into difficulties.
5  They talk about shipping goods, and finally reach a deal.

### RECORDING SCRIPT

🌐 3:17–3:21

1
A: Bruno, have you seen this letter from those people in Slovakia?
B: No, what do they want?
A: Well, they say they're ready to place a large order now if they can pay next year.
B: Well, you'd better do some research on the company. Make sure they can pay! But be discrete. We don't want to upset them.

2
C: I'm still worried about sending these parts by sea. They're quite fragile, you know.
D: Well, don't worry. We're meeting the insurance people tomorrow. If anything goes wrong, we'll be covered.
C: But the insurance premium will be expensive, won't it?
D: Probably. But we have to do it anyway. It's one of the conditions in the contract. No insurance, no deal.

3
E: Francesca, have we received a payment from Kawasaki?
F: No. And I've already sent two reminders.
E: Two? Listen, could you give them a call? If we're not careful, they'll be late every month, and I don't want to have the same problems we had last year.

4
F: So, could you send the payment as soon as possible, Mr Takahashi?
G: Well, it's just that there seems to be a small problem with your invoice. It's more expensive than we expected.
F: I'm sorry, Mr Takahashi, but the invoice is for exactly the same amount as our quotation, which you accepted.
G: Ah, yes. Well, exceptionally, as we are regular customers, could you perhaps wait two or three weeks? We just have a small cashflow problem at the moment. I'm sure you understand, Ms Trevi. It's nothing to worry about …

5
H: Well, we'll accept your terms providing you deliver direct to our factory.
I: Hm. Our customers normally collect the goods from the port of entry.
H: But you said yourself these parts are fragile, so surely it would be better for the same forwarder to deliver all the way to the door? That way there's less risk of damage.
I: Well, you have a point there, I suppose.

H: And this will be a regular order, so it means a lot of business for the forwarder. I'm sure you can negotiate good terms with them.
I: Yes. Yes, you're right. OK, then. It's a deal.

## Collocations

**5**  Do this as a whole-class activity, listing the collocations on the board. Make sure that you have listed the collocations needed for exercise 6.

**ANSWERS:**

credit line, credit terms, credit period, credit sales, credit card, credit insurance, credit policy
insurance claim, insurance policy, insurance sales
customer credit, customer loyalty, customer portfolio

**6**  Students complete the sentences individually. Check answers by getting students to read the complete sentences aloud.

**ANSWERS:**

1  customer loyalty
2  credit policy
3  insurance policy
4  customer portfolio
5  credit insurance
6  insurance claim

## Defining words

**7**  Student A's information is on the page so ask Student Bs to cover the crossword until they are ready to start.

To help students get started, do a few definitions with the whole class. Choose one of the terms in exercise 1, e.g. *negotiate a deal*, and give students a simple definition, e.g. *this means that two people or companies discuss things until they reach an agreement*. Students have to guess the term. Continue with one or two more terms, e.g. *vet an application*, *ship goods*, and get students to suggest definitions.

Students could use a dictionary or thesaurus to help them with any new words or phrases. While students are completing the crossword, circulate and assist where necessary.

When they have finished, get students to practise using the expressions by forming sentences of their own which include them.

**ANSWERS:**

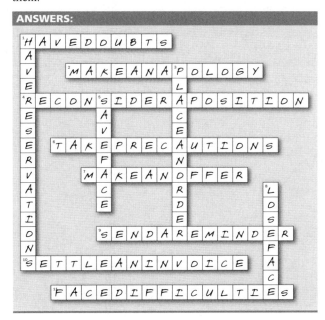

## FURTHER PRACTICE

Get students to close their books. Using some of the key words in this module, write a list of scrambled words on the board and get students to unscramble them, e.g.:

| | |
|---|---|
| *oeiivnc* | (invoice) |
| *napmyet* | (payment) |
| *rditec* | (credit) |
| *rdirmnee* | (reminder) |
| *oontiaemcpsn* | (compensation) |
| *mlaci* | (claim) |
| *lyocip* | (policy) |
| *olptfroio* | (portfolio) |
| *poverpa* | (approve) |
| *uniacenrs* | (insurance). |

When they have unscrambled the letters, get students to suggest collocations for them.

## 8.3 Grammar

### Prepositions

This module practises prepositions of time, verb + preposition and noun + preposition combinations in the context of international trade.

### Internet research

A search for "*how to become a millionaire*" will reveal several websites offering advice. The words that students choose will vary, but some possible answers might be *take control of, decide on, make good use of, be certain of, willingness to, the best strategy for.*

Students could do this research before they do the speaking activity in exercise 7 or after they have completed this module.

### Test yourself: Prepositions

**1** Start by reading the notes on prepositions in the *Refresh your memory* box with the class. Get them to make simple sentences using some of the phrases in the box.

Students work alone to complete exercise 1 and then compare their answers with a partner. Check answers with the whole class by getting individual students to read the sentences or parts of the sentences aloud. If students seem unsure of the prepositions or would like further practice, work through some or all of exercises 1–8 in the *Grammar and practice* section (page 132 of the Student's Book, answers on page 119 in this book).

**ANSWERS:**

| | |
|---|---|
| 1 | from |
| 2 | During |
| 3 | by |
| 4 | until |
| 5 | on |
| 6 | for |
| 7 | in |
| 8 | within |
| 9 | at |
| 10 | after |

**2** Follow the same procedure as in exercise 1. Check answers by getting students to read the complete sentence aloud. For further practice, students could complete exercises 9–11 in the *Grammar and practice* section (page 133 of the Student's Book, answers on page 119 in this book).

**ANSWERS:**

| | |
|---|---|
| 1 | about, no preposition |
| 2 | no preposition, to |
| 3 | on, on |
| 4 | in, to |
| 5 | no preposition, on |
| 6 | to, from |
| 7 | no preposition, to |
| 8 | for, for |

## FURTHER PRACTICE

To consolidate use of the prepositions, get students to group the verbs according to the preposition used, e.g.:

about: *hear about*
for: *apologize for, wait for*
from: *hear from*
in: *succeed in*
on: *insist on, comment on, rely on*
to: *look forward to, complain to, consent to, conform to*

Get students to explain the difference between *hear about* (you hear about something) and *hear from* (you hear from a person) and between *complain about* (you complain about something) and *complain to* (you complain to a person).

**3** Follow the same procedure as in exercise 1. For further practice, students could complete exercises 12–13 in the *Grammar and practice* section (page 133 of the Student's Book, answers on page 119 in this book).

**ANSWERS:**

1 International negotiators should always show <u>respect</u> for other cultures.
2 Transparency in all dealings with foreign governments is essential to <u>success</u> in export.
3 Exporters should remember that certain countries levy special <u>taxes</u> on imports.
4 Any <u>involvement</u> with illegal trading practices can permanently damage a company's image.
5 Late payment can have a very damaging <u>effect</u> on a company's cash-flow.
6 The seller's bank may have <u>access</u> to information about the buyer's credit-worthiness.
7 In a confirmed documentary credit, the seller's bank takes <u>responsibility</u> for obtaining payment.
8 Bills of exchange and letters of credit are no <u>substitute</u> for careful credit checks.
9 Credit ratings and reports are a practical <u>solution</u> to the problem of evaluating risk.
10 Credit insurance can eliminate the <u>need</u> for letters of credit.

## Listening for detail

**4** 3:22 Get students to read the schedule and try to predict the prepositions. In most cases, there is more than one possibility. Play the recording. Pause at appropriate places to allow students time to note down their answers. Check answers by getting students to say the complete sentence aloud.

**ANSWERS:**

2 by 6.30
3 at 23.10
4 not until 9.15 / at 9.15
5 at 7.30 or later
6 by 7.45
7 until Saturday
8 between tomorrow morning and Friday
9 on Saturday evening
10 before flying back / on Saturday
11 within three weeks
12 during the flight

## RECORDING SCRIPT

3:22

Paul: Oh, Jenny, did you pick up my tickets?
Jenny: No, I'm picking them up this evening. I have to be there before 6, so I'll be able to drop them off here by 6.30.
P: That's great! What time's the flight?
J: It's at 23.10. But it's OK – check-in doesn't open until 21.15. You've got plenty of time.
P: Hm. I've got the finance committee tonight. That usually goes on until at least half seven. I'll only just have time to go home and pick up my suitcase. I probably won't see the kids for a week now. They'll be in bed by quarter to eight. When do I get back from the States again?
J: On Sunday morning. You've got six meetings between tomorrow morning and Friday. That leaves you a day to visit New York, and you fly back late on Saturday evening.
P: Well, I don't think I'll have much time to visit New York. I've got the Merosom pitch to prepare for next Monday. I'm going to be jetlagged on Sunday, so I'll have to do it before flying back.
J: Oh, yes, that's right. When do you expect Merosom to announce their decision?
P: Well, they said within three weeks. By the way, have you got the files for the New York meetings?
J: Yes, they're all ready. Do want to look at them now?
P: No, I've got another meeting!
J: Well, you'll have to read them during the flight, then.
P: Hm. I suppose so.
J: OK. Well, I'll get on, then, unless you've got any other questions?
P: Er, yes, just one. When am I going to sleep?

## Dependent prepositions

**5** Students work with a partner. They should refer back to the earlier exercises to remind them of some of the prepositions. Check answers with the whole class.

**ANSWERS:**

1 agree ~~ask~~ consent refer (to)
2 comply sympathize ~~resort~~ associate (with)
3 vote pay allow ~~object~~ (for)
4 depend rely insist ~~attend~~ (on)
5 result invest ~~borrow~~ succeed (in)
6 suffer emerge hear ~~account~~ (from)
7 ~~discuss~~ apply look apologize (for)
8 consist ~~react~~ approve think (of)
9 access call ~~comment~~ tell (ø)
10 insure fight protect ~~conform~~ (against)

See next page for an extension activity on dependent prepositions.

## EXTENSION ACTIVITY

Divide the class into pairs and get each pair to draw two 3x3 grids, each one on a separate piece of paper like this:

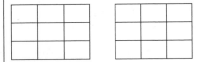

In the squares of one grid they should write nine verbs, and in the other grid nine prepositions, selected from the exercises in this module.

Collect all the completed grids and put the verb grids in one pile and the preposition grids in another pile. Mix each pile up and distribute them around the class so that each pair receives one of each.

The pairs see how many combinations of verb + preposition are possible from the words on the grids and make a list on a separate piece of paper. They can use their dictionaries to check their answers, if necessary.

When students cannot think of any more combinations (or you could set a time limit), they should pass their grids to the pair on their left and repeat the procedure again with a new pair of grids. They continue in this way until they have found 20 correct combinations. (You can adjust this total according to the level of your students or the time available.) The game stops when the first pair reaches this total. Circulate while students are working and check their answers.

Get the winning pair to read out their verb + preposition combinations.

## Listening for gist

**6** 3:23–3:32 Play the ten short dialogues. Allow students to choose the correct words and add the prepositions individually, before checking answers with the whole class. Get students to pick out the words or phrases they heard which helped them arrive at the answer.

With lower-level classes, do this as a whole-class activity. Give students a few minutes to check the meanings of the words, using their dictionaries or referring back to earlier exercises. Play one conversation at a time and get students to choose the best word from the box, adding the correct preposition.

To consolidate understanding, students work with a partner to produce similar short conversations to show the meaning of these expressions.

### ANSWERS:
1. investing in property
2. apologizing for saying something which upset someone
3. damage to a car
4. aptitude for languages
5. dependence on one customer
6. complying with regulations
7. insuring against non-payment
8. satisfaction with results
9. not hearing from Taiwan
10. access to data

## RECORDING SCRIPT

3:23–3:32

**1**
A: It seems to me that with interest rates so low, property is still a better choice than the stock market.
B: Yes, you're right. I think a small flat in the town centre should give a good return.

**2**
C: I think you should talk to her. She's still upset.
D: OK, OK. I'll call her and tell her I'm sorry. I didn't mean what I said.

**3**
E: What state is it in after the accident?
F: Well, it could have been worse. Apart from a broken windscreen and headlights, there are only a few scratches on the paintwork. I was lucky.

**4**
G: It's amazing. She already speaks seven different languages, and she's picking up Chinese really fast!
H: Yeah, some people just have a gift, I guess.

**5**
I: You desperately need to get some more contracts. Relying on just one big firm is so dangerous.
J: Yes, I know. But we've always done most of our turnover with them.

**6**
K: The Americans are much more demanding. The food and drug administration are terribly strict. But if you want to sell in the States, there's no other way.
L: Yes, there's no choice. We'll have to adapt the product to their norms.

**7**
M: What if we deliver the goods, but they don't pay?
N: Well, we have a policy which covers that risk. For a small percentage of the value of the goods, we will guarantee to pay you if the customer defaults.

**8**
O: Well, sales are up 300%, we've reduced costs, our stock price has almost doubled and shareholders are delighted! Everything's worked out perfectly!
P: Yes. It doesn't get any better than this.

**9**
Q: Have you had any news from Taiwan?
R: No, not a word. It's strange. Usually they're in touch at least once a week.

**10**
S: Hey, Terry. Have you changed the passwords? I can't get into the database!
T: No, I'm having the same problem. I've tried everything, but the system won't let me in.

## Speaking

**7** Read the instructions with the whole class, including the instructions at the back of the book to make sure that students understand what to do. Each group should then choose one of the topics to discuss, or you could allocate a topic to each group.

Circulate while students are speaking and assist where necessary. Make a note of any mistakes in the target language for remedial teaching later.

Higher-level classes or groups who finish early could repeat the activity using a different subject and/or by choosing different words to put on another six slips of paper.

## 8.4 Speaking

## Negotiations – diplomacy

This module explores the intercultural aspects of negotiating style and practises ways of using language diplomatically in negotiations to achieve a successful outcome.

### Internet research

The anthropologist, Edward T. Hall, describes what are known as high- and low-context cultural factors. In a high-context culture, many contextual elements help people to understand the rules of society. In a high-context culture, meaning is not always put into words, and, for example, non-verbal clues will be as important. As a result, a lot of things are taken for granted. This can be confusing for people outside the culture who do not understand these 'unwritten rules'.

In a low-context culture, very little is taken for granted. Meaning is made explicit and put into words. This means that more explanation is needed, but there is also less chance of misunderstanding, particularly for people from outside the culture.

'Chronemics' is the term given to cultural attitudes towards time. In a monochronic culture, time is tightly controlled and measured. Punctuality is seen as a virtue and careful planning and scheduling are common. Monochronic cultures tend to be low context. In a polychronic culture, time is regarded more flexibly; meetings may not start on time and there is less concern for getting things done according to a schedule. Polychronic cultures tend to be high-context.

It would be best if students did this research before they start this module as it provides useful input for exercises 1–4.

## Discussion

**1** Read the information in the box with the whole class. If students have limited experience of these countries or regions, do this exercise with the whole class, encouraging them to share experiences they have from business trips, holidays, reading, etc.

Get students to describe the kind of culture they live in, according to the descriptions in the box and the information they found in their Internet research.

### SUGGESTED ANSWERS:

China H, USA L, Australia L, N Europe L, Middle East H, Latin America H, UK L, Japan H

The following scale is suggested in GLOBALWORK: Bridging Distance, Culture, And Time by Mary O'Hara-Devereaux and Robert Johansen

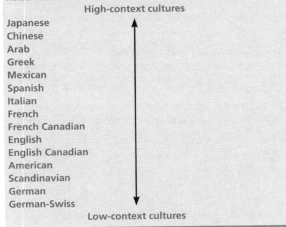

High-context cultures

Japanese
Chinese
Arab
Greek
Mexican
Spanish
Italian
French
French Canadian
English
English Canadian
American
Scandinavian
German
German-Swiss

Low-context cultures

## Listening for gist

**2** 🌐 3:33–3:35 Play each extract one by one, getting students to note down what went wrong in each case. Check answers by getting students to give you at least one cultural factor and one example of a phrase which might have caused difficulties. Higher-level classes could also be asked to say how the individuals might have felt at the end of the conversation.

### ANSWERS:

1 They fail to understand each other's different cultures regarding time and decision-making.
2 Frau Meier does not understand that Amal does not share her concern for deadlines and pushes Amal into an extreme position.
3 Misunderstandings lead to conflict, made worse by the use of undiplomatic language.

## RECORDING SCRIPT

🌐 3:33–3:35

1
A: I'm afraid I think we might need more time to explore all the implications, and perhaps to include some of our senior management in the discussions.
B: Look, Mr. Yamada, I've already been here a week, and I have a plane to catch this evening. If you don't want to do this deal, just say so! I mean, when I get back, I have to tell my boss we have a contract, or explain why I failed to get one!

2
C: We feel there are still quite a large number of difficulties to face in this project, and these will take a very considerable amount of time and money to resolve.
D: OK, Amal, let's sit down and work out a schedule.
C: I am not sure that at this stage a schedule is appropriate, in view of the considerable, er, cultural differences between our companies.
D: Well, we need to start work soon if we want to meet the deadlines.
C: Frau Meier, perhaps we should talk again in a few days, by telephone?
D: Are you saying you're quitting the project?!
C: If you insist on putting it in those terms, then, yes, I think probably that is best.

3
E: And you pay the shipping costs.
F: No, as I told you, our prices are ex works. You pay for shipping.
E: So you don't want to sell us your machine tools?
F: No, why do you say that? I never said that!
E: Your terms with Auckland Industries last year included shipping, I believe.
F: Yes, but that was a much larger contract.
E: So our order is not very important for you?

**3** 🌐 3:36–3:38 Play the recordings and get students to listen for the ways in which the negotiators changed their language and approach in order to avoid misunderstandings, e.g. they use less direct language and a less confrontational approach.

### ANSWERS:

This time they check and correct misunderstandings and reformulate their positions; in this way they are able to defuse potential conflict.

## RECORDING SCRIPT

🔊 3:36–3:38

**1**

A: I'm afraid I think we might need more time to explore all the implications, and perhaps to include some of our senior management in the discussions.

B: Uh-huh. Yamada-san, correct me if I'm wrong, but you seem to be saying that you're not completely convinced by this deal.

A: I'm afraid there seems to be a slight misunderstanding, Mr Bryson. Let me put it another way. We are as enthusiastic about this deal as ever, but here in Japan, it is very important to take the time to consult everybody, and to be sure there is a consensus.

B: Ah, yes, I understand. It's important for me to keep my Board informed too.

**2**

C: I'm afraid we feel there are still quite a large number of difficulties to face in this project, and these will take a very considerable amount of time and money to resolve.

D: OK, Amal, have I got this right? You're saying that you're not sure we have the time or the money to make this project a success?

C: That's right. Especially in view of the considerable, er, cultural differences between our companies.

D: So, would I be right in saying that you are considering withdrawing from the project?

C: No, I'm sorry, Sabine, that isn't quite what I meant. What I was trying to say was, we need to take our different approaches to these problems into account, but I'm sure we can find solutions.

D: Yes, I'm sure we can. Perhaps we should talk again in a few days, by telephone?

C: Yes, that would be fine.

**3**

E: And if I've understood correctly, you will pay the shipping costs.

F: I'm sorry, perhaps I haven't made myself clear. The price we quoted was ex works. But we can quote including shipping if you like.

E: But didn't you say you would give us the same terms as for Auckland Industries last year?

F: Ah, I see, yes. Well, allow me to rephrase that. What I meant was, we would be very happy to give you the same terms as Auckland, if you were in a position to order the same volume.

## Listening for detail

**4** 🔊 3:36–3:38 Play the recordings again, pausing if necessary to allow students time to complete the phrases. Check answers with the whole class. Get students to repeat the phrases, using the appropriate pronunciation, stress and intonation.

**ANSWERS:**

1  Correct me if I'm wrong, but you seem to be saying that …
2  I'm afraid there seems to be a slight misunderstanding
3  Let me put it another way
4  Have I got this right?
5  Would I be right in saying that …
6  I'm sorry, that isn't quite what I meant …
7  What I was trying to say was …
8  If I've understood correctly …
9  Perhaps I haven't made myself clear.
10  Allow me to rephrase that.
11  What I meant was …

## Diplomatic language

**5** Do this as a whole-class activity. Get one student to say the direct statement and another to say the matching diplomatic statement. Make sure students use appropriate stress and intonation in the diplomatic statements. Play 🔊 3:36–3:38 again so that students can hear the diplomatic statements in context.

**ANSWERS:**

1  b)   2  d)   3  a)   4  c)

**6** Do this as a whole-class activity. Get students to review the phrases in exercises 4 and 5 to help them complete the summary.

As preparation for exercise 7, get students to identify the characteristics of the direct language, e.g. short sentences, absence of qualifiers or softeners, unambiguous messages.

**ANSWERS:**

Diplomatic language often uses:
modal verbs like *could, would, might, should*
softening adverbs like *maybe* or *perhaps*
qualifiers like *a bit, rather, a little* or *quite*
introductory warnings like, *I'm sorry, actually, I'm afraid*
(negative) questions rather than statements.

**7** Students work with a partner. Remind students to use the features of direct and diplomatic language they have practised. Circulate and assist where necessary. Check answers by getting students to read out the statements they have written, using appropriate stress and intonation. Accept any reasonable answers.

**SUGGESTED ANSWERS:**

| Direct | Diplomatic |
|---|---|
| 1 I don't want to risk going to Columbia for a meeting. | I'm sorry, but wouldn't it be easier for everybody if we held the meeting here rather than in Columbia? |
| 2 If you don't want to do business, just say so! | Perhaps you feel that it's a little too soon to formalize our relationship, if not everybody is convinced? |
| 3 You must be able to make a better offer than that. | Actually, I was wondering whether you might possibly reconsider your position? |
| 4 So you don't want to sell us your products? | Do you perhaps have some reservations about doing business with my company? |
| 5 If you people can get out of bed earlier we'll actually get some work done! | I'm sorry, but couldn't we start a little earlier than 11 tomorrow? We might find we would make a bit more progress. |
| 6 That's not true. I never said that! | I'm afraid I don't remember actually using those words. |
| 7 Look, I know lots of people think business trips are essential, but mostly they're a waste of time. | To be perfectly honest, I'm inclined to think that business trips aren't quite as essential as everybody says they are. |
| 8 So you don't trust us to pay? | You wouldn't have doubts about our ability to pay our debts, would you? |

## Negotiating

**8** With lower-level classes, read the instructions with the whole class and elicit from them the kinds of things they might want to negotiate about. You could also remind students of the work they did in Unit 5 on bargaining in negotiations and the value of trying to reach a win-win conclusion.

While students are speaking, circulate and assist where necessary. Check that they are using the target language appropriately.

Allow students time to prepare and practise their conversation. Then take whole-class feedback. Ask what students agreed to do. Get one or more confident pairs to present their conversation to the rest of the class.

Alternatively, with higher-level classes, get one or two pairs to do their negotiating in real time, i.e. without preparing it beforehand. The rest of the class listens and comments on the performance and the outcome, giving two things that worked successfully and two things that could be improved.

## 8.5 Writing
### Requests and reminders

This module explores formal and informal language use in the context of correspondence to do with payments.

**Internet research**

A search for *factoring receivables* will reveal that this is one way companies can improve their cash flow. For a fee, a factor provides a business with an advance payment based on their accounts receivable and invoices. The factor then waits to collect payment on the invoice and accepts any risks attached to it. This allows the company to get the cash flow and working capital it needs, without having to wait. Many businesses use factoring, among other things, to generate instant working capital; to help them predict and manage cash flow; and to increase sales by offering customers competitive extended credit terms.

Students could do this research as a follow-up to the work done in this module.

### Discussion

**1** Encourage students to give reasons for their answers, and to add any stories or anecdotes of their own to illustrate their answers. Take feedback from the whole class.

### Reading and analysis

**2** Read the instructions with the whole class. If necessary, explain or elicit the meanings of the four terms.
Students do the exercise with a partner. Check answers by getting students to give you the number of the email and the phrases that helped them decide.

**ANSWERS:**

a request 4   a reminder 1   a refusal 2   a final demand 3

**3** Students work with a partner. They can use their dictionaries to check any unknown words. Check answers with the whole class by getting students to read the sentences aloud and to tell you in what kind of correspondence it would be found.

To check that students have fully understood these formal sentences, get them to rephrase them in a less formal style, e.g. (1) *Could you extend credit terms of 60 days?*, etc.

**ANSWERS:**

1 I am writing to enquire whether you would be able to extend credit terms of 60 days.
2 I am afraid group policy does not allow us to give more than 30 days' credit.
3 We are pleased to agree to the terms you propose.
4 May I remind you that the sum of €21,552 is still outstanding?
5 We wrote to you on November 4 regarding the balance of €12,650 which is still outstanding.
6 Would you let us know your decision as soon as possible?
7 We would appreciate your early settlement of this outstanding balance.
8 We shall have no alternative but to pass the matter on to our legal department.

a request 1, 6   a reminder 4, 7   a refusal 2
an agreement 3   a final demand 5, 8

**4** Do this exercise with the whole class. Get students to read out the more formal phrase or sentence.

**ANSWERS:**

| 1 a) | 2 b) | 3 b) | 4 a) |
| 5 b) | 6 a) | 7 a) | 8 a) |

**5** Students work with a partner to complete these emails. Remind students to check that they have the correct spelling of the words they use. Circulate while students are working and assist where necessary. Check answers by getting students to read the complete emails aloud.

**ANSWERS:**

1
In view of the increase in our volume of business, I am writing to enquire whether you would be prepared to extend credit terms of 60 days.
Would you let us know your decision as soon as possible?

2
With regard to your request for improved credit terms, I am afraid that group policy does not allow us to extend more than 30 days credit.

3
Further to your email of 17 July, we are pleased to agree to the terms you propose, and we look forward to receiving your order.

4
May I remind you that the sum of €101,000 is still outstanding on your account.
We would appreciate your early settlement of this outstanding balance.

5
We would like to apologize for the delay in sending the enclosed cheque. This was an unfortunate oversight due to circumstances beyond our control, and we can assure you that it will not recur.

6
We wrote to you on 11 April regarding the balance of €15,550 which is still outstanding.
Unless we receive payment within seven days, we shall have no alternative but to pass the matter on to our legal department.

a request ☐1  a reminder ☐4  a refusal ☐2
a final demand ☐6  an apology ☐5  an agreement ☐3

---

**FURTHER PRACTICE**

Get students to rephrase the emails in exercise 5 in a less formal, but still polite way.

---

## Writing

**6** Give students a few minutes to read the instructions so that they can see the context for the correspondence they will write. Then get each student to read part 1 of their instructions.

While students are writing the first email, circulate and assist where necessary. Remind students to check what they have written for the best choice of vocabulary and formality of language before they deliver their correspondence. They should refer back to the exercises in this module if they need help.

With higher-level classes you could set a time limit for each phase of the correspondence.

---

When students have finished, get them to group each set of correspondence, i.e. three sets of four pieces of writing, and review them. Did they use and maintain an appropriate level of formality? Were there any grammatical errors? Are there any parts they could improve?

---

**EXTENSION ACTIVITY**

This activity practises some useful money idioms. Write the idioms and their explanations on the board in random order and get students to match them. The idioms and the explanations are given below:

| Idiom | Explanation |
|---|---|
| loaded | have a lot of money |
| hard up | don't have much money |
| nest egg | money that someone has saved |
| on a shoestring | with very little money to spend |
| pay through the nose | pay a high price for something |
| tighten your belt | live on less money than usual |
| ready cash | money that is available to spend |
| spend money like water | spend too much |

Once students have correctly matched the idioms and explanations, they can be used in various ways, e.g.:
- one student says the idiom, another says the matching explanation
- one student gives the explanation, another says the matching idiom
- students work with a partner or small groups to make short dialogues which include the idiom
- students pick an idiom and describe a situation which illustrates it.

Ask students if similar money idioms exist in their own language; get them to translate them into English and explain them.

---

# 8.6 Case study

## Jeddah Royal Beach Resort

This case study explores issues to do with credit and cash flow at an international resort hotel. Students practise writing letters to customers about credit facilities.

### Internet research

An Internet search for *collecting debt* will provide information on how to recover debts, including how to act within the law to contact a debtor; what to do if a debtor disputes the debt or refuses to pay; how to go about taking legal action. Students will also find websites for debt collection agencies who, for a fee, will undertake to recover debts on behalf of clients from debtors all over the world and who will provide legal advice if the client needs to pursue a debt through the courts.

Students could do this research before they start this module or after they have finished it, as a follow-up task.

## Discussion

**1** Do this as a whole-class activity. Make a list of the ideas on the board or get a student to do it.

## Reading for detail

**2** Students read the article silently and answer the questions, then compare their answers with a partner. Check answers with the whole class. You could also ask students to consider the disadvantages of an in-house credit card for customers (e.g. it encourages them to spend more than they can afford; they lose track of how much they have spent; they don't pay attention to how much things cost).

**ANSWERS:**

1 Giving credit develops customer loyalty and makes it easier for customers to spend freely on the hotel's additional services.
2 To develop customer loyalty to their hotel or group and to avoid paying commision to credit card companies
3 It's easier to make bookings, it speeds up check-in and check-out, there are no exchange problems, no need to carry cash.
4 Credit Manager of the Jeddah Royal Beach Resort: his responsibilities include vetting applications, credit control and debt recovery.

## Listening for detail

**3** 3:39 Read the instructions aloud. Get students to look at the database records and predict what the conversation is going to be about.

Play the recording through once so that students can complete the database entries. Check answers by getting students to form sentences, e.g. *Ms Koepple works for Cool Breeze, a record company. Her company credit rating is unknown. She doesn't have a current credit limit*, etc.

**ANSWERS:**

Customer: Ms Koepple
Company: Cool Breeze, record company
Company credit rating: good / average / poor / <u>unknown</u>
Current credit limit: 0
Credit limit requested: $20,000
Notes: very friendly, wants to organize a big conference for executives

Customer: Mr Kobayashi
Company: Kobayashi Auto Sales
Company credit rating: <u>good</u> / average / poor / unknown
Current credit limit: $50,000
Credit limit requested: $100,000
Notes: difficult, unpleasant, Frederick doesn't trust him

Customer: Mrs Saman
Company: Black Nile
Company credit rating: good / average / <u>poor</u> / unknown
Current credit limit: $30,000
Credit limit requested: $100,000
Notes: charming old lady, very influential

## RECORDING SCRIPT

3:39

Frederick: Good evening, Riaz!
Riaz: Oh, hello Frederick. Everything OK?
F: Yes, fine, thanks. I just wanted to give you these applications, if you've got a moment?
R: Yes, of course. Have a seat.
F: Thanks.
R: OK, so what have we got here?
F: Well, first of all, there's Ms Koepple in room 406. She's with Cool Breeze. It's a record label based in Buenos Aires. Now, I know you don't like record companies, but …
R: Yes, Frederick, and you know very well why I don't like record companies and those vulgar rock groups they send us, always causing damage and disturbing the other guests: Argentina, you say?
F: Yes. But Ms Koepple says they want to organize a big conference for their executives. There won't be any rock groups or that kind of thing, just corporate executives. So, they're applying for our credit card.
R: Well, it's true we need to develop in the conference market. It's good business, and it often brings in more business by word of mouth. But Argentina … OK, leave it with me and I'll look into it. How big is Ms Koepple's bill?
F: Well, she's been here for four nights. Leaving on Saturday. She's spending a lot of money – maybe six thousand dollars so far. But she's very nice, very friendly. I'm sure she won't leave without paying.
R: Hm, she's applying for a credit limit of twenty thousand. Let's keep an eye on her, anyway. Let me know if her account goes over ten thousand dollars, OK?
F: Sure.
R: What else have you got there?
F: The next one is Mr Kobayashi from Tokyo. Remember him?
R: Oh, yes. The second-hand car salesman?
F: Yes. He's a really difficult customer. We've had to move him to a different room three times this week because he didn't like the view, or it was too far from the restaurant …
R: Well, he may be difficult, but his credit's good. He seems to have built himself quite an empire over there. Kobayashi Auto Sales is doing very well. We've never had any problem with his people.
F: Well, I wouldn't buy a car from him. He never looks you in the eye, never smiles, never says thank you. He wants us to raise his credit limit, but I don't trust him.
R: Let me see. From fifty up to a hundred thousand, eh? All right, I'll think about it.
F: Right. And this last one is our old friend Mrs Saman and her

team from Egypt.

R: Oh, no. Are they still coming here? I thought we stopped their credit last year.

F: No, the company paid up in the end, remember?

R: Yes, I do now. Charming lady, of course, but that company – what's it called? Black Nile, that's it. They invented the concept of the slow payer! I think it took 18 months to get them to pay their last invoice. What does she want now?

F: Well, she wants us to raise their credit limit to a hundred thousand, too.

R: Oh, no way!

F: But there are ten of them this time, and she's such a wonderful little old lady!

R: I should really suspend their credit and insist on cash in advance. They're on, let's see … (types on keyboard) thirty thousand dollars. It's just too big a risk. Have you seen the latest cash-flow figures? Our customers are taking longer and longer to pay, and uncollectibles have gone over 3%! I'm getting a lot of pressure from management to take firm action.

F: Well, be careful: Mrs Saman told me yesterday that her brother is a very senior government official. And remember, we have a lot of guests from Egypt now. We don't want to upset them.

R: Yes, that's true. You never know who Mrs Saman might talk to. She's a very influential old lady. All right, leave it with me, Frederick. I'll let you know what I decide tomorrow.

**4** Read the questions aloud. Students try to answer them, on the basis of what they remember from the first listening. Play 3:39 again. Pause if necessary to allow students to note down their answers. Check answers with the whole class.

**SUGGESTED ANSWERS:**

1 Because they are vulgar, cause damage and disturb other guests.
2 About $6,000
3 $10,000
4 Because he has changed rooms three times.
5 He never looks you in the eye, never smiles, never says thank you.
6 The hotel almost stopped their credit because they took 18 months to pay.
7 Mrs Saman's brother is a senior government official; they are both influential in a country which is an important market for the hotel.

## Discussion

**5** Do this as a whole-class activity. You could remind students of the work they did in Unit 7, and encourage them to use some of the vocabulary they practised there, e.g. *fall, drop, jump, rise*, etc.

With lower-level classes you may need to remind students of adverbs which can be used to describe the nature of the change, e.g. *rapidly, slightly, significantly, sharply*. These were practised in Unit 7.

**ANSWERS:**

1 decreasing rapidly
2 increasing slightly
3 increasing significantly
4 increasing sharply

**6** Give students a few minutes to discuss the three questions. In question 3, review the situation for each of the three customers by looking at the database entries in exercise 3. Students should also take into account the circumstances surrounding each customer and the likelihood of further business mentioned in the conversation.

Students could listen to the conversation again or read it in the recording script on page 147 in their books. Circulate and assist where necessary. Take whole-class feedback.

**SUGGESTED ANSWERS:**

1 Cash payments are decreasing; this is probably the price of the hotel's policy of offering credit cards to encourage customer loyalty.
Credits of less than 4 weeks are only increasing slightly; almost 40% of customers pay within 30 days of reception of their invoices.
Longer credits are increasing significantly, perhaps because a number of (larger?) customers are taking advantage of a competitive market to exploit the hotel's credit policy and pay more and more slowly. The increase in uncollectibles suggests some poor decisions have been made in allowing credit to unreliable customers.

2 The hotel could improve its cash flow by:
• reducing credit to existing customers
• avoiding giving credit to new customers
• vetting customers more carefully before giving credit
• paying suppliers more slowly
• invoicing more quickly
• giving discounts for cash payments
• using a debt collection agency
• factoring (selling invoices to a factor or agent in return for cash – the factor collects payment for the invoices and accepts any credit risk attached to them).

## Writing

**7** Remind students of the language they practised in module 8.5, i.e. the level of formality required in this kind of correspondence; the useful phrases in exercises 3 and 4 that they could reuse.

Students write a first draft, which they exchange with another student for feedback. When they are reading each other's drafts, students should check for grammar, spelling, appropriate use of language, and a clear message. Circulate while students are writing and assist where necessary.

Students then revise their texts using the feedback. Display the finished texts on a table or on the wall so that students can read them all. If you wish, get them to choose the best two or three letters and give reasons for their choice.

# Review 7 and 8 answers

## Review 7

(page 108 in the Student's Book)

### 7 Mergers and acquisitions

**1**

1 due diligence
2 liabilities
3 merger
4 acquisition
5 variable costs
6 fixed costs
7 assets
8 liquidity
9 economies of scale
10 turnover

**2**

1 variable costs
2 fixed costs
3 liquidity
4 liabilities
5 turnover

**3**

1 climb
2 dip
3 fluctuate
4 stabilize
5 deteriorate
6 slide
7 rise
8 soar
9 jump
10 peak

**4**

1 considerable
2 dramatic
3 moderate
4 sharp
5 significant
6 slight
7 sudden

**5**

because of / due to / thanks to / as a result of

**6**

1 we're going to enter
2 you'll
3 I'm meeting
4 I'll

**7**

1 let's move on
2 next slide shows
3 notice from the chart
4 seem to suggest
5 as a result of
6 resulted in
7 However
8 whereas

## Review 8

(page 109 in the Student's Book)

### 8 International trade

**1**

1 Don't sell on price rather than quality.
2 Be proactive with local distributors.
3 Make a firm commitment to export.
4 Think outside the box.
5 Trade on open account.
6 Sign an exclusive deal.
7 Be prepared to modify product specifications.
8 Invest time, effort and money.
9 Ask a credit agency about a customer's creditworthiness.
10 Chasing payments can be done by the credit agency.
11 Focus on one market, rather than trying to sell all over the world.
12 Don't assume that what works in your domestic market will also work abroad.

**2**

1 creditworthiness
2 chasing

**3**

1 ~~reach~~
2 ~~assume~~
3 ~~chase~~
4 ~~state~~
5 ~~check in~~
6 ~~move behind with~~

**4**

1 reach
2 ship
3 issue
4 comply with
5 chase
6 get behind with
7 check up on

**5**

1 During
2 In
3 from
4 until
5 within
6 at

**6**

1 Let me put it another way.
2 Correct me if I'm wrong, but you seem to be saying that you are not convinced.
3 I'm afraid there seems to be a slight misunderstanding.
4 Perhaps I haven't made myself clear.
5 Would I be right in saying that you want to withdraw from the project?

**7**

1 I think we might need more time.
2 I'm afraid there are still quite a large number of difficulties.
3 Perhaps we should renegotiate one or two parts of the contract.
4 Won't that be rather expensive?

**8**

1 According to
2 now overdue
3 early settlement
4 outstanding balance
5 Further to
6 regret to inform
7 have no alternative
8 pass this matter

**9**

1 overdue
2 outstanding

**10**

outstanding

# Grammar and practice answers

116 *The* **Business**

## 1 Corporate culture

(page 118 and 119 in the Student's Book)

**1**

past simple: said, happened, recognized, was, had, saw, didn't mention
past continuous: was doing, was working, was filling in, was entering
past perfect: had asked, had given, had applied for, hadn't found out

**2**

You use the <u>past perfect</u> to show that one event happened before another.
You use the <u>past continuous</u> to describe an activity in progress that gives the background to the main events.
You use the <u>past simple</u> to describe the main events of the story.

**3**

1 was revising / called
2 didn't hear / was reading
3 saw / was talking
4 was working / met

**4**

3 (we only know by the context)

**5**

1 got / had already worked
2 had just finished / called
3 was / hadn't seen
4 hadn't met / listened

**6**

1 finished / had finished
2 had already started
3 was / had been
4 had bought

**7**

1 b)    2 c)    3 a)

**8**

2 (return to a previous subject)

**9**

actually = in fact
after that = the next thing that happened was
apparently = it seems that
eventually = in the end
obviously = of course

**10**

1 was working
2 had just left
3 was serving
4 hadn't arrived
5 came
6 asked for
7 wanted
8 took
9 was sitting
10 placed
11 had never been
12 saw
13 was
14 had become

**11**

1 from *One day* to *naive*
2 from *Anyway* to *my life*
3 from *Of course* to *them all*
4 from *But, even today* to *that day*

**13**

1 You should t̶o̶ do it today.
2 You ought <u>to</u> do it today.
3 He should̶s̶ do it today.
4 D̶o̶ ̶I̶ ̶s̶h̶o̶u̶l̶d̶ Should I do it today?

**14**

1 You should speak …
2 You must speak …

**15**

1 apply
2 applying
3 to apply
4 apply

**16**

1 That sounds like a good idea.
2 That might be worth trying.
3 I'm not sure about that because …
4 No, that's not a good idea.

## 2 Customer support

(page 120 and 121 in the Student's Book)

**1**

| | |
|---|---|
| Present simple | <u>Do</u> you work there? |
| | <u>Does</u> she work there? |
| Present continuous | <u>Are</u> you working there now? |
| | <u>Is</u> he working there now? |
| Past simple | <u>Did</u> you work there before? |
| | <u>Did</u> she work there before? |
| Past continuous | <u>Were</u> you working there then? |
| | <u>Was</u> he working there then? |
| Present perfect | <u>Have</u> you ever worked there? |
| | <u>Has</u> she ever worked there? |
| Past perfect | <u>Had</u> you already worked there? |
| | <u>Had</u> she already worked there? |
| Modals | <u>Would</u> you work here next year? |

Rule:
You form *yes/no* questions using:
auxiliary verb + subject + main verb

**2**

1 Did you buy
2 Do you have
3 Have you tried
4 Are you sitting
5 Will you reinstall

**3**

1 Yes, I do.
2 Yes, I am.
3 No, I didn't.
4 No, I haven't.

**4**

1 How much does
2 Why are
3 how far will
4 How do
5 what will

**5**

1 What
2 Which
3 Which
4 What

**6**

1 d)
2 c)
3 b)
4 a)

**7**

1 Who did you meet
2 Who met you
3 Who spoke
4 What did he speak

**8**

1 I wonder if I could <u>possibly</u> leave a few minutes early today?
2 a) grateful
  b) appreciate

**9**

1 b)
2 a)
3 d)
4 c)

**10**

1 of course
2 certainly
3 sure

**11**

1 c)
2 a)
3 b)

**12**

Actually / To be honest

**13**

1 b)    2 e)    3 c)    4 d)    5 a)

**14**

1  You mustn't do it.
2  You have to do it.
3  You don't have to do it.

**15**

1  don't have to
2  mustn't
3  have to
4  mustn't
5  don't have to
6  have to

## 3 Products and packaging

(page 122 and 123 in the Student's Book)

**1**

1  an / a / a
2  the / the / the
3  - / - / -

**2**

1  a
2  the
3  no article

**3**

1  a / the
2  the / a
3  the / an
4  a / the

**4**

1  - / the
2  The / -
3  - / the
4  - / the

**5**

1  FedEx is an international company that / which operates in the transportation business.
2  Charlie Wang is a dynamic man who / that runs the New China Packaging Company.

**6**

Here is the package we designed last week.

**7**

You can leave out *who*, *which* or *that* in a defining relative clause if they are followed immediately by a pronoun or noun.
You must keep *who*, *which* or *that* if they are followed immediately by a verb.

**8**

1  These are the views of the consultants whose report was used by the government.
2  Look at this article about that German manufacturing company whose production was outsourced to Slovakia.

**9**

2  ✓
4  ✓

**10**

A non-defining relative clause simply adds extra information.
In a non-defining relative clause you use commas around the clause.
In a non-defining relative clause you cannot leave out who or which.
In a non-defining relative clause you cannot use *that*.

**11**

2  task force / focus group
3  sales forecast / hearing aid
4  market leader / stock control
5  price range / customer feedback

**12**

1  product design team
2  action film hero
3  staff development strategy
4  computer software engineer
5  customer feedback program
6  bridge construction project

**13**

2  a nice-looking action film hero
3  a long-term staff development strategy
4  a self-employed computer software engineer
5  a web-based customer feedback program
6  an over-budget bridge construction project

## 4 Careers

(page 124 and 125 in the Student's Book)

**1**

1  d)
2  c)
3  b)
4  a)

**2**

1  Do you work on Saturdays? / No, luckily I don't work on Saturdays.
2  Are you going for an interview today? / No, I'm not going today – the interview is tomorrow.

**3**

1  comes / is coming
2  have / am having

**4**

1  am doing
2  have
3  check
4  is staying
5  am waiting
6  do

**5**

1  The soup tastes delicious!
2  The soup is boiling. ✓
3  Sorry, I'm not following you. ✓
4  Sorry, I don't understand you.
5  What are you saying? ✓
6  What do you mean?
7  This book belongs to me.
8  This book is selling for €15 on Amazon. ✓
9  Please don't interrupt me – I'm doing a grammar exercise. ✓
10  This grammar exercise is easy – I know all of the answers.

**6**

1  c)
2  b)
3  a)

**7**

The present perfect has several uses, but it shows that the speaker is looking back from the present to the past.
The present continuous has several uses, but it shows that a present action or situation is temporary.
The present simple has several uses, but it shows that a present action or situation is permanent.

**8**

1  since
2  for
3  during
4  for
5  many years ago

**9**

for: used with periods of time; used with the past simple and present perfect; answers the question 'how long?'.
during: used with periods of time; used with the past simple; answers the question 'when?'.
since: identifies the point an event began; used with the present perfect.
ago: used to say how far back in the past something happened; used with the past simple.

**10**

1  just
2  already
3  yet
4  ever
5  never

**11**

When you talk about people's experiences up to now, you use the present perfect or present perfect continuous.
When you focus on the action itself, not the result, you use the present perfect continuous.
When you focus on the result, not the action, you use the present perfect.
When you say *how many* you use the present perfect.

**12**

1 have been sending off / haven't had
2 have sent off / have been applying
3 has just received / has failed

**13**

1 went up
2 have gone up
3 go up
4 have worked
5 worked
6 work

**14**

1 want
2 applied
3 have been waiting
4 have decided
5 am sleeping

## 5 Making deals

(page 126 and 127 in the Student's Book)

**1**

1 b)
2 c)
3 a)
4 a)

**2**

1 Sentence a) is called the zero conditional and the time reference is general.
2 Sentence b) is called the first conditional and the time reference is future.
3 Sentence c) is called the second conditional and the time reference is future.

**3**

1 If we continue talking, I'm sure we'll find a compromise.
2 If I agree to that price, can you sign today?

**4**

1 b)
2 c)
3 a)

**5**

The first conditional refers to a likely event in the future. In the *if* clause you use any present tense (simple, continuous or perfect) and in the main clause you use *will* or other modals or the imperative.

**6**

1 I'll
2 we might be able to
3 I should be able to

**7**

When the *if* clause comes at the end, you leave out the comma in writing.

**8**

1 S
2 D
a) uncertainty
b) certainty

**9**

1 Unless
2 If
3 If
4 Unless

**10**

1 Unless we leave now, …
2 Unless he agrees to our terms, …

**11**

1 a)
2 d)
3 c)
4 b)

**12**

1 If I was the boss of this company, I would improve communications by having regular meetings.
2 If we paid a 50% deposit now, would you reduce the price to €25,000?

**13**

The expressions *providing, provided, as long as* and so long as all mean if and only if. They emphasize the condition. They have a second conditional form, so they are followed by a verb in the past simple.

**14**

1 I suggest we to buy the cheaper model.
2 I recommend it that we have a short break.
3 I advise that you to look again at the figures.
4 What do you suggest me?
5 I recommend you not parking here.

## 6 Company and community

(page 128 and 129 in the Student's Book)

**1**

1 a)
2 b)
3 b)
4 A lot of illegal immigrants were employed last year.

**2**

1 b)
2 a)
3 d)
4 c)

**3**

ending 1 makes a better link

**4**

1 Car parts are made here.
2 The river is being polluted.
3 The law was obeyed.
4 I have been offered the job.
5 Fake goods were being sold.
6 This policy can be changed.
7 We might be fined.
8 This will be decided later.

**5**

1 The environment has been put at the centre of our future planning.
2 The idea of corporate social responsibility was introduced by Johnson & Johnson.
3 The elevator is serviced every week.
4 The elevator was serviced last week by that guy with the crazy look in his eyes.
5 A hundred new employees are being hired this month.
6 My flight was delayed.
7 My flight was delayed by a major security alert involving 80 Chechnian terrorists.
8 The environment must be protected.

**6**

A terrible gas leak occurred in Bhopal in 1984 – it seems that the disaster was caused by an act of sabotage.

**7**

1 e)
2 b)
3 c) and d)
4 a)
5 g)
6 f)
7 h)

**8**

1 ✓
2 ✓
3 ✓
4 ✓

**9**

She said that they'd give me their answer today.

**10**

1 She said that she would do that.
2 She told me that she would do that.
3 She said to me that she would do that.
4 She asked me what I would do.
5 She asked me if I would do that.
6 She asked me what I was doing.
7 She asked me when I would arrive.

**11**

2 She announced that they were stopping all production.
3 He reassured me that they had fitted new filters.
4 She replied that they could do absolutely nothing.

## 7 Mergers and acquisitions

(page 130 and 131 in the Student's Book)

**1**

1 b)　2 a)　3 e)　4 c)　5 d)

**2**

'Good morning, ladies and gentlemen. I've called this press conference because of the rumours circulating in the media about our M&A strategy. Over the next few years our bank <u>will</u> become a major player in Central Europe, and naturally we <u>will</u> look at strong local banks as possible targets for acquisition. But we <u>won't</u> make any decisions until we have studied the market carefully. There has been much comment about possible job cuts, but I want to reassure you that the staff of a bank are amongst its most valuable assets. When we do make a move, there <u>won't</u> be significant job losses at the bank we acquire. In any case, we <u>will</u> deal with this issue at the time, and I have no further comment to add now.'

**3**

1 There <u>will probably</u> be significant job losses.
2 There <u>probably won't</u> be significant job losses.

**4**

1 b)
2 e)
3 a)
4 c)
5 d)

**5**

1 d)
2 b)
3 e)
4 a)
5 c)

**6**

1 prediction
2 plan
3 prediction
4 plan

**7**

1 Citibank are going to make a bid for Tatra Banka.
2 We're not going to have enough time.

**8**

am flying / are coming / are giving

**9**

1 are going to make
2 will probably start
3 I'll come back
4 we're going to go

**10**

1 it will definitely
2 it's almost certain to
3 it's likely to
4 it might
5 it might just
6 there's not much chance it will
7 there's no way it will

**11**

1 There's a <u>good</u> chance the merger will go ahead.
2 The merger will <u>definitely</u> go ahead.
3 The merger <u>definitely</u> won't go ahead.
4 The merger might <u>just</u> go ahead.
5 The merger is <u>almost</u> certain to go ahead.
6 It's <u>highly</u> likely the merger will go ahead.
7 We <u>fully</u> expect the merger to go ahead.

**12**

1 T
2 F ('could not' means 'it is impossible')
3 T

## 8 International trade

(page 132 and 133 in the Student's Book)

**1**

1 at / after
2 from / until
3 on
4 by
5 for / during
6 within

**2**

1 ~~by~~
2 ~~at~~
3 ~~during~~
4 ~~While~~
5 ~~During~~
6 ~~In the last year~~
7 ~~Last year~~

**3**

1 lunch
2 the summer
3 the morning

**4**

1 Ø
2 Ø
3 Ø
4 Ø
5 Ø
6 Ø

**5**

1 by
2 until
3 until
4 By
<u>until</u> means 'up to'
<u>by</u> means 'on' or 'before'

**6**

1 on time
2 in time
3 in time
4 on time
<u>in time</u> means 'with enough time'
<u>on time</u> means 'at the right time'

**7**

<u>in the end</u> means 'eventually' or 'finally'
<u>at the end</u> refers to the last part of something
<u>by the end</u> means 'at' or 'before the end'
<u>towards the end</u> means 'near the end'
<u>at last</u> shows pleasure because something happens that you have been waiting for

**8**

1 S
2 S

**9**

1 e)
2 c)
3 d)
4 a)
5 b)
6 g)
7 j)
8 f)
9 h)
10 i)

**10**

1 complained to / apologized for
2 rely on / hear about
3 conform to / succeeded in
4 insist on / look forward

**11**

1 invest in
2 consists of
3 comply with
4 depends on
5 insure against
6 apply for
7 suffer from
8 agree with

**12**

1 in
2 for
3 for
4 to
5 with
6 on
7 for
8 on
9 to
10 for

**13**

1 involvement
2 substitute
3 ratings
4 dealings
5 damaging
6 levy
7 tax
8 credit-worthiness

# Additional activities

## Speaking: Qualities of a good manager

**Type of activity:** Ranking activity followed by a presentation activity. Students have to substantiate why they think certain managerial qualities are more important than others.
**Preparation:** Make one photocopy of page 121 for each group of two or three students. Cut each sheet into 14 strips.

1   Ask students to write down at least four key attributes of a good manager.
2   Students then take it in turns (working in pairs or in groups of three) to say *one* necessary attribute each, without repeating what anyone else has said. For example:
   Student A: *A good manager can be trusted.*
   Student B: *A good manager is always fair.*
   They should continue until they can't think of any more to add.
3   Give out the ranking exercise, cut up into strips. In pairs or threes, students select the top five most important attributes and order / prioritize these, justifying their choices to each other. Tell students they can make short notes about what is decided, but that they should not write down the sentences word-for-word.
4   A representative from each group then reports back to the whole class, giving clear justifications for their top three choices. Encourage students to give two justifications for each choice, for example:
   *A good manager needs to have a good sense of humour, as humour can be used to calm down awkward situations. It also creates a positive working environment, which in turn can make the company more effective.*
5   Ask students which managerial attributes they think they possess at present, i.e. would they make good managers?

## Reading: New bosses, new rules

**Type of activity:** Information exchange. Half the class reads one text and the other half reads another. Students then exchange information with a partner who did not read the same text as them.
**Preparation:** Make enough photocopies of page 122 for half of the class. Cut the photocopies in half.

1   Elicit ways in which inequalities manifest themselves at work (pay differences, holidays, treatment by boss in terms of work allocation, etc). Also elicit possible reasons for inequalities (gender, age, etc.). Pre-teach a few words such as: *undermine(d), suspicious, anxious, unjust, outraged, deteriorate.*
2   Give half of the class the text about Catherine (*Text A*) and the other half, the text about Vincent (*Text B*). They will both need to make notes in a grid format. Write this up on the board or make it into a hand-out without the answers in grey.
3   Ask students to read their texts alone or with another student who is reading the same text and complete their part of the grid. Circulate and assist where necessary.
4   Then ask students to work with a partner who read the other text and to exchange information orally and complete the rest of the grid. Make sure that the initial texts are covered, and that they only use their grids and memory.

|  | Details of employee (age, name, job) | Problems met at work and why (the unwritten rules) | The employee's personal reaction | Steps taken by them | Consequences |
|---|---|---|---|---|---|
| Text A | Catherine Albery, 29, manager of small graphics company | New boss gave more interesting work to her colleagues; she didn't see eye to eye with him; didn't get any recognition; felt it was because of being a woman; very competitive work culture. | She felt undermined and lost interest in her work. | She resigned. | She now has a job in a smaller company where company culture suits her better. |
| Text B | Vincent Prior, 49, office manager | Colleagues who'd joined the company many years after him were receiving much better benefits. Created a culture of suspicion and he felt the company culture favoured younger employees. | Very angry. Felt it was unjust. | He resigned even though risky at his age. | He found a less well-paid job in a smaller company where a culture of trust is encouraged. |

5   Ask students to tell you / each other what they would have done if they were Catherine or Vincent.
6   For homework, get students to read their partners' texts. They should make a record of new words and phrases.

✂

**A good manager is able to listen effectively.**

**A good manager is able to keep calm under pressure.**

**A good manager is able to motivate employees.**

**A good manager is able to see the whole picture, not just the detail.**

**A good manager has good ideas and vision for the company.**

**A good manager prioritizes equality and transparency between staff.**

**A good manager has a good sense of humour.**

**A good manager has a wealth of experience and expertise.**

**A good manager has good qualifications.**

**A good manager commands respect.**

**A good manager is relatively young.**

**A good manager is able to prioritize and focus effectively.**

**A good manager is able to identify talents in each of his/her employees, and exploit them appropriately.**

**A good manager delegates effectively.**

*The Business Intermediate Teacher's Book* © Macmillan Publishers Limited 2007. This page may be photocopied and used within the class. *The* **Business**

# Text A

Catherine Albery, 29, was working in a well-paid position as an assistant manager in a large printing company, when she started to feel that things were going wrong. Although she had been reasonably happy at her place of work for over six years, a new boss meant great changes. 'I realized that I was working at least as hard as my male equivalents, and certainly wasn't getting the same recognition.' Her new boss then started to assign the more interesting and innovative work to her colleagues. Catherine began to feel undermined and her commitment to the job started to wane.  After discussing the issue with her line manager, she talked to her boss directly and things improved slightly for a few months. However, soon after, the situation deteriorated further.

'I just knew that I was never going to see eye to eye with my boss. He just didn't like me for some reason. I am sure it was because I am a woman – he questioned my loyalty. I simply didn't have the energy to fight.' Feeling completely disillusioned, Catherine resigned from her post last spring, and was unemployed for six months. She was eventually offered a position as manager in a small graphics company and has not looked back since. Working for a smaller company, being in the position of decision-maker, has turned out to be a very positive move for her. She works shorter hours, and does not feel the need to prove herself all the time, or compete with colleagues.

Catherine looks back positively at the events of the last year. 'As a manager, I have made a self-pledge to listen to my employees; to treat them with equality and fairness; to create a very positive culture in the workplace. I feel this experience has made me into a better manager, and arguably a better person!'

# Text B

Ironically, it was at his firm's Christmas party that Vincent Prior, 49, discovered that he was being treated unfairly, after being employed by the company for 17 years. He was the office manager in a leading car rental company, and found out in casual conversation that his younger colleagues of a similar position were all receiving far greater benefits.  These ranged from a slightly larger Christmas bonus to longer holidays. In one case, a colleague had been given a very substantial pension plan, considerably larger than the average. These had all been introduced since the arrival of a new boss, 12 months earlier.

'I was absolutely outraged,' he said. 'One sits in the same open-plan office with these people, works the same long hours and to similar deadlines.  These managerial decisions seem totally unjust and encourage suspicion between colleagues.' Vincent was convinced that the cause was due to age differences.  The next working day, Vincent went to speak directly with his manager. He was informed that his colleagues were new to the company, and that the various benefits had been part of their initial packages. In recognition of Vincent's good work, his manager promised to reappraise some of Vincent's own benefits.

'At that point, something just snapped inside me,' said Vincent. 'I decided I couldn't work in a culture like that any more.' After considering the issue very carefully, he decided not to take his case further, but simply to resign. Realizing that this was a very risky decision at his age, he was understandably anxious. However, immediately after resigning, he was fortunate enough to meet an old friend who was able to offer him a similar post in his own small company, a company which hires out heavy-duty gardening machinery. Although his new job is slightly less well-paid, he is now working in an environment of trust. 'All in all, I feel very positive about what happened. These events have made me re-assess what is important in my working life.'

## 2 Customer support   Teacher's notes & answers

### Speaking: Difficult, but important customers

**Type of activity:** Roleplay.
**Preparation:** Make enough photocopies for each pair to have one roleplay situation. Cut each sheet into the four roleplays.

1   To introduce the topic, ask students what they think 'the customer is always right' really means (even when the customer is wrong, sometimes companies and services have to agree with them to maintain the company's reputation in the community).
2   Write the four roleplay situations on the board, i.e. the names of the two roles in each case. Ask pairs to choose which one they would like to do. Warn students that the 'customer' in each case is fussy, and makes some rather strange requests. Pre-teach *fussy*.
3   Distribute the role cards.
4   Allow students to read their cards and remind them of key points, e.g. if they are not sure what the customer actually wants / means, they should ask for clarification. Remind students about making polite requests and promising help (see 2.4 in the Student's Book). You could also remind students how to complain in a reasonably polite manner by writing these phrases on the board:
    *I'm afraid I wasn't too happy with the ...*
    *I was rather surprised to see ...*
    *I was disappointed to find ...*
    *Could you tell me why ...*
    *Personally, I feel that ...*
5   While students are doing their roleplay, circulate and make notes of any points for remedial teaching.
6   When they have finished, each pair can then do a different roleplay and swap roles – i.e. a different person plays the customer.

### Reading: A letter of complaint

**Type of activity:** Reading comprehension.
**Preparation:** Make one photocopy of page 125 for each student.

1   To introduce the topic, ask students which broadband services they use / know of and what their main advantages are, e.g. speed. Ask if they, or anyone they know, have had any problems.
2   Ask students to read the first paragraph quickly to find out why Patricia Henry is writing. (She wanted to change from a 'normal' Internet service, Anytime, to a broadband service.) You may need to pre-teach a few words like: *cancel a contract, authorization, authorize (v), reimburse, incur, gender, conflicting information.*
3   Ask students to read the letter then work through the exercises with a partner. Circulate and give help where needed.

**ANSWERS:**

**1**
1   the first paragraph
2   the rest of the letter apart from the last two paragraphs
3   the penultimate paragraph
4   the last paragraph

**2**
1   for speed
2   for unknown technical reasons
3   technical support supervisor
4   £59.96 + £152.68 = £212.64
5   yes
6   because the cancellation had come from an overseas call centre and this was not therefore valid
7   money back; apology; the company to do something about the customer service problems

**3**

| Noun ( thing) | Noun ( person) | Verb |
|---|---|---|
| cancellation | - | cancel |
| advice | adviser | advise |
| authority | authorizer | authorize |
| inconvenience | - | inconvenience |
| acceptance | - | accept |
| reimbursement | - | reimburse |

4   As a follow-on task, or for homework, you could ask students to reply to the letter, having brainstormed some ideas for the content, as well as the starter sentence(s), in class. Decide as a class what Hoorah's position is first, i.e. are they going to give in to the requests or not ? Will there be a compromise?

## Roleplay A

**Student A: Unreasonable guest in hotel**
*Situation*:
You have been staying in this 5-star hotel for 6 days. You are a regular guest here.
*Complaints*:
- You do not like having cream-coloured towels in your room.
- You can't see the sun rise from your room (though you can see the sun set).
- The mini-bar does not stock your favourite brands of water / whisky / crisps.
- You don't like the music in the lift.

Speak to the receptionist or manager and make your complaints. You feel very strongly about these aspects.

## Roleplay A

**Student B: Hotel manager**
You are about to speak to an important guest, who frequently stays at your hotel. However, he/she is very fussy. Remember that the customer is always right! Try to remain calm and helpful at all times.

## Roleplay B

**Student A: Unreasonable traveller on an airplane**
*Situation*:
You are travelling on a long-distance flight. You regularly travel with this airline and always go business class.
*Complaints*:
- You want to sit next to the window (though you did not book a window seat).
- You would like a larger TV screen.
- You are sure that there is slightly less leg-room than normal.
- You would like a fresh set of earphones every time you use them.

Speak to one of the in-flight crew and make your complaints. You feel very strongly about these aspects.

## Roleplay B

**Student B: In-flight crew member**
You are about to speak to an important traveller, who frequently uses your airline and stays in business class. However, he/she is very fussy. Remember that the customer is always right! Try to remain calm and helpful at all times.

## Roleplay C

**Student A: Unreasonable customer in a restaurant**
*Situation*:
You are having lunch with some business colleagues at a top-class restaurant. You eat here regularly.
*Complaints*:
- You prefer cloth napkins to paper ones.
- The other customers are very noisy.
- Your favourite dish was not on the menu tonight.
- Your coffee was too hot – it burnt your tongue.

Speak to the head waiter and make your complaints. You feel strongly about these aspects.

## Roleplay C

**Student B: Waiter**
You are about to speak to an important guest who regularly dines at your restaurant, and who often brings business colleagues. However he/she is very fussy. Remember that the guest is always right! Try to remain calm and helpful at all times.

## Roleplay D

**Student A: Unreasonable events manager**
*Situation*:
You have organized a conference on human resources at a high-class conference centre. However, there are aspects of the centre and its facilities that you are not satisfied with. You decide to complain to the conference centre manager after the event.
*Complaints*:
- The water for delegates was sparkling, not still.
- The soap in the bathrooms was not perfumed.
- You did not like the waitresses' uniforms.
- The spaces in the car-park were very narrow.

Speak to the conference centre manager and make your complaints. You feel very strongly about these aspects.

## Roleplay D

**Student B: Conference centre manager**
You are about to speak to the events manager from an important firm. They held their annual conference at your centre this year, and you are hoping to retain their custom for future years. However, he/she is very fussy. Remember that the client is always right! Try to remain calm and helpful at all times.

## 2 Customer support   Reading

38 Heath Road
High Wycombe
HP18 8LM

Hoorah Customer Care
Hoorah UK plc
PO Box 486
Rotherham
S63 5ZX

20th February 2007

Dear Sir / Madam

Customer: Patricia Henry
Username: pathen.fsworld.co.uk
Tel: 01494 586290

Re: Claim for reimbursement and compensation

I am writing to complain about the poor service and inconvenience I have suffered and the expenses I have incurred in trying to terminate my contract with Hoorah Broadband.

In September 2005, I changed from Hoorah Anytime to Hoorah Broadband, having decided that I wanted a faster Internet service. However, I was unable to get a reliable broadband connection, for unknown technical reasons. For several months I tried to go back to my original service, Anytime. After spending at least 50 hours trying to resolve the problems, including numerous, lengthy phonecalls to technical support, my Hoorah Broadband contract was finally cancelled on 8th February 2006.

As I was unable to make use of the Broadband service from 9th October 2005 to 8th February 2006, I expect to be reimbursed for that period. This amounts to four months at £14.99, totalling £59.96.

In addition to this, I expect to be compensated for the considerable costs incurred by me in (a) contacting technical support and (b) using the pay-as-you-go 'Dial-up service' to connect to the Internet as I was unable to use the broadband service. The two Dial-up charges amount to £140.20 and the technical support phone charges amount to £12.48, making a total of £152.68. I enclose copies of my telephone bills for this period.

I would also like to express my extreme dissatisfaction with your customer services department. I was originally told by patient and polite technical support staff that there was indeed no technical solution and that we could therefore break the contract. When I contacted Customer Services, however, the man I spoke to at this point was extremely rude and aggressive. He said that the technical support officer who had authorized the cancellation was 'in the overseas call-centre' and 'had no authority' to do this. I was told that I should have asked to be put through to a UK-based call centre when phoning about Hoorah Broadband contracts. He ended the conversation without any warning, hanging up on me!

It is unacceptable to be given conflicting information by your employees and to be dealt with in such a rude manner. It is also unacceptable as a customer to be expected to know which call-centres to contact for certain matters. This is not effective 'customer service'.

I have been shocked and angered by the attitude of Hoorah in refusing to release me at an earlier stage from a service that was not functioning and was causing me considerable inconvenience. I have also been totally dismayed by the unwillingness of a major company such as yours to adhere to basic customer service policies and attitudes. As a consequence, I intend to take the matter up with consumer rights groups, if necessary.

I look forward to a positive response from you regarding the reimbursement detailed earlier in this letter, as well as to receiving an apology. I would also like you to consider and act on the facts mentioned in relation to your company's customer service problems.

Yours faithfully
Patricia Henry

**1** Skim read the text. Which paragraphs contain: 1) the summary of events; 2) the details of the events and the customer's demands; 3) a summary of the customer's feelings about the events; 4) the customer's overall demands.

**2** Answer the following questions.

1 Why did the customer want to change to Hoorah Broadband initially?
2 Why was it not possible to switch to Hoorah Broadband?
3 Who said that she could cancel the contract initially?
4 What is the total amount that the customer wants to be reimbursed from Hoorah?
5 Was the service from the technical support staff satisfactory?
6 Why did the customer service adviser say that the authorization for the cancellation of the contract was not valid?
7 What three steps does the customer want Hoorah to take in response to her letter?

**3** Complete this table.

| Noun (thing) | Noun (person) | Verb |
| --- | --- | --- |
| | - | cancel |
| | | advise |
| authority | | |
| | - | inconvenience |
| | - | accept |
| | - | reimburse |

## Speaking: Compound adjectives

**Type of activity:** Pelmanism. Revises and introduces more compound adjectives.
**Preparation:** Make enough photocopies of page 127 for one set of cards between each group of three students. Cut each sheet up into a set of 24 cards.

1   Ask students to work in groups of three. Shuffle the 24 cards in each set and give each group a set.
2   Get students to match the two halves of each compound adjective. New compound adjectives that are not in the Student's Book are: *long-lasting, hard-wearing, cost-efficient*. The first two are different in form as they are actually adjective + adjective. Clarify the meaning and form of the new ones at the end of the matching activity, if necessary. Make sure that students match the correct ones for this activity – there are one or two other possibilities in some cases, e.g. *water-saving, child-proof*, but if students match these, the game will not work!
3   Students then re-shuffle the cards, and spread them out onto the desk – word-side down. Students take it in turns to turn over two cards, one at a time. If they do not match, they turn them back over, face down, slowly enough for the other two players to see the two upturned cards and try to remember where they are. Then the next player does the same. If the two cards turned over match e.g. *labour + saving*, then the player keeps that pair if they can name one thing that could be described by the compound adjective they have 'won', e.g. *A washing machine is a labour-saving device*. If they give a noun which team members deem to be inappropriate, they lose that pair and have to turn them face down again onto the desk. If the example is correct they have another turn.
4   The player with the most pairs wins.

## Reading: Warm as toast

**Type of activity:** Reading comprehension
**Preparation:** Make one photocopy for each student.

1   To introduce the topic, ask students how they find out weather forecasts.
2   Write *Use your loaf* on the board. Ask students what they think this means, and draw attention to the double meaning of 'use your loaf' (use your loaf of bread – literal; use your brain – figurative, colloquial British English).
3   Ask students to read the text then do exercise 1.

| ANSWERS | | | | | | |
|---|---|---|---|---|---|---|
| **1** 1 b) | 2 a) | 3 a) | 4 c) | 5 c) | 6 c) | 7 a) |

4   Before doing exercise 2, allow students to re-read the text and think of some possible responses, as if they were Robin. Ask students to work with a partner and to take turns asking and answering the questions.
5   A possible extension task is to ask students to give a presentation based on this toaster (see page 39 in the Student's Book). This could be written as homework, embellished as appropriate with their own ideas.

| | | | |
|---|---|---|---|
| energy | saving | labour | saving |
| cost | efficient | water | resistant |
| hard | wearing | shock | proof |
| child | resistant | tamper | resistant |
| fool | proof | eye | catching |
| attention | grabbing | long | lasting |

# Forget your eggs sunny-side up or even clouds in your coffee … use your loaf!

THOSE keen for a glimpse of the morning weather forecast could soon be examining their breakfast toast.

Design student Robin Southgate 5 has come up with a toaster that burns the day's weather into each slice. Perfectly browned and emblazoned with a shining sun, cloud or raindrops, every one 10 tells a weather story. (And tastes delicious with butter and jam.) The toaster prints the symbols on the toast using stencils that mask part of the slice while the rest continues 15 to be toasted. When the bread is first inserted into the toaster, it is browned in the normal way. But in the last 20 to 30 seconds, an electric motor inside rolls out the appropriate 20 stencil in front of the bread. 'It works with brown, but best with white,'

advised Mr Southgate, who is in his final year at Brunel University in London. But how does his toaster 25 know whether the day will pop up as hot as the breakfast bacon or as soggy as scrambled egg? To find out the weather, the toaster uses an in-built modem, a gadget normally 30 used by computers to process data from the Internet. Using a telephone line, the modem connects to 23-year-old Mr Southgate's personal computer which, in turn, connects to 35 the Met Office website. A software program on his computer then interprets the weather details. It can tell which area of Britain the toaster is in by the telephone code. If the 40 local forecast is for rain, for example, the computer sends a message to the toaster to release the cloud and

raindrop stencil. Mr Southgate, who developed his toaster under 45 the guidance of tutor Professor Stan Swallow, is keen to spread each slice with even more information. He is experimenting with an array of heating elements that can create 50 a much more detailed design on the bread. This could be used to stencil on elaborate weather maps or advertising logos. He can even envisage a day when breakfast toast 55 becomes textfast toast, popping up with mobile phone messages. Mr Southgate, however, is not optimistic that his toast will replace a quick look at the paper, TV news or even 60 out the window for the weather.

'I did it because it was an interesting challenge,' he said. 'There is no practical application for it.'

---

**1** Read the text then choose a), b), or c) to complete these sentences.

1 Robin Southgate is _____ student.
   a) an engineering     b) a design     c) a physics
2 The gadget has _____ possible weather symbols.
   a) three     b) five     c) seven
3 The symbol is burned on to the toast _____ the toast is browned.
   a) while     b) before     c) after
4 The gadget works with _____ types of bread.
   a) white     b) brown     c) both
5 The toaster uses _____ to function.
   a) its own in-built software     b) a battery     c) a modem
6 The toaster can tell where you are in Britain by _____.
   a) an in-built global-positioning device     b) pre-recorded instructions     c) using the telephone code
7 Robin thinks that his toaster _____.
   a) is fun, but of little use in real life     b) could be better than the TV or newspaper forecasts
   c) could be as good as the TV or newspaper forecast

**2** Respond to these questions, as if you were Robin:

1 Why did you decide to invent this?
2 Where did the idea come from?
3 Was it an enjoyable project for you, and why?
4 What other things have you invented?
5 Do you think this gadget might have some potential in certain markets, e.g. overseas?
6 What did your family think of your achievement?
7 Where do you see yourself in 15 years' time?

## 4 Careers  Teacher's notes & answers

### Speaking: Quirky jobs

**Type of activity:** Roleplay. Students roleplay a radio interview about having an unusual job.
**Preparation:** Make enough photocopies of page 130 for each student to have a role card. Cut out the role cards.

1  Give one or two examples of unusual jobs, particularly from your own experience, e.g. someone you have met. Ask students to tell you about any unusual jobs they know of.
2  Write the four job titles from page 130 on the board, checking any vocabulary as necessary. Be prepared to change the jobs slightly, to fit in with the local context more if necessary. Ask students to choose just one job that appeals to them.
3  Tell students they are going to take part in an interview for a radio programme, *Quirky ways to earn a living*, that interviews people with unusual jobs.
4  Give students the rolecard for the job they have chosen and ask them to read the information carefully, helping with any difficult vocabulary. Give students a set amount of time (at least 10 minutes) to a) complete the missing parts with their own ideas, using their imagination; b) consider how to make whole-sentence answers in each case; c) consider what the questions will be. Break these stages up, as appropriate.
5  Ask students to work with a partner and take turns to play the role of the interviewer. Explain that interviewers will have to use full questions. If necessary, ask pairs to orally make the prompts on the cards into full questions, e.g. *Where do you work?* and take quick class feedback on this.
6  Say or write the following starter on the board:
   *Interviewer: Good morning and welcome to our weekly programme,* Quirky ways to earn a living. *Here in the studio today is (name) , a (job) from (place).* Also remind interviewers that they need to respond appropriately to the responses, either with appropriate exclamations or back-channelling devices (*uh uh, right,* etc.) or by asking further questions. If necessary, model the start of an interview with a confident student, with you playing the interviewer.
7  While students are doing the roleplay, circulate and make a note of any problems for remedial work after the activity. When they have finished the first interview, students work in pairs (or threes, with two interviewers), and carry out the interview. When they have finished, students change roles.

### Reading: Book reviews

**Type of activity:** Scan reading and comprehension.
**Preparation:** Make one photocopy of page 131 for each student.

1  To introduce the topic, tell students that the books are all related to job-hunting. If possible, show an example of a similar type of book. Tell students that they were reviewed orally by two new graduates, as well as a careers adviser. This was then placed in the 'Jobs' section of a national newspaper, to help graduates choose. Check students know the meaning of *blurb* (information about a product printed on its packaging – e.g. the back cover of a book – to make it sound interesting and worth buying).
2  Ask students to work through the exercises individually then to check their answers with a partner before you take whole-class feedback.

**ANSWERS:**

| | | | | | | | | | | | | |
|---|---|---|---|---|---|---|---|---|---|---|---|---|
| **1** | 1 | book E | 2 | book B | 3 | book D | 4 | book C | 5 | book A | 6 | book C | 7 book B |
| **2** | 1 | book C | 2 | books B & D | 3 | book A | 4 | book A | 5 | book E | | |

3  Ask students if they would like to read any of the books. Ask them to discuss their choice with a partner and to explain why.
4  For an additional language-focused activity, ask students to select and categorize adjectives used to describe the books, e.g. *invaluable, accessible*, as positive or negative.
There are also numerous examples of compound adjectives such as: *thought-provoking, touchy-feely, user-friendly*. Students could record these, with the example sentence and include a note on style and use. For example:
Style: *touchy-feely* is more commonly used in spoken / informal English.
Use: *thought-provoking* could be applied to a book, a film, etc.

## A Toy designer

- *Where work?*

- *Experience / training?*
  Art college as a student; worked as a graphic designer for a small company

- *Length of time in this particular job?* 14 years

- *Biggest challenges?*
  Coming up with new ideas, trying to widen the market beyond Europe; developing exciting designs for a range of age groups (0-2 year olds, 3-4 year olds, etc.)

- *How got into the job?*

- *Most enjoyable aspects of the job?*

- *Greatest achievement?*

- *Any negative aspects?*

- *Job prospects / plans for future?*

## C Hat designer

- *Where work?*

- *Experience / training?*
  Fashion college, Paris; apprenticeship to established hat makers.

- *Length of time in this particular job?* 12 years

- *Biggest challenge(s)?*
  Coming up with different ideas suitable for different occasions; being diplomatic with 'clients', i.e. if they want a style which does not suit them.

- *How got into the job?*

- *Most enjoyable aspects of the job?*

- *Greatest achievement?*

- *Any negative aspects?*

- *Job prospects / plans for future?*

## B Crocodile breeder

- *Where work?*

- *Experience / training?*
  Learnt from father and grandfather on their farms.

- *Length of time in this particular job?* 11 years

- *Biggest challenge(s)?*
  Controlling the larger animals, particularly the males; security.

- *How got into the job?*

- *Most enjoyable aspects of the job?*

- *Greatest achievement?*

- *Any negative aspects?*

- *Job prospects / plans for future?*

## D Tatooist

- *Where work?*

- *Experience / training?*
  Art school for a year then trained with professional tatooist for 18 months. Father was a doctor.

- *How long in this particular job?* 7 years

- *Biggest challenges?*
  Some of the designs customers want are very difficult to get right; some customers want their tatoos on delicate areas such as eyelids!

- *How got into the job?*

- *Most enjoyable aspects of the job?*

- *Greatest achievement?*

- *Any negative aspects?*

- *Job prospects / plans for future?*

## 4 Careers  Reading

**A**
*Is this it?*
Isabel Mirth, 2005  £9.99
Blurb: *'This is a life-changing book, giving several accounts of people who have gone on the voyage of self-discovery, and found new, fulfilling paths to follow.'*
Shirley Miller (SM), careers adviser: 'For me, this book was rather annoying in terms of the style. It was over-romanticized. However, there were one or two stories that moved me, particularly the one about the high-powered businessman who turned to small-time chicken-farming.'
Sarah Rupert (SR), university graduate: 'I thought this was a really thought-provoking read. I read it as I was going to bed at night, as it made me feel really positive and ready to face new challenges. In this way I think it could help you indirectly. It was inspiring.'
Paul Lees (PL), university graduate: 'I found this interesting, but I'm not convinced it's really useful for new graduates. Perhaps it would be more suited to people going through a mid-life crisis! The way the book is written is not to my personal taste – it's almost like a story for a film, a book on miracles, it's too much.'

**B**
*Finding a job that's perfect for you*
Jemima Pannell, 2005–2006 edition
£12.99
Blurb: *'If you want to know how to find out your talents and then the ideal career for you, then read this book.'*
SM: 'This is a user-friendly and practical book for young people who don't know which direction to take. By getting you to list and mind-map your strengths and talents, you can come to a fuller understanding of yourself. The list of resources is useful too.'
SR: 'I found this helpful and very accessible. It's really practical and gives several concrete ways to help to know yourself.'
PL: 'There were lots of quizzes, ticklists and surveys and I thought this was a really practical approach to this area. It really helped you to see the wood for the trees in terms of knowing yourself and where you should start to focus.'

**C**
*Staying cool*
Michael L. Bolinger, 2006    £7.99
Blurb: *'This is a book crammed full of handy tips for how to relax before and during an interview, and also in the first few days of a new job.'*
SM: 'This book is probably useful for some. It's certainly packed full of different ideas. However, I personally found the area too 'touchy-feely' and emotional. It's like yoga for job-seekers, but also includes lots of practical tips such as what food to eat before an interview!'
SR: 'I didn't really go for this one. It's just not me. It assumes that everyone is practically a nervous wreck before an interview, and that isn't necessarily the case.'
PL: 'This was an unusual book, and I think it's a new take on this area. However, it's not my thing really. I can't really see myself using any of the calming techniques, except for the breathing.'

**D**
*How to do brilliantly at interview*
Clark Lowess and Pamela Smythe, 2005
£8.99
Blurb: *'This pocket-sized book is invaluable for job-hunters. You'll wonder how you survived without it.'*
SM: 'This is a great little book, with some very useful suggestions. It could really help graduates feel confident before an interview if they learnt some of the possible responses and sentence starters.'
SR: 'I loved this book! The examples are easy to work with. Obviously you have to adapt the answers to your own situation, but this book saves you a lot of work and energy, trying to guess what might come up.'
PL: 'This was an engaging read and it could be very useful at the interview stage to certain people. After reading this, you'd actually want to get some difficult questions, so that you could show off!'

**E**
*Irresistible CVs*
Joseph King 2005 £11.99
Blurb: *'Once you have mastered how to write a good CV, be prepared for the numerous requests for interview. This book will not let you down.'*
SM: 'This is a very good guide, with several concrete and realistic examples of different sorts of CVs. Some might find it a little over-simplistic in approach, and as part of it deals with American résumé-writing, it's not all relevant.'
SR: 'I can see myself using this when I come to write my own CV. It's very thorough and realistic, and tells you in great detail which parts are probably going to be more important to potential employers.'
PL: 'Having read this, I'm definitely going to change my current CV. It tells you what to put in, and how to say things in a convincing yet brief manner.'

**1**  Scan read the reviews quickly to find a book:

1  on how to make a successful written application for a job.
2  which can help you if you are lost in terms of choosing a career.
3  which specifically helps you to answer questions successfully.
4  which gives you mental calming techniques.
5  on how to make big but positive changes in your working life.
6  which is cheaper than all the others.
7  which each of the three reviewers describe as 'practical'.

**2**  Now read the texts more carefully. Which book(s):

1  has received negative comments from each of the three reviewers?
2  received no negative review comments, only positive ones, from all three reviewers?
3  was thought to be more suited to older candidates by one reviewer?
4  book was thought to be problematic in terms of style, by two of the reviewers?
5  did two of the reviewers say they will actually use?

## Speaking: What would you do if ... ?

**Type of activity:** Group discussion.
**Preparation:** Make enough photocopies of page 133 for each student in the class.

1 Write the first problem on the board / an OHT and see what the students think. Encourage them to focus on accuracy in their responses in terms of using the conditional.
2 Give out the sheet of problems and ask students to look at all six, and consider individually what they would do in each situation. They should write notes.
3 After a few minutes' preparation, put the students into groups of three and allow them to compare answers orally. Circulate and remind students to aim for accuracy.
4 Get full class feedback on some of the problems at the end, if you feel students would benefit from this.
5 Alternatively, if your students are quite strong and do not need preparation time, cut up one set of situations per group, and put these face down in front of them. Allow one person in turn to pick up a problem and read it out to the others then to say what they would do. Ensure that they look at one problem only at a time.

## Reading: Weird buys on the Internet

**Type of activity:** Group discussion.
**Preparation:** Make enough photocopies of page 134 for each student in the class.

1 To introduce the topic, ask students what things they would / would never buy on the Internet.
2 Ask students to read the text then work through exercise 1 individually or with a partner.

**ANSWERS:**

**1** 1 T    2 F    3 T    4 F    5 T    6 F    7 F    8 T    9 F    10 T

3 For exercise 2, make sure that students spend time considering the meaning in the context of the text. They should also identify what part of speech they are. After working alone, get students to compare their answers with a partner.

**ANSWERS:**

**2**

1 *be taken off the market (phrase)*: no longer for sale
2 *asking price (n)*: the ideal price that the seller wants
3 *rash (adj)*: risky, not thought through
4 *turn down (phrasal verb)*: rejected, not accepted
5 *devastated (adv)*: very, very upset and disappointed
6 *turn out (phrasal verb)*: be (in the end)

4 Ask students to discuss in pairs what they would have done if they'd been Nicky and Harvey. Then take whole-class feedback.

## Situation A

Tom Hissop gets on really well with his boss and has learnt a great deal from him. His boss is now leaving the company and has asked Tom to join him, working for a larger company in a similar role with slightly more money. Tom is considering the matter carefully. He loves working with his boss, but there are still lots of opportunities in this present company. He knows he will feel disloyal whichever option he chooses.

What would you do in this case?

## Situation B

Fiona Hank's senior colleague resigned a few months ago. Although Fiona applied for the job, an external candidate was recruited. Since the departure of the ex-colleague, Fiona has taken on approximately 40% of his job and it appears that this is not going to be given to the new employee. Fiona has also had to do most of the training of the new colleague herself. This does not seem fair, though Fiona does enjoy the new responsibilities.

What would you do in this situation?

## Situation C

Sebastian Pannell's boss has offered him the possibility of working from home for two days a week, but with a slight reduction in salary, i.e .10% less per day (a total reduction of 20% per week). He likes the idea in many ways, especially as he has to commute for two hours each day. However, the reduction in salary is problematic.

What would you do if you were in this person's shoes?

## Situation D

Charlie Hughes has worked for a small local firm for the last 21 years and has been very happy there. All profits are currently being poured into R&D, to keep up with competitors. Twenty-five per cent of staff have been made redundant in the last 18 months. The boss is very concerned and has asked the remaining staff if they will all accept a 15% pay-cut for the next 12 months, until the new product is on the market. This way the company can survive.

What would you do if you worked for this company?

## Situation E

Robert Gammon has been informed from a secret but extremely reliable source that the company he works for is about to go bankrupt. He has been there for nearly two years, working as an engineer and has been very happy there. The job market is not very good at the moment.

What would you do if you were in this situation?

## Situation F

Della Appleby's boss is giving her some fantastic opportunities to develop and she thinks she may be offered a promotion soon. Her boss has asked her to go to a conference in Vancouver and give a talk on behalf of the company. She wants to say 'yes', but she has a very deep fear of flying, which she has kept secret.

What would you do if you were Della?

# Weird buys on the Internet

## Purchasing their dream house on the Internet nearly turned into a nightmare for Nicky and Harvey Lyons.

Nicky and Harvey decided they wanted to move from their small two-bedroomed terraced house in Liverpool to a cave in southern Turkey. 'We had talked about moving to Turkey for ages, and wanted somewhere really interesting to live after we'd retired,' Harvey explained. 'As we weren't able to travel to Turkey for long enough to go house-hunting, we decided to research our dream house on the Internet, and found loads of relevant sites. We actually first saw our new 'cave house' in our living-room in Liverpool, just browsing. We had looked at some fascinating properties, ranging from wooden huts to mini-castles, but we both adored the cave houses we came across!'

Having found a couple of attractive-sounding cave houses – 'all mod cons, freshly decorated, spacious, light and airy and well-situated for shops and beaches' – they decided they had to go and see them. However, as it turned out, they didn't actually manage to get to Turkey as they'd had some family problems. Then, one of the caves was taken off the market for some reason, and then they were informed that some very good offers had been placed on the second one. 'It seemed very affordable,' said Nicky. 'We would be getting a four-bedroom house for half of the asking price for our two-bedroom Liverpool home! It looked cool and calming. So, we decided to be rash and agreed to buy it without seeing it; thereby taking the biggest risk of our lives!'

'We contacted the Turkey-based agency who sent us more details and photos of the property. We were even more impressed with how it looked in the photos, so we quickly made an offer before anyone else snapped up our bargain buy. Our first offer was turned down so we immediately increased our bid and a few days later received a contract to sign. A couple of weeks later, when the sale was completed, we arranged to come out and see our new home,' said Harvey.

'When we first saw it for real, we were so excited. It looked like a small, attractive bungalow from the front, but the back of it was built into the hillside. We were not so excited when we went inside though – in fact, we were devastated! It was cold and damp, with no running water or electricity and the paint was peeling off the walls and ceiling. In fact it looked nothing like it did in the pictures. It turned out that the agency had used pictures taken in our neighbour's houses to show what it *could* be like! We found out that there was nothing we could do about it legally. Buying a house on the Internet is not like buying a laptop – you can't just exchange it or return it because it's faulty!'

The cave also cost them quite a lot more than they'd agreed to pay. This was a result of all the hidden costs, such as agency fees and administration charges that they were unaware of at the time of signing the contract.

As there was little choice in the matter, Nicky and Harvey decided to stay and make a go of it. 'It was still a bargain at the price,' said Nicky. 'So we moved out there and spent a tough year renovating and decorating. Our new neighbours were wonderful and helped us out at every opportunity. In the end, it has worked out fabulously for us and we truly feel we now have our dream house – though it was so nearly a nightmare. We do miss our children and grandchildren, but they love coming to stay. We certainly never want to go back to the UK.'

---

**1** Mark these sentences *T* (true) or *F* (false). Then, check your answers with a partner.

1 Harvey and Nicky decided they wanted to spend their retirement abroad.
2 They wanted to live in a mini-castle.
3 They searched for suitable properties on the Internet.
4 They made an offer on two caves that they found.
5 They arranged to go and see the properties in person.
6 Their first offer was accepted.
7 They went to Turkey to see their cave before they signed the contract.
8 They found out that the photos they'd seen weren't actually of the cave they bought.
9 The price they agreed on was what they finally paid.
10 They had a lot of support from their new neighbours.

**2** Find these words in the text. Try to guess their meaning. Compare your answers with a partner then check in your dictionary.

1 *be taken off the market* (line 30)
2 *asking price* (line 36)
3 *rash* (line 39)
4 (*be*) *turned down* (line 49)
5 *devastated* (line 61)
6 *turn out* (line 66)

## 6 Company and community  Teacher's notes & answers

### Speaking: Logging

**Type of activity:** Roleplay / debate. This is based on real-life, current events. It is an opportunity for students to use the passive in natural situations, e.g. *our home is being destroyed,* and possibly reported speech, *e.g. you promised us that ...; we asked you if ....*

**Preparation:** Make enough photocopies of page 136 for each pair of students to have fact sheet. Cut out enough role cards for students to have one each and for the chairperson to have a copy of all the role cards that are being used.

1 To introduce the topic, you could perhaps show students a map of the area (Peru, Brazil and Bolivia) and show something made of mahogany to stimulate interest.
2 Pre-teach some vocabulary, such as: *native people, tribe, log + logging, legal + illegal, corrupt + corruption, isolation.*
3 Ask students to read the fact sheet and to ask any questions. Invite reactions: *What do you think about this ? If you were a native tribesperson, how would you feel and what would you do?*
4 There are seven role cards so divide up your class accordingly, giving out fewer role cards if necessary. Alternatively, repeat one or two of the cards e.g. *Tribesperson 1.* If you have a relatively small class, e.g. nine students, then you could allow all the students to participate, but otherwise put the students into groups of 4–7 around the room.
  If you have a large class, first of all get students with the same role cards to work together. Each student should only get their own role card, except for the chairperson who should read all of them.
5 Ask your students to read their role card and to tell you whether they are supposed to be 'for' or 'against' in their roles. Remind them that they have to play this role, even if they disagree with it personally.
6 Allow students preparation time, to decide what they are going to say. Encourage them to add more ideas to their role cards. Tell them that they are going to have a formal debate.
7 Remind students that first of all they need to introduce themselves and say what their position is, e.g. *I'm X, I'm a X and I strongly believe that ....*
8 Start the debate. Tell students that they should aim to try and reach some sort of 'compromise' in about 20 minutes, having heard each person's argument. Explain *compromise* if necessary.
9 At the end, allow students to express their personal opinions on the matter, if appropriate.

**Alternative suggestion**: Put a group of students in the middle of the class in an inward-facing circle, with the 'audience' outside. Let them start the debate, then change students with the same role every few minutes, at random, e.g. change the lawyers – this way all students get the opportunity to talk in a formal, full-class debate.

### Reading: Ethical futures

**Type of activity:** Reading comprehension and ranking activity with discussion.
**Preparation:** Make enough photocopies of page 137 for each student.

1 To introduce the topic, ask students if they can think of a job which is 'ethical' and also 'unethical'. Ask what kind of things make a company more or less 'ethical' than others ?
2 Ask students to read the article and to work individually or with a partner to answer the questions. Take whole-class feedback.

#### SUGGESTED ANSWERS:

**1**
1 No. Graduates nowadays are concerned that companies they will work for have a good ethical track record.
2 No. She does not believe in companies that exploit people for profit.
3 A CSR programme is often used to promote a company and create an image that might not actually be true.
4 1) Because it can improve the image of the company which in turn means that people will want to do business with them, which in turn means their profits will increase; 2) they will be able to attract the best graduate recruits to work for them.

3 Ask students to work individually first and to rank the list in order of importance for themselves (1 = most important, etc.). Then ask students to work with a partner and explain why they have ordered them as they have done. Then, take whole-class feedback to find out what some of the arguments were. You could then try to do this as a whole-class ranking exercise on the board to stimulate whole-class discussion.
4 As a follow up, ask students to think of a company they would like to work for. For homework, they could do some 'digging around' to find out what that company's ethical policies 'really mean' as suggested in the last paragraph of the text. Students can then report back to the class on their findings in the next lesson.

**The facts:**

There is an area of the rainforest in Peru, near the border with Brazil and Bolivia, where people such as the Yaminahua and the Amahuaca tribes live. These people are natives to the region and their lives are being threatened by logging. These tribes like to live in (semi-) isolation.

Now their jungle-home is being destroyed by the US and other foreign timber industries, who are pulling down the huge mahogany trees for export. This wood is then made into high-quality furniture and car dashboards. Each tree can fetch up to $100,000 once exported.

Local tribespeople say that the destruction is not legal – most of the logging is illegal and there is a lot of corruption amongst officials.

### Tribesperson 1

Consider the following issues:
- Destruction of your way of life / culture.
- Loss of your home and means of survival.
- Danger to your tribespeople.
- The companies have broken promises.

### Representative of SD (Stop the Destruction)

SD is a campaign group to defend the native people and their lifestyle.
Consider the following issues:
- These native people choose to live in isolation.
- Their culture and way of life is being destroyed.
- People have a moral duty to respect other cultures.
- These tribes will die out if this continues.

### Tribesperson 2

You are a young man / woman who wants to live in America.
Consider the following issues:
- You want your people to move into the modern age. Time changes – now is the time to move forward.
- Your people have a very basic, hard life. People rarely survive beyond 50.
- Life in the jungle is limited. It is not a place for young people.

### Environmental campaigner

Consider the following issues:
- We need to preserve the rainforest: it is the world's 'lung'.
- Many rare and unique species of animal and plants live in the rainforest.
- The jungle is also a great source of drugs and research.

### Manager of a US timber factory

Consider the following issues:
- US laws allow you to do this – it is legal.
- You provide work for several hundreds of men.
- You provide opportunities for local people to work with you.
- Before logging, you have discussions with the local people.

### Lawyer for one of the US timber factories

Consider the following issues:
- The logging companies are following the current US law.
- Unless the law is changed, the logging can continue.
- Logging companies discuss which areas of the jungle to log with the locals before moving in.
- The companies are considering ways of replanting trees in logged areas.

### Chairperson

You need to consider <u>both</u> sides of the story and to make sure that everyone's voice is heard. Think how you will do this in English, e.g. *What do you think, X?*
It is also your job at the end, to try and find some kind of compromise. Again, think of the kind of language that you will be using, e.g. *I suggest that …; One option is to …; Are you happy to agree to this?*

# Ethical futures

Twenty years ago, the only factors that graduates took into consideration when seeking employment were whether prospective employers could offer them good career prospects, a decent salary, training opportunities and benefits like holidays and pension plans. Today, though, they also want to know if the companies they are interested in working for have a good track record in corporate social responsibility. In fact, a company that doesn't, is very likely to be struck off the list.

The current student population and those in their first years of employment have a much keener sense of how their life choices, from where they buy their clothes and food to where they choose to work, can have an impact on far-flung societies. They also feel that they will be more at ease with the company culture of an ethical employer as they will be able to see eye to eye with their colleagues and managers. This is putting pressure on employers to become more ethical in their trading and day-to-day operations in order to attract new recruits.

Gemma Stevens, 21,  has recently started working for a company that sources fair-trade food products such as fruit, tea, coffee and chocolate, from around the world. 'I knew I wanted to work for a company that was not trashing people's lives in trying to please its shareholders. It was a much more important consideration for me than getting a big salary and lots of perks. In fact, I'm very lucky, because of our company's ethical policies, we as members of staff are treated very well – we have a good benefits, including discounts on the fair-trade products we sell, we get lots of useful training, good career prospects and we are certainly not underpaid. And the best thing is to think that the people that are working hard all around the world to produce the goods we buy in are also getting a fair deal!'

When people are looking for prospective employers, though, they should really do some digging around to find out what some companies' 'ethical policies' really mean. Beware of annual reports and glossy advertising – these  are not sources to be trusted. People in charge of corporate social responsibility in a company often work closely with marketing departments: boasting about good deeds can gain a company lot of admiration and respect and boost its reputation and profits.

**1**  Read the text and answer these questions.

1   Can non-ethical companies attract as many new employees now as they did twenty years ago? Why (not)?
2   Would Gemma work for, e.g. a clothing manufacturer that pays its workers in China very low wages? Why (not)?
3   Why are some companies' CSR programmes not transparent?
4   Why do companies want to promote their ethical policies? (2 reasons)

**2**  Look at the list of factors that people consider when selecting a prospective employer. Put them in order of importance to you. Then, work with a partner and explain your reasons.

– Pay
– Holiday entitlement
– Work environment (i.e. office / place of work)
– Company's commercial success
– Promotion prospects
– Pension scheme
– Company's ethical policy
– Perks – company phone, company car, gym-membership, etc.

## Speaking: Your predictions

**Type of activity:** Game. This game links to Unit 7 page 88 in the Student's Book (future forms and expressing likelihood), and acts as an extension to materials on page 89. It should therefore be done as a follow-up to these pages.

**Preparation:** Make enough photocopies of page 139 for each student to have a copy of the target language box. Cut enough sets of the speaking points into strips for each group of three to have a set.

1   Ask students to work in groups of three. Give each group a set of the speaking points and tell them to arrange them face-down on their desk.
    Also give out a copy of the box with the target language to each student. This is virtually a copy of the box on page 88 in the Student's Book, but it's briefer and therefore more demanding.
    Ask students to give their opinions about the speaking points, using the language from the box, e.g. *There is not much chance that classrooms will die out.* Focus on accuracy when eliciting examples.

2   Establish the rules of the game. After giving the basic rules, a demonstration with a strong group is probably most effective. The two main aims are: for each group member to use one different language item in each turn and for each group member to talk on each topic for at least 30 seconds.

3   One student starts the game, turning over one of the discussion strips, and then gives his/her opinion, using just one of the target items in a full sentence. They should then carry on talking about the topic for at least 30 seconds, e.g. giving reasons for their views, expanding their points.

4   The first speaker records the language item he/she used on his/her grid, in the 'used' column, with a tick. He/she cannot use this item now in the rest of the game at all, though other group members can.

5   When the first speaker has finished, the second and third players take their turns to talk separately on the *same* discussion point for 30 seconds. The other players both have to use one *different* piece of language each, again recording the phrase they use on their own grids.

6   As they discuss the topic, the other group members are allowed to rephrase their partners' words if they acknowledge them, e.g. *As X said, ...., and I also believe this.*

7   Once each member has spoken on the discussion point, they go on to the next topic. The teacher needs to ensure that students are on-task, using the target language effectively and keeping a clear tally of their scores. Either correct on the spot, or take notes for remedial teaching after the task.

## Reading: A beneficial takeover

**Type of activity:** Comprehension and discussion.
**Preparation:** Make enough photocopies of page 140 for each student.

1   As a lead-in to this topic, take in some (pictures of) Body Shop and L'Oreal products if possible. Introduce the article by writing the headline on the board, and finding out if anyone knows anything about it. Clarify the word *cosmetics* here, if necessary.

2   Ask students to read the first three paragraphs of this article to find out: a) who started Body Shop (Anita and Gordon Roddick) and b) how much money the couple will make from the sale (£130 million).

3   Write these numbers on the board one at a time and ask students to scan the first four paragraphs and tell you what they represent:
    *54* (Body Shop exists in 54 countries.)
    *300* (L'Oreal bought the shares for 300p each.)
    *30* (Body Shop was set up 30 years ago.)
    *419* (The company turned over £419 million in 2005.)
    *652* (Body Shop was bought for £652 million.).

4   Ask students to read the rest of the article and do exercise 1 individually or with a partner. Take whole-class feedback.

**ANSWERS:**

**1**   1 a)    2 a)    3 c)    4 c)    5 c)    6 b)    7 a)    8 b)

5   For exercise 2, try to focus students on the ethical issues here, mentioned in several of the paragraphs (2, 5, 7, 8, 11, 12).

**SUGGESTED ANSWER:**

**2**

Many supporters of Body Shop are concerned that it will lose some of its values, once joined with the larger company of L'Oreal, which is not based on the same ethical principles.
L'Oreal is also part-owned by Nestlé, a company with a very poor ethical record.

## 7 Mergers and acquisitions  Speaking

✂

| | |
|---|---|
| **People will have fewer and fewer children worldwide, and also in your country.** | **Your country will become increasingly important in the international market.** |
| **People will be far less dependent on oil for fuel.** | **China and India will be the world's economic giants, governing the global markets.** |
| **There will be a far greater number of female politicians in your country.** | **The standard of living will improve for some people in your country, but the gap between rich and poor will grow.** |
| **You will be a successful businessperson with few financial problems.** | **Hundreds of languages will die, as the use of English grows even more.** |

| | USED | | USED |
|---|---|---|---|
| a 50/50 chance | | could | |
| unlikely | | bound to | |
| no way | | a good chance | |
| definitely | | highly (un)likely (that ...) | |
| possible | | may | |
| might (just) | | likely to | |
| not much chance | | fully expect | |
| almost certain | | a (good / remote) possibility | |

# L'Oreal buys Body Shop for £652m

COSMETICS retailer Body Shop today agreed to a £652.3 million takeover by L'Oreal. Body Shop accepted an offer of 300p a share from the French firm – a large premium on its closing price of 268p.

5 It is expected that Anita and Gordon Roddick, who set up Body Shop 30 years ago, will make £130 million from the sale. Dame Anita said: 'For both Gordon and I, this is without doubt the best 30th anniversary gift the Body Shop could have received. L'Oreal has displayed 10 visionary leadership in wanting to be an authentic advocate and supporter of our values.'

L'Oreal said the Body Shop brand would be retained and the company would continue to be based in and run independently from the UK.

15 The French firm said Body Shop would enhance its business because of its 'sizeable and complimentary brand' across 54 countries, which delivered revenues of £419 million last year.

It also said the deal would give it increased presence 20 in the 'masstige' sector – mass market combined with prestige – which Body Shop has worked hard to exploit over the last four years.

In a statement to the stock market today, the two companies said the proposed takeover depended on 25 regulatory clearance.

L'Oreal chief executive Sir Lindsay Owen-Jones, who was born in Wallasey, Merseyside, said: 'We have always had great respect for the Body Shop's success and for its strong identity and values created by its outstanding 30 founder, Dame Anita Roddick.

A partnership between our companies makes perfect sense. Combining L'Oreal's expertise and knowledge of international markets with the Body Shop's distinct culture and values will benefit both companies.'

35 Iain McGlinn, one of the original investors and an old friend of Dame Anita and Mr Roddick, will make around £140 million from his 21% stake in the company. The Body Shop board today urged other shareholders to back the sale. Shares in Body Shop surged more than 10% 40 today towards the 300p mark offered by L'Oreal. They were as low as 56.5p three years ago.

The Roddicks started Body Shop with a store in Brighton in 1976 to help support their two young daughters, Justine and Samantha. They opened a second 45 store six months later and now have 2,085 branches around the world, including 304 in the UK.

Body Shop, which is based in Littlehampton, West Sussex, represented an ethical alternative to the traditional approach to cosmetics and was against animal testing.

50 Throughout her career, Dame Anita has campaigned passionately around ethical issues such as fair trade and sustainable development.

**1** Choose the correct alternative to complete these statements.

1 L'Oreal is a/an _____ company.
   a) European   b) American   c) Asian
2 Under L'Oreal, the identity and 'look' of Body Shop _____.
   a) will not change   b) will change slightly   c) will change a great deal
3 L'Oreal's CEO said that Body Shop had _____.
   a) knowledge of international markets   b) respect   c) a distinct culture and values
4 As a result of the merger, shares in Body Shop _____.
   a) went up slowly in value   b) remained more or less the same   c) went up very quickly in value
5 _____ of the Body Shop stores are based in the UK.
   a) Just over 30%   b) Half   c) A relatively small percentage
6 The Roddicks set up the Body Shop to _____.
   a) add to their already large business empire   b) provide an income to help the family survive   c) as an adventure
7 Body Shop differs from other cosmetics companies because _____.
   a) it is based on sound values   b) it started very small   c) it tests its products on animals
8 From the comments in the article, it seems that the Roddicks are _____.
   a) slightly disappointed   b) very happy   c) rather nervous

**2** Why do you think some former Body Shop supporters, in particular those supporters of its ethics, are very worried about this takeover and what it means to the brand?

## 8 International trade   Teacher's notes & answers

### Speaking: Half the story

**Type of activity:** Jigsaw speaking. This is a controlled practice of verbs and their dependent prepositions and so it links with page 101 in the Student's Book.  It demands clarity of pronunciation and intensive listening.
**Preparation:** Make one photocopy of page 142 for each pair. Cut the page in half so each student has card A or card B.

1   To introduce the topic, ask students what stresses and problems a housewife / stay-at-home mother might face. Tell them they are going to read about one such person called Sally Mills.
2   Divide the class into pairs (As and Bs) and give out the relevant 'card' to each partner. Students must not show their partner their card. Students read their card and check if there are any words they do not know how to pronounce.
3   Tell students that they need to find out what the problem is with Sally. Tell A to start with *d) Sally Mills objected …*, and ask  B to read the rest of the sentence that follows on from this. Then A does the same and then let students continue like this in pairs. Then, without looking at each other's cards, get students to work alone to complete the story in their own words from what they can remember. Remind students that if they are not sure about something, they should ask their partner to repeat the sentence(s).
4   At the end, they should check with the teacher that they have the correct version. Then they can look at their partner's card.

**ANSWER:**

**1** d) , k) , e) , j) , a) , i) , f) , h) , c) , g) , b)

### Reading: Is China a threat?

**Type of activity:** Reading comprehension.
**Preparation:** Make one photocopy of page 143 for each pair.

1   To introduce the topic, you could get students to look at their clothes / possessions and see where the items come from.
2   Before you start, make sure students know the meaning of: *threat, source of information, make an impression, develop / make contacts, bureaucracy, opportunity.*  Try to keep the pre-teaching of lexis to a minimum.
3   Ask students to look at the headline / title of the article and to answer the question in exercise 1 and say why they think so or not. Then ask them to do exercise 2.

**ANSWERS:**

**1** no     **2** Photolink

4   Ask students to work through exercise 3 with a partner to find the answers as quickly as they can. Get students to justify their answers from the text.

**ANSWERS:**

**3** 1D     2C     3E

5   Ask students to work through the questions in exercise 4 individually and then get them to check their answers with a partner.

**ANSWERS:**

**4**
1   Very fast. The economy has grown by 9% every year for the past 25 years.
2   All sizes.
3   The press portrays China as a threat to the UK's economy because it is a market for cheap labour and production costs which UK firms can't compete with.
4   The local chamber of commerce organized a trade mission.
5   To find local business partners and clients.
6   Dealing with bureaucratic problems can be time-consuming and there are language and cultural hurdles to get over too.
7   Getting better.

**A**

a) of actually leaving the company. He applied …

b) in dealing with his problems, simply by talking the matter over with his boss.

c) from the meeting feeling much happier, confident that this time, everything would work out well. And it did. The meeting resulted …

d) Sally Mills objected …

e) to this, as Jim was a valued employee. However, within a few weeks, he was travelling as much as before. Sally was very angry as she relied …

f) for not keeping his word. Having explained in more detail about his situation at home, Jim felt his boss really sympathized …

**B**

g) in a much happier employee, husband and father, and of course, a very happy wife and mother. Jim was also proud that he had succeeded …

h) with him, for the first time in his working life. As a result, he actually emerged …

i) for a few jobs with other firms, but nothing happened. So he decided to speak to his boss again, who apologized …

j) on Jim being at home at weekends to help with their three children. She herself was a working mother and needed time to relax. She was so upset that Jim began to think …

k) to her husband Jim spending 50% of his time abroad on business. After discussing the problem together, Jim asked his boss if he could reduce the number of foreign trips he was making. His boss agreed …

## 8 International trade Reading

# Is China a threat to Britain's small businesses?

### By Gareth Chadwick

**A** THE EMERGENCE of China is an epoch-defining change in the global economy. This country of 1.3 billion people has in the last 10 years built enough roads to circle the equator 16 times. It already makes 90 per cent of the world's toys, 40 per cent of the world's socks and 80 per cent of the world's DVD players. Its economy has grown by around nine per cent every year for the past 25 years and is now worth more than US$2 trillion.

**B** With statistics like these, it is perhaps no surprise that China is usually perceived as a threat to the UK's economy; a country of cheap imports and even cheaper labour. However, for businesses that are prepared to look beyond the headlines, China's growth is actually an enormous opportunity, not a threat. And it is not just a market for the multinationals. Small and medium-sized businesses are finding a huge new market for their products and services.

**C** Photolink, a creative services agency in Manchester, sees huge potential for developing its business in China, both helping Chinese-based companies market themselves internationally, and also helping UK or European businesses trade in China. It is planning to open an office in either Beijing or Shanghai by 2007. But Claire Robinson, the company's China Trade Director, says that the lack of information for smaller British businesses interested in trading in China means that many do not realise the opportunities that are available. 'It is estimated that by 2030 China will be the largest economy in the world and yet there is relatively little information about doing business there in the UK press,' she says.

**D** Photolink's first exposure to China was via a part-funded trade mission organized by the local chamber of commerce, often a good source of initial information. Another invaluable resource is the China team at UK Trade & Investment in London, the international trade arm of the Department of Trade and Industry. They can also liaise with the British Embassy and the various consulates in major cities throughout China, which can help British companies of all sizes find local business partners and clients.

**E** It would be a mistake to think that China can offer a quick-fix for any businesses which are struggling in the UK, however. As well as the different culture, language and business environment, Chinese bureaucracy, in particular, is often cited as a hindrance to doing business. Says Pearson: It can take months to get the right paperwork or even find out the best procedure for doing what you want to do, but it is getting better. And when you look at the opportunities, there's no question it is worth the effort.

---

**1** Look at the title of the article. Read the first two paragraphs of the article and find out if the answer is *yes* or *no*.

**2** Scan the article very quickly to find the name of a British business which is trading successfully with China.

**3** Match these headings to the correct paragraph.

1 Where to start and who to contact when trying to create links in China
2 Opportunities for small businesses
3 Possible problems of doing business in China

**4** Answer these questions.

1 Exactly how fast is the Chinese economy growing?
2 Is the Chinese market more suited to large or small companies overseas?
3 What is the problem with the British press in relation to these growing opportunities?
4 How did Photolink get into the Chinese market?
5 Why might you go to the British Embassy?
6 Why is China not a 'quick-fix' for struggling UK businesses?
7 Are bureaucratic problems improving or getting worse?

---

Macmillan Education
Between Towns Road, Oxford OX4 3PP
A division of Macmillan Publishers Limited
Companies and representatives throughout the world

ISBN 978-1-4050-8186-3

Original design by Keith Shaw, Threefold Design Ltd
Cover design by Keith Shaw, Threefold Design Ltd

The authors and publishers are grateful for permission to reprint the
following copyright material:

p128 Extract from 'As warm as toast' by Paul Kendall first published
in *Daily Mail* 07.06.01, reprinted by permission of the Solo
Syndication; p 140 Extract from 'L'Oreal buys Body Shop for £652m'
copyright © The Independent 2006, first published *The Independent
website* 17.03.06, reprinted by permission of the publisher; p 143
Extract from 'Is China a threat to Britain's small businesses?' by
Gareth Chadwick copyright © Gareth Chadwick 2006 first published
*The Independent website* 23.04.06, reprinted by permission of the
publisher.

Although we have tried to trace and contact copyright holders before
publication, in some cases this has not been possible. If contacted
we will be pleased to rectify any errors or omissions at the earliest
opportunity.

Printed and bound in Spain by Cayfo-Quebecor

2011  2010  2009  2008  2007
10  9  8  7  6  5  4  3  2  1

PIANO / VOCAL / GUITAR

# JUSTIN BIEBER

# MY WORLD

Photos by Pamela Littky

ISBN 978-1-4234-9241-2

## HAL•LEONARD® CORPORATION
7777 W. BLUEMOUND RD. P.O. BOX 13819 MILWAUKEE, WI 53213

Visit Hal Leonard Online at
**www.halleonard.com**

6     One Time

15    Favorite Girl

21    Down to Earth

29    Bigger

39    One Less Lonely Girl

48    First Dance

56    Love Me

# ONE TIME

Words and Music by JAMES BUNTON,
CORRON TY KEE COLE, CHRISTOPHER STEWART
and THABISO NKHEREANYE

down semitone

Moderately slow groove

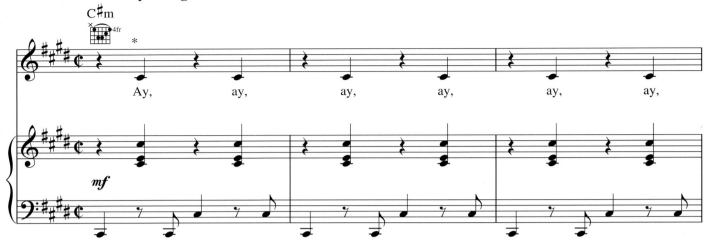

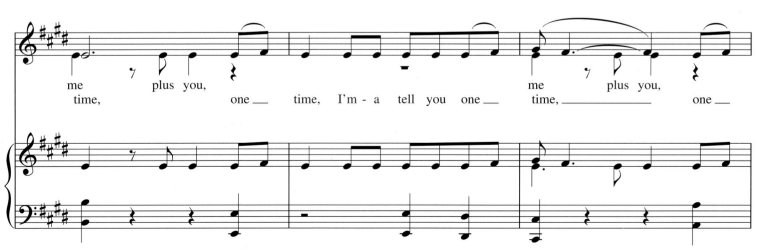

*Male vocal written at pitch.*

time, ___ I'm - a tell you one ___ time,    one time,    one ___ time,    one ___ time.

# FAVORITE GIRL

Words and Music by ANESHA BIRCHETT,
ANTEA BIRCHETT, DERNST EMILE
and DELISHA THOMAS

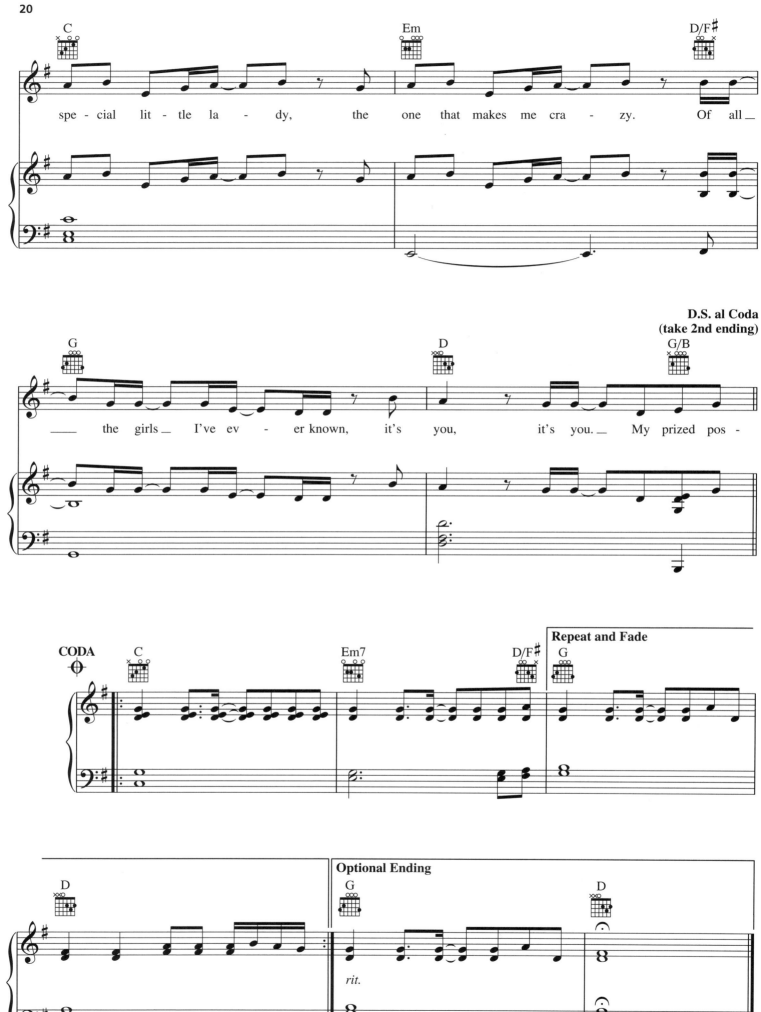

# DOWN TO EARTH

Words and Music by JUSTIN BIEBER,
CARLOS BATTEY, KEVIN RISTO,
WAYNNE NUGENT, MASON LEVY
and STEVEN BATTEY

# BIGGER

Words and Music by JUSTIN BIEBER,
LONNIE BREAUX, KEVIN RISTO,
WAYNNE NUGENT and OLADAPO TORIMIRO

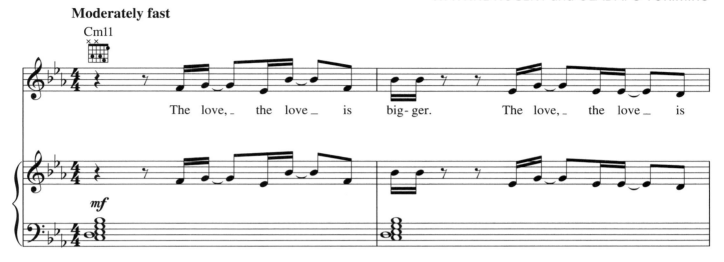

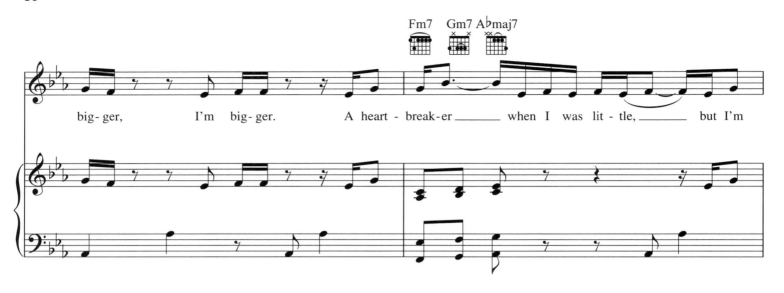

big - ger, I'm big - ger. A heart - break - er _____ when I was lit - tle, _____ but I'm

big - ger, I'm big - ger. And all the hit - ters, I swear they look so ___

___ small ___ from up here, 'cause we're big - ger, love's big - ger, I'm

big-ger, and you're big-ger. I was a play-er_____ when I was lit-tle,_____ but now I'm

big-ger, I'm big-ger. A heart-break-er_____ when I was lit-tle,_____ but I'm

big-ger, I'm big-ger. And all the hit-ters, I swear they look so_____

# ONE LESS LONELY GIRL

Words and Music by EZEKIEL LEWIS,
BALEWA MUHAMMAD, SEAN HAMILTON
and HYUK SHIN

# FIRST DANCE

Words and Music by USHER RAYMOND,
RYON LOVETT, ALEXANDER PARHM JR.,
JESSE WILSON and DWIGHT REYNOLDS

It's your chance, take her hand, to the floor, to the floor. Girl, if you

see some-thing you like, then let him know, 'cause you on-ly got one ___

___ chance, your first ___ dance. So take ad-

*Recorded a half step lower.*

# LOVE ME

Words and Music by PETER SVENSSON
and NINA PERSSON